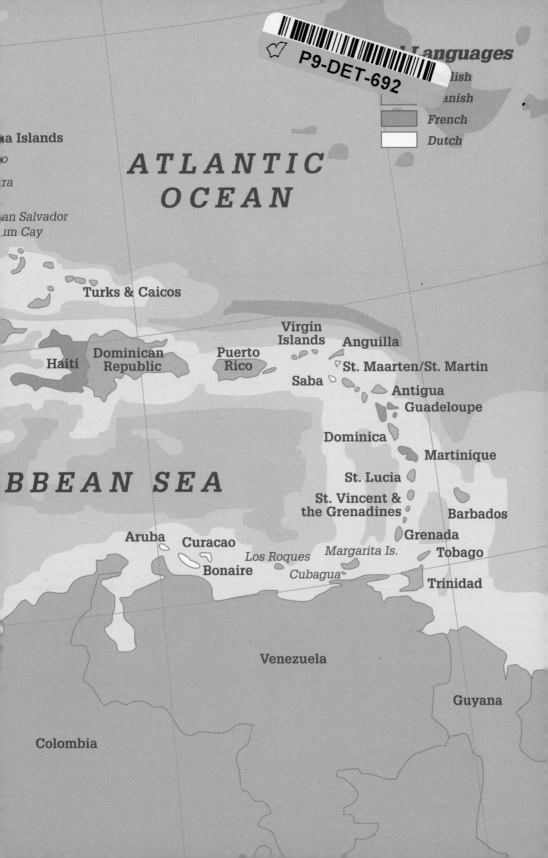

Languages

English

Spanish

French

Dutch

P9-DET-692

a Islands
o
ra

an Salvador
m Cay

ATLANTIC
OCEAN

Turks & Caicos

Virgin
Islands   Anguilla

Haiti   Dominican   Puerto   St. Maarten/St. Martin
         Republic   Rico
                              Saba   Antigua
                                          Guadeloupe

                                   Dominica
BBEAN SEA   Martinique

                                   St. Lucia

                              St. Vincent &
                              the Grenadines   Barbados

Aruba   Curacao   Grenada
                        Los Roques   Margarita Is.   Tobago
              Bonaire   Cubagua
                                                     Trinidad

                         Venezuela

                                                Guyana

Colombia

REEF
CREATURE
Identification

FLORIDA CARIBBEAN BAHAMAS

PAUL HUMANN
NED DELOACH
LES WILK

NEW WORLD PUBLICATIONS, INC.

Jacksonville, Florida USA

Acknowledgments

We wish to express our gratitude to the many individuals who have generously provided photographs and species identifications for the hundreds of animals included in this volume. The nearly 75 percent increase in species from the previous edition of *Reef Creature Identification* is due in large part to Les Wilk who spent three years canvassing the underwater photography community for images of new animals. Many of the contributing photographers are devoted underwater naturalists, who spend hundreds of hours below the surface hunting for rare, and often, cryptic species. Of special note are the "Mucksters," a group of passionate South Florida divers who regularly hunt the murky waters of the Intracoastal Waterway beneath the Blue Heron Bridge near West Palm, Florida. This shallow sand and rubble bottom has produced a wealth of unusual inshore species.

The comparison of photographs with scientific literature to determine a species names can be a tedious task. A special thanks to the many scientists who have given freely of their time, advice and knowledge. Every attempt has been made to keep species identification as accurate as possible; however, certainly a few errors crept in, and they are the authors' sole responsibility.

CREDITS
Editor: Ken Marks
Photography Editor: Eric Riesch
Art Director: Michael O'Connell
Print Consultant: D'Print Pte. Ltd., Singapore
ISBN 978-1-878348-53-1
First Edition, 1992; Second Edition, 2002; Third Edition, 2013; Second Printing 2015, Third Printing 2019.
First Edition Copyright, ©1992; Second Edition Copyright, ©2002; Third Edition Copyright, ©2013 by New World Publications, Inc.
All rights reserved. No part of this book may be reproduced without prior written consent.
Published and Distributed by New World Publications, Inc., 1861 Cornell Road, Jacksonville, FL 32207,
Phone (904) 737-6558, www.fishid.com, orders@fishid.com

Scientific Acknowledgments

The invaluable assistance of Dr. Walter Goldberg of Florida International University deserves special mention. He undertook the Herculean task of principle scientific adviser, and coordinator of the project. Following are the scientists who assisted with identifications and information. Their specialty and institution are listed after their names. Those taking the time and effort to make laboratory examination of photographed and collected specimens are noted with an asterisk.

Dr. Roland C. Anderson, Seattle Aquarium, WA – Cephalopods
Dr. Arthur Anker, Florida Museum of Natural History University of Florida, Gainesville, FL – Shrimp
Mike Bacon, North Palm Beach, FL – Gastropods
Dr. Rolando Bastida-Zavala, Laboratorio de Sistemática de Invertebrados Marinos (LABSIM), Ciudad Universitaria, Puerto Angel, Oaxaca, México – Segmented Worms
Dr. Raymond Bauer, University of Louisiana at Lafayette – Shrimp
David Behrens, Gig Harbor, WA – Nudibranchs
Dr. Anita Brinckmann-Voss – Hydromedusa
Dr. Temir A. Britayev, A.N. Severtzov Institute of Ecology & Evolution, Moscow, Russia – Scale Worms
Phil Bush, Cayman Islands Department of Environment, Cayman Islands – General Assistance
***Dr. Dale Calder**, Royal Ontario Museum, Toronto, Canada – Hydroids
Dr. Luis F. Carrera-Parra, El Colegio de la Frontera Sur, Unidad Chetumal, Quintana Roo, México – Bobbit Worms
Dr. Kerry Clark, Florida Institute of Technology, Melbourne, FL – Sea Slugs
Dr. Charles E. Cutress, University of Puerto Rico, Mayaguez, PR – Anemones, Zoanthids, Corallimorphs
Dr. Sammy De Grave, Oxford Museum of Natural History , Oxford, UK – Shrimp
Anne DuPont, Delray Beach, FL – Sea Slugs
Dr. Kristian Fauchald, National Museum of Natural History, Smithsonian Institute, Washington, DC – Segmented Worms

Dr. Daphne Fautin, University Of Kansas, Lawrence, KS – Anemones, Zoanthids, Corallimorphs
Dr. Josh Feingold, Nova Southeastern University, Dania Beach, FL – General Assistance
John W. Forsythe, National Resource Center for Cephalopods, Galveston, TX – Cephalopods
Charles H.J.M. Fransen, National Museum of National History Naturalis, Leiden, The Netherlands – Shrimp
Dr. Lisa-ann Gershwin, University of California at Berkeley – Jellyfishes
Dr. D.I. Gibson, Natural History Museum, London, England – General Assistance
Dr. Ivan Goodbody, The University of the West Indies, Kingston, Jamaica – Tunicates
Dr. Joseph Goy, Harding University, Searcy, AR – Shrimp
Dr. Robert H. Gore, BIO-ECON, Inc., Naples, FL – Crustaceans
Dr. Ken Grange, National Institute of Water and Atmospheric Research, Nelson, New Zealand – Mollusks
Jeff Hamann, El Cajon, CA – Sea Slugs
Dr. Roger T. Hanlon, Marine Biological Laboratory, Woods Hole, MA – Cephalopods
Leslie Harris, Natural History Museum of Los Angeles County, Los Angeles, CA – Segmented Worms
Dr. Gordon L. Hendler, Natural History Museum of Los Angeles County, Los Angeles, CA – Echinoderms
Dr. Alexandra Hiller, Smithsonian Tropical Research Institute, Panama – Porcelain Crabs
Marlo F. Krisberg, letstalkseashells.com, Merritt Island, FL – Mollusks
Ronald Larson, US Fish and Wildlife Service, Klamath Falls, Oregon – Jellyfishes, Comb Jellies
Dr. Rafael Lemaitre, National Museum of Natural History, Smithsonian Institution, Washington, DC – Hermit Crabs
Dr. Marian K. Litvaitis, University of New Hampshire, Durham, NH – Flatworms
Dr. Felix Lorenz, www.OVULIDAE.com – Allied Cowries
Dr. Larry Madin, Woods Hole Oceanographic Institute, Woods Hole, MA – Hydromedusa
Dr. Christopher Mah, Smithsonian National Museum of Natural History, Washington, D.C.– Sea Stars
Dr. Raymond B. Manning, National Museum of Natural History, Smithsonian Institution, Washington, DC – Mantis Shrimp
Dr. Richard Mariscal, Florida State University, Tallahassee, FL – Anemones, Zoanthids, Corallimorphs
Dr. George I. Matsumoto, Monterey Bay Aquarium Research Institute, Moss Landing, CA – Comb Jellies
***Dr. Patsy A. McLaughlin**, Shannon Point Marine Center, Western Washington University, Anacortes, WA – Hermit Crabs
Dr. Charles G. Messing, NOVA University Oceanographic Center, Dania, FL – Echinoderms, General Reference
Dr. Claudia Mills, Friday Harbor Laboratories, University of Washington – Hydromedusa
Dr. Francoise Monniot, Muséum National d'Histoire Naturelle, Paris, France – Tunicates
Dr. Jon L. Norenburg, Smithsonian National Museum of Natural History, Washington, D.C. – Ribbon Worms
Dr. Hazel A. Oxenford, University of West Indies, St. Michael, Barbados, W.I. – General Assistance
***Dr. David L. Pawson**, National Museum of Natural History, Smithsonian Institution, Washington, DC – Echinoderms
***Thomas H. Perkins**, Florida Marine Research Institute, St. Petersburg, FL – Segmented Worms
Dr. Marian H. Pettibone, National Museum of Natural History, Smithsonian Institution, Washington, DC – Scale Worms
Dr. John F. Pilgra, Agnes Scott College, London,Decator, GA – Spoon Worms
***Dr. Shirley Pomponi**, Harbor Branch Oceanographic Institute, Ft. Pierce, FL – Sponges
Dr. Stephen Prudhoe, Natural History Museum, London, England – Flatworms
Dr. Philip Pugh, National Oceanographic Centre, United Kingdom – Siphonophores
Beatriz Yáñez Rivera, Universidad Nacional Autónoma de México, Unidad Académica Mazatlán, Sinaloa, México – Fire Worms
Dr. Clyde Roper, National Museum of Natural History, Smithsonian Institution, Washington, DC – Cephalopods
Dr. Bill Rudman, Australian Museum, Sydney – Opisthobranchs
Dr. Patricia Salazar-Silva, Instituto Tecnológico de Bahía de Banderas, Nayarit, México – Scale Worms
Dr. Guillermo San Martin, Universidad Autonóma de Madrid, Spain – Syllidae Worms
Dr. Scott Santagata, Post Campus of Long Island University, Brookville, NY – Phoronids
Dr. Shaila Van Sickle, Ft. Lewis State College, Durango, CO – Phonetics
Dr. Daniel Martin Sintes, Consejo Superior de Investigaciones Cientificas, Catalunya, Spain – Segmented Worms
Dr. Robert Van Syoc, California Academy of Sciences, San Francisco, CA – Barnacles
Dr. Angel Valdes, California State Polytechnic University, Pomona, CA – Sea Slugs
Dr. Nancy Voss, Rosenstiel School Of Marine Sciences, University of Miami, FL – Cephalopods
***Dr. Mary K. Wicksten**, Texas A & M University, College Station, TX – Crustaceans
Dr. Gary Williams, California Academy of Science, San Francisco, CA – Sea Pens
Dr. Judith E. Winston, Virginia Museum of Natural History, Martinsville, VA – Bryzoans
Dr. James B. Wood, Waikiki Aquarium, University of Hawaii-Manoa, Honolulu, HI – Cephalopods
Dr. Sven Zea, Universidad Nacional de Colombia, Centro de Estudios en Ciencias del Mar, Sede Caribe, Santa Marta, Colombia – Sponges
Dr. Russel L. Zimmer, University of Southern California, Los Angeles, CA – Phoronids

The authors made every effort to keep text and identifications accurate, however, we are sure a few errors crept in and they are our sole responsibility.

Photo Credits

Leopoldo Moro Abad, 222b; *Cindy Abgarian,* 39mr, 67bl, 69bl, 71mr, 106mr, 119ml, 120t, 121br, 123tr&br, 131br, 132br, 136b, 142br, 149tl, 155ml, 170ml, 174mr, 175m&br, 176bl, 181t, 182mr, 183tl&br, 187mr, 188tl, 193bl, 194bl, 197bl, 207ml,mr&br, 214ml, 224tr&bl, 232ml, 233br, 234t, 236bl, 237mr, 238ml, 254bl&br, 255t&ml, 273br; *Jose Alejandro Alvarez,* 113ml; *Mike Bacon,* 72mr, 105bl, 135mr, 148ml, 168bl, 240bl, 262ml, 263tl; *Marjorie Bank,* 55br, 156ml, 158ml, 184br; *Bud Barr,* 45br, 112t; *Cor Bosman,* 220ml; *Jim Brandon,* 70b, 103br, 111t, 187br, 229tl; *Frank Burek,* 221mr; *John Carter,* 123tr, 175bl; *Chuck Catlett,* 110t, 126t; *Jim Chambers,* 103m, 209tr; *Florent Charpin,* 109b, 246br; *Jenfu Cheng,* 72ml; *Robyn Churchill,* 95bl, 218ml, 238bl; *Rick Coleman,* 134bl; *Susan Coleman,* 233tr; *Carol Cox,* 21ml, 107bl, 114ml&br, 116b, 146br, 176m, 188tr&bl, 213tr, 242mr; *Alan Cressler,* 246tl; *James Dailey,* 122br; *Sarah Davies,* 270bl; *Helmut Debelius,* 239b; *Peter deGraaf,* 18mr, 22tr, 24br, 39br, 41ml&mr, 105br, 122ml, 126mr, 159ml, 222mr, 240ml, 270tl; *Jonathon DePelos,* 226tr; *Deb Devers,* 68bl, 107mr, 118bl, 131ml, 152ml; *Anne DuPont,* 67br, 68t&br, 69t, 70ml&tl, 72br, 73m&br, 87ml, 88ml, 90mr, 169mr, 170tr&mr, 172tr, 178t, 180tl&bl, 181mr, 183tr, 189tl, 190mr&bl, 191mr, 193tr&mr, 194br, 195bl&br, 196tl,tr&br, 198br, 204tr&bl, 205br, 208ml&b, 211b, 218bl, 220tl,bl&br, 221ml, 229br, 232bl, 238t, 240br, 241br, 246tr, 247bl, 262mr, 267bl; *Sandra Edwards,* 94br, 285bl; *Josh Feingold,* 162tl; *Joao Feitosa,* 135b; *Bill Frank,* 223ml; *Ryan Frimel,* 226br; *Steven Frink,* 255b; *Dr. John Forsythe,* 254ml; *Jim Garin,* 86bl, 223tl&tr; *Valeri Gast,* 70tr, 104ml, 117tl, 159bl, 199tl; *Johanetta Gordijn,* 118tr; *Gretchen L. Grammer,* 213br; *Michael Greenmeier,* 221tl; *Ray Haberman,* 29br, 73tr, 104mr, 123tl, 142bl, 146bl, 225br, 227tr, 229m, 236tl, 266bl, 270tr, 274mr, 278mr, 284row4r; *David Hall,* 125tl, 212t, 267t; *Jeff Hamann,* 193tl, 210tr&ml, 211m, 216m&br, 218br, 219tr, 220tr&mr, 222t&ml, 224tl, 227tl, 234mr; *Dr. Roger Hanlon,* 248bl&br, 253br; *Larry Harris,* 205ml; *Gordon Hendler,* 274b, 282ml; *Alicia Hermosillo,* 203tl,m&br, 204ml&mr, 219mr, 230tl, 237t; *Dave Holladay,* 181ml, 206br, 208tr, 216tr, 275tl; *Linda Ianniello,* 117br, 134tl, 184tl, 192ml, 202t&ml, 212ml, 214tr, 217ml, 218mr, 221tr, 224m, 225ml,mr&bl, 226m&bl, 230tr, 231t, 234ml, 235mr, 236tr, 237ml, 239ml, 249tr; *Jim Jeup,* 262t&b; *Kevin Johnson,* 213ml; *Douglas A. Kahle,* 176tl, 215br, 228ml; *Jim King,* 268ml; *Steve Kovacs,* 117bl, 118br, 224br, 225tl; *Frank Krasovec,* 174bl, 195ml; *Marlo F. Krisberg,* 193br; *Marge Lawson,* 43ml, 94bl, 172m, 216tl; *Diane Leazenby,* 115tr; *Tom Lindner,* 17mr, 20tr, 28t&br, 81bl, 129ml, 130ml, 169ml, 200bl, 238br, 241ml, 261mr, 285ml; *Robert Lipe,* 170bl, 171br, 172tl&bl, 179br, 182t, 185ml&mr; *Barry Lipman,* 144mr; *Jim Lyle,* 170tl, 209m, 211mr, 266t; *Donald MacKinnon,* 17t; *Ken Marks,* 50tl, 69mr, 89tr, 108m, 147br, 169br, 189m, 237b, 281bl; *Andrew Martinez,* 24t, 132ml, 168br, 171tl, 180m&br, 182ml, 232mr, 243t, 253t, 278br, 282br; *Fred McConnaughey,* 125mr, 130mr; *Scott McDuff,* 145b, 210br, 225tr, 284row4l; *Greg McFall,* 21t, 159br, 215bl, 284row4r; *David McRee,* 137ml; *Suzan Meldonian,* 59ml, 138ml, 221br, 245br; *John Miller,* 265m, 274t, 278t; *Ryan Moody,* 56br; *Doug Moyer,* 61bl; *Ellen Muller,* 39tr, 43mr, 56br, 73tl, 123ml, 133br, 145ml, 152bl, 171ml, 181br, 184ml, 212b, 217b, 223b; *Brent Murdoch,* 67mr; *Geri Murphy,* 5t, 285mr; *Randy Newman,* 148bl, 149tr; *Jo O'Keefe,* 129ml, 132ml; *Michael Ormiston,* 138b; *Doug Perrine,* 144b, 248ml, 251bl, 269ml; *Lee Peterson,* 105tr, 280t; *Mike Phelan,* 201mr; *Marina Poddubetskaia,* 209bl&br; *Larry Polster,* 16bl, 19bl&br, 21ml, 154bl; *Sharon Pool,* 39bl; *Steve Powell,* 239mr; *Diane Randolph,* 142mr; *Brian Ricker,* 213bl; *Susan Riegner,* 105mr; *Eric Riesch,* 15ml, 69br, 113t, 116t, 127br, 136t, 143bl, 156mr, 157tl&br, 194tr, 201t, 249ml, 250ml, 272mr, 279tl; *John Roach,* 155mr; *Dr. Carolina Rogers,* 254ml; *Jeff Rotman,* 269tl; *Lazaro Ruda,* 210bl; *Rob Ruzicka,* 26tl; *Wolfram Sander,* 16t, 152ml, 269tr; *Geoff Schultz,* 20mr, 30br, 57t; *Dr. Gus Schwartz,* 59mr; *Paul Selden,* 17br, 23m, 49bl, 139t, 276mr; *Nancy Sheridan,* 219tl; *Aaron Smith,* 141ml; *David Snyder,* 133mr, 281mr; *Jason Spitz,* 118tl, 141ml, 171bl; *Stephen Spotte,* 110ml, 117tr; *Sipke Stapert,* 125tl, 142ml; *Walter Stearns,* 265t, 267mr; *Matt Sullivan,* 88mr, 145ml, 146ml, 172mr, 195ml, 214tl&br, 217mr, 231ml, 250mr; *Graeme Teague,* 267ml; *Bill Tipton,* 58b, 130t, 135t&ml; *Judy Townsend,* 87t, 89br, 128mr, 129tr, 134tr, 149bl, 154bl, 159mr, 188ml, 202mr, 203bl, 214mr, 226tl, 234b, 235bl, 236ml&mr, 242tr, 245bl; *Everett Turner,* 67ml, 71bl, 72mr, 89bl, 91tl, 94ml, 116ml, 139mr, 151bl&br, 152tr, 153tl, 159t, 171tr&mr, 173bl, 174ml&br, 176br, 177ml, 179bl, 183bl, 184bl, 185bl&br, 187t, 191ml, 193ml, 194mr, 200ml&mr, 208mr, 210mr, 211tl, 212mr, 231br, 233m&bl, 236mr, 241ml, 243mr, 246bl, 247tr,mr&br, 252br, 254tr, 269mr, 271m; *Louis Usie,* 70br, 112mr; *Peter Vermeul,* 219ml; *Patrick Weir,* 117m; *Rudy Whitworth,* 16br, 18tr, 95tl&tr, 119br, 122tr, 191tr, 196mr, 197tl; *Keri Wilk,* 67t, 68ml&mr, 71tl, 72tl, 73bl, 80tr, 81ml&mr, 82bl&br, 91b, 94mr, 95m, 96b, 104bl, 105tl, 107t, 113bl, 114mr, 116mr, 119mr, 122bl, 123bl, 127mr, 128br, 131t, 147ml, 148mr, 149br, 150mr&b, 154tl, 157ml&mr, 175tl, 177mr, 178ml, 181bl, 187ml, 192bl&br, 195t, 196bl, 197ml&br, 199bl, 202b, 207bl, 209tl, 210tl, 211tr, 216bl, 217t, 221bl, 223mr, 227m, 228mr, 229bl, 230b, 231mr, 232t, 235t&ml, 238mr, 239tl, 260t, 267br, 268mr, 273bl, 284row3r; *Kris Wilk,* 132tl, 260mr; *Bryan Willy,* 251t, 264mr; *Tom Wineman,* 186ml; *Peter Wirtz,* 43tr; *Lawson Wood,* 177t; the remaining photographs were taken by the authors.

About the Authors

Ned DeLoach & Paul Humann

Paul Humann and Ned DeLoach published their first marine life identification field guide *Reef Fish Identification—Florida, Caribbean, Bahamas,* in 1989. Since then the pair have published eight more guides for fishes and invertebrates around the world. In 1990, they co-founded the Reef Environmental Education Foundation (REEF), an active group of volunteer divers who have built the world's largest fish sighting database, housing more than 175,000 marine wildlife surveys.

Paul began photographing underwater in 1964. In 1972 he left his law practice in Wichita, Kansas to become the owner/operator of the *Cayman Diver,* the Caribbean's first successful live-aboard dive cruiser. He sold the vessel in 1979 to devote more time to travel, photography and writing. When not on the road, Paul lives in Davie, Florida.

Ned moved from his childhood home in West Texas to Florida so that he would be able to do what he loves best—dive. In 1971 he completed his first diving guide to the state, *Diving Guide to Underwater Florida,* which is now in its 11th edition. Through the 1970s and 80s, he was active in Florida's cave diving community, and dive/travel writing. Ned and his wife Anna live in Jacksonville, Florida.

Les Wilk

As an avid diver and underwater photographer, Les Wilk has been studying and documenting marine life for more than three decades. His passion for marine creatures is very much a family affair. Les along with his wife Any and sons, Kris and Keri, have made dozens of extended trips to Florida and the Caribbean to photograph marine species, and spent untold hours comparing the images with scientific literature. He is co-owner of ReefNet, Inc. and the content developer for the company's electronic field guides to Caribbean fishes. A nuclear physicist, Les works and resides near Toronto, Canada.

Authors' Note

Too often in the past, the underwater naturalist's enthusiasm was tempered by his inability to identify the many unfamiliar life forms encountered on the reef. This frustrating situation stemmed from the fact that published scientific descriptions, the majority completed well before the advent of scuba, relied on laboratory examinations of preserved specimens dredged from the depths. Such studies found it impractical to take into account colors and markings displayed by creatures in the wild. To obtain correct identification, it was often necessary for the authors to collect photographed specimens for laboratory examinations by specialists. This process has, for the first time, made it possible to identify many invertebrates by their visual characteristics.

As divers are becoming more conscious of the reef's natural history, marine biologists are also spending more time underwater. Both groups understand the importance of bridging the gap between laboratory taxonomy and field identification. *Reef Creature Identification* represents a collaboration between the scientific community and underwater photographers.

Even though an unknown animal can't be given species status from a photograph, an image does establish that a new species exists and indicates where it might be found. Photography is also beneficial for recording and monitoring a region's biodiversity as well as confirming a species' range extension, information essential for establishing sound management practices.

Ten Identification Groups
Common & Proper Phylum Names

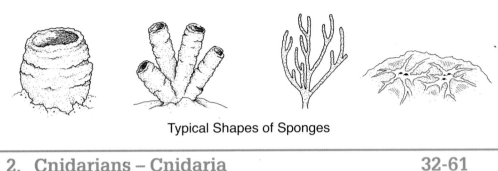

Typical Shapes of Sponges

Sea Anemones   Zoanthids   Corallimorphs   Tube-dwelling Anemones

Hydroids   Hydromedusae   Siphonophores

Jellyfishes   Box Jellies

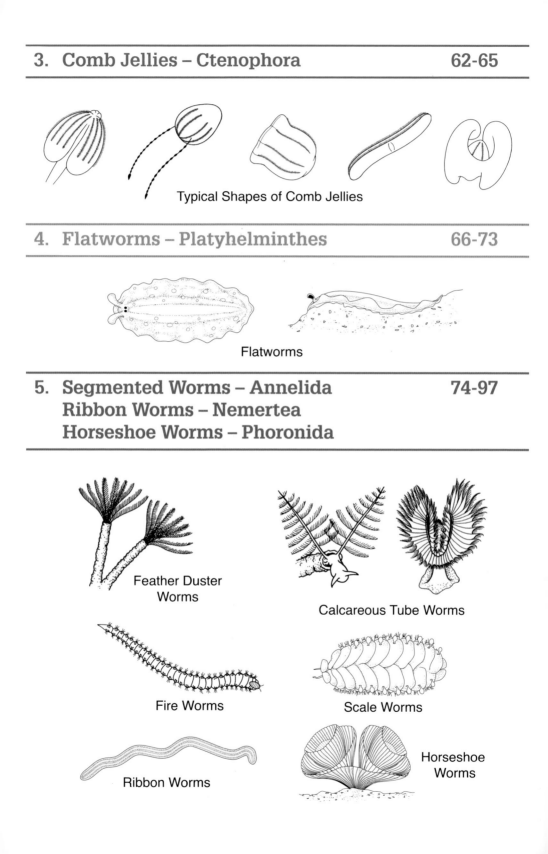

3. Comb Jellies – Ctenophora

Typical Shapes of Comb Jellies

4. Flatworms – Platyhelminthes

Flatworms

5. Segmented Worms – Annelida
Ribbon Worms – Nemertea
Horseshoe Worms – Phoronida

Feather Duster
Worms

Calcareous Tube Worms

Fire Worms

Scale Worms

Ribbon Worms

Horseshoe
Worms

6. Crustaceans – Arthropoda 98-159

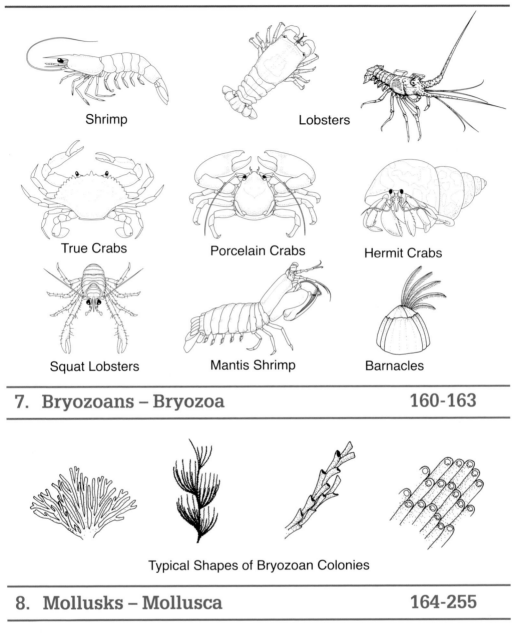

Shrimp

Lobsters

True Crabs

Porcelain Crabs

Hermit Crabs

Squat Lobsters

Mantis Shrimp

Barnacles

7. Bryozoans – Bryozoa 160-163

Typical Shapes of Bryozoan Colonies

8. Mollusks – Mollusca 164-255

Snails

Headshield Slugs

Seahares

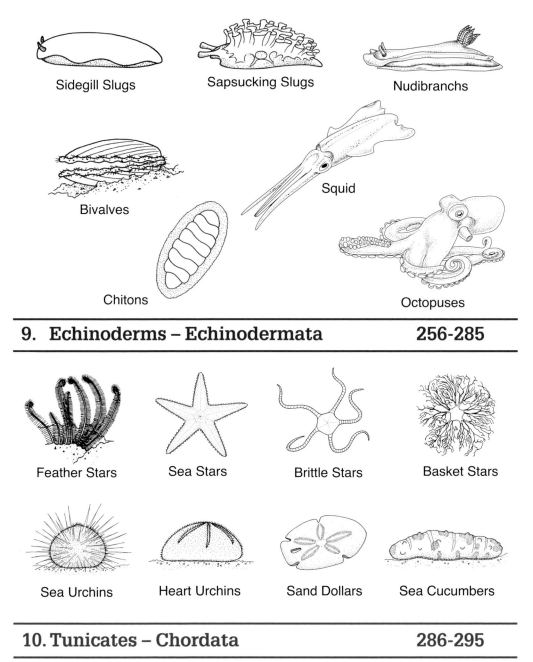

Sidegill Slugs

Sapsucking Slugs

Nudibranchs

Bivalves

Squid

Chitons

Octopuses

9. Echinoderms – Echinodermata 256-285

Feather Stars

Sea Stars

Brittle Stars

Basket Stars

Sea Urchins

Heart Urchins

Sand Dollars

Sea Cucumbers

10. Tunicates – Chordata 286-295

Typical Shapes of Tunicate Colonies

Planktonic
Tunicates

How to Use This Book

Over one million species of animals have been described in the Animal Kingdom. Of these, approximately seven percent are single-celled animals. The remainder are multicellular animals that fall into two large groups: the vertebrates – animals with backbones, and the invertebrates – animals without backbones. Vertebrates make up only four to five percent of the multicellular species but, in the sea, they include significant animals such as fishes, dolphins, whales, seals, turtles and, of course, divers. The remaining and overwhelming majority, approximately 88 percent, are invertebrates. In the sea these include many commonly known groups, like corals, sponges, jellyfishes, shrimp, crabs, snails, nudibranchs, octopuses and sea stars.

This book primarily focuses on the identification of marine invertebrates inhabiting shallow water reefs and adjacent habitats in Florida, the Bahamas, and Caribbean that are most likely encountered by divers with the exception of the animals commonly known as coral, which are included in a separate volume.

Order of Identifications

Identifications begin with an animal's major scientific classification group known as a phylum (plural: phyla). A brief explanation of the predominant anatomical features that distinguish the animals in each phylum is presented at the beginning of each of the ten Phylum/Identification Groups. It is important to note that although organisms within a phylum share basic anatomical similarities, some appear distinctly different from their relatives. As standard practice, phyla are presented from the least complex organisms advancing to the more complex, also considered the basic order of evolution. The animals within a phylum are classified further into increasingly smaller groupings, such as class, order, family and genus, which, for the most part have been displayed together within this text.

Names

Information about each species begins with the animal's common name – that used by the general public. Generally the scientific community does not favor the use of common names because many animals are known by several common names leading to confusion. The common names used in this book generally resulted from research of published material about the species and web usage. If more than one common name was found, which was often the case, the most frequently used name was usually chosen. If no common name could be found an English equivalent of the scientific species name was normally selected.

In addition to the common name, the two-part scientific name is given in italics. The first word (always capitalized) is the genus. The genus name is given to a group of animals with very similar physiological characteristics. The second word (never capitalized) is the species. A widely held definition characterizes species as animals that are sexually compatible and produce fertile offspring. Scientific names, traditionally rooted in Latin and Greek, are universal, avoiding the confusion of multiple common names and translations in various languages.

Typically, members of a genus tend to have similar visual features. As an identification aid, an attempt has been made to place similar appearing species in the same genus close together, as well as placing similar appearing genera within a family on adjoining pages. In many cases, the original scientific description of an animal was based on microscopic or obscure features not readily observable in life or photographs, a factor often making visual identification difficult or impossible. When an identification is probable, but not certain, "Identification tentative." has been inserted in the text. Occasionally "cf." appears between the genus and the species name, this indicates that the animal is very similar to the species, but unlikely the same.

Occasionally in place of the common name either the word "UNDESCRIBED" or "UNDETERMINED" appears. UNDESCRIBED means that the animal has yet to be formally described in scientific literature. UNDETERMINED indicates that the species may have been described, but that it is impossible to determine an identification from the photograph. If only the genus of an animal is known, its scientific genus name will be given followed by "sp." indicating the lack of a species name. If the genus is not known the entire area is left blank, and the closest identification for that particular animal will be the family listed just under where the genus and species name should go. If there is more than a single unknown species from the same genus, "sp." is followed by a numeral, such as "*Doto* sp.1, *Doto* sp.2". The numerical order of unidentified species in a genus is arbitrary, and only relates to this book.

For quick reference, both common and scientific group names, color coded for each Phylum/Identification Group, have been placed at the top of each identification page indicating the animal group or groups appearing on the two-page spread – common names are placed on left pages, and scientific on the right. The scientific headers often consist of multiple group names separated by a "/", with the phylum name always listed at the far right, preceded, to its left, by lesser group names. When multiple families appear on a spread, the common name of the first family to appear is listed at the far left of the left-hand page followed to the right by subsequent families.

Size

An animal's estimated largest size appears under a species' common name, written in both centimeters "cm", which has been converted and rounded off to inches "in." to the right. If not otherwise specified, sizes refer to an organism's overall length or width.

Descriptive Information, Distribution and Abundance

A species description is given for each animal. This, as a rule, lists visual details used to augment a photograph for identification purposes. The information lists subtle, but often overlooked facets of an animal's anatomy, markings or color. It might also emphasize details not shown clearly in the photograph, or describe variations not shown in the identification image(s). At times portions of descriptive text appear in bold type indicating an important diagnostic key that will help differentiate an animal from a similar-appearing species.

In cases where a species' habitat provides a clue for identification purposes, such as a commensal relationship between the species and a specific host, or assists in locating a particular species underwater, this information has been included. When a species is represented by multiple photographs, reference in the text to a particular image is indicated with bold initials: **T**-top, **M**-middle, **B**-bottom, **L**-left, **R**-right. As an example, a photograph appearing on the top right of a page is indicated with **TR**.

Distribution (range) among species varies widely from endemic organisms that live only within a confined geographical region to circumtropical species that inhabit warm waters around the globe. Although this text only list a species' distribution in Florida, Bahamas, Caribbean, and in appropriate circumstances the Gulf of Mexico, a given species' range might extend outside this region, such as south to Brazil or north along the eastern seaboard to the Carolinas or New York. In a few instances, species are circumtropical meaning that they might be encountered in water around the equator.

In many cases, information about an animal's range is incomplete, or in the instance of a rare or recently discovered species, known only from one or a few collected or photographed specimens. In circumstances where a species is known only from the image displayed in this text, the distribution reads: "Known from" followed by the country of the photograph's origin. Typically the distribution information is preceded by an animal's relative abundance: Abundant, Common, Occasional, Uncommon or Rare. This rather ambiguous data often varies significantly in both time and space. For instance a species might be rare in one area of its range while, at the same time, common in another. Such distribution patterns also might change significantly over the years.

IDENTIFICATION GROUP 1
Phylum Porifera
(Por-IF-er-uh / L. hole-bearing)
Sponges

Sponges are the simplest of the multicellular animals. The individual cells display a considerable degree of independence, and form no true tissue layers or organs. However, depending on a cell's location within the sponge, they do perform somewhat specialized functions. A sponge's surface is perforated with numerous small holes called **incurrent pores** or ostia. Water is drawn into the sponge through these pores and pumped through the interior by the beating of whiplike extensions on the cells called flagella. As water passes through the sponge, food and oxygen are filtered out. The water exits into the body's interior cavity and out the animal's one or more large **excurrent openings** or oscula.

Sponges come in many sizes, colors and shapes. Some are quite small, less than half an inch across, while the Giant Barrel Sponge may attain a height of over six feet. Their colors range from drab grays and browns to bright reds, oranges, yellows, greens, and violets. The shape of what can be considered a typical sponge resembles a vase. However, growth patterns vary tremendously. Those with one large body opening form bowls, barrels and tubes. Sponges with multiple body openings may form irregular masses, or shapes like ropes, candles, branching horns or, in the case of encrusting sponges, take the shapes of what they overgrow.

Although sponges come in many forms, they can usually be recognized as a group by their excurrent openings that are generally large and distinct. Another key is their lack of any evident movement. Nearly all animals react with an obvious protective movement when approached or touched, but sponges show no reaction when disturbed. Sponges may occasionally be confused with tunicates (Identification Group 10), which often have similar-appearing body openings and grow in comparable patterns, shapes and colors. Tunicates, however, are highly evolved animals, having a nervous system and relatively complex muscles that can rapidly close their body openings.

While sponges are easy to recognize as a group, many individual species are difficult to identify. This is because the same species may grow in different shapes and patterns, which is the consequence of several factors, including age, location, depth and water movement. Color is often another poor clue to identification. Variations of color within the same species may result from the water chemistry, depth, light conditions and the presence of algae living in symbiosis with the sponge. For these reasons, correct identification of many species can only be made in the laboratory, by microscopic examination of the tissue or the shape of tiny interior structural elements called spicules. Fortunately, a number of the more common sponges found on reefs grow in relatively consistent patterns, shapes and colors, making visual identification possible.

For the convenience of visual reference this Identification Group is arranged by shape rather than scientific classification. The order of these shape/categories: tubes, vases and barrels, balls, irregular masses, ropes, encrusting, boring, and finally, the calcareous sponges.

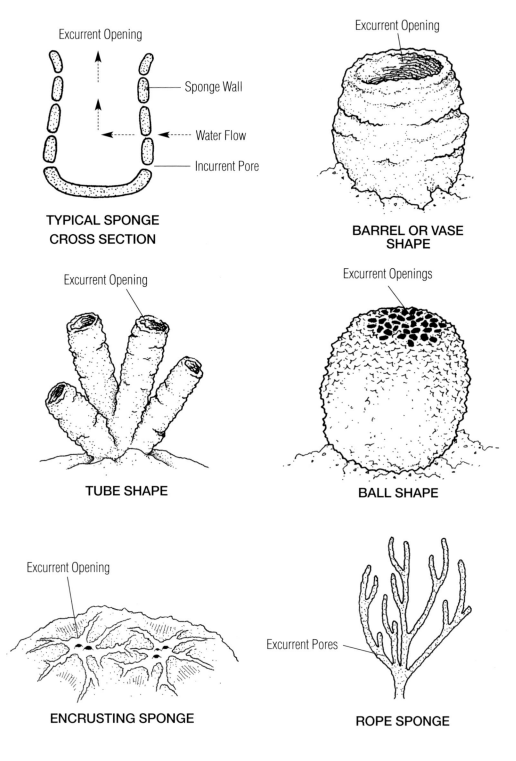

TYPICAL SPONGE CROSS SECTION

Excurrent Opening

Sponge Wall

Water Flow

Incurrent Pore

BARREL OR VASE SHAPE

Excurrent Opening

TUBE SHAPE

Excurrent Opening

BALL SHAPE

Excurrent Openings

ENCRUSTING SPONGE

Excurrent Opening

ROPE SPONGE

Excurrent Pores

Aiolochroia crassa

Tube Sponges – Aplysinidae

SIZE: to 45 cm (18 in.)

ID: Clusters of yellow, purple, orange or olive green tubes fan out from a common base; stippled exterior occasionally with fiberlike projections; yellow interior; occasionally grow in fan shape in areas with consistent current. Coral reefs and walls from 20 to 80 ft. Abundant Caribbean; common Bahamas; occasional S. Florida.

ROUGH TUBE SPONGE   *Oceanapia bartschi*

SIZE: to 120 cm (4 ft.)   Tube Sponges – Phloeodictyidae

ID: Solitary gray to black tubes, globes or barrels; thick-walled rough exterior with numerous projections; thin collar rises slightly from openings; heavily encrusted. Walls and ledges from 60 to 130 ft. Occasional Bahamas, Caribbean; rare Florida.

CONVOLUTED BARREL SPONGE   *Aplysina lacunosa*

SIZE: to 1 m (3 ft.)   Barrel Sponges – Aplysinidae

ID: Form into thick-walled barrels or clusters of tubes; deep grooves with greenish ridges and yellow valleys; tubes taper toward base; surface often encrusted with debris. Lagoons, reefs and sand. Occasional Bahamas, Caribbean.

STOVEPIPE SPONGE
Aplysina archeri
Tube Sponges – Aplysinidae
SIZE: to 2 m (6 ft.)
ID: Solitary or clusters of long slender lavender, brown or tan soft-walled tubes often taper toward base; interior paler often cream-colored. Reefs and walls from 50 to 100 ft. Common to occasional Bahamas, Caribbean.

BRANCHLET SPONGE   *Aplysina insularis*
SIZE: to 50 cm (20 in.)   Tube Sponges – Aplysinidae
ID: Short to elongated yellowish tubes crowned with irregular projections (branchlets); branchlets can be longer than tubes; typically rough, convoluted surface. Patch reefs to 50 ft. Occasional W. Florida, Bahamas, E. and S. Caribbean.

GOBLET SPONGE   *Aplysina bathyphila*
SIZE: to 30 cm (12 in.)   Tube Sponges – Aplysinidae
ID: White to tan or brown goblet-shaped tube often with extremely narrow base; small central opening. Deep reef slopes and caves from 70 to 500 ft. Uncommon Bahamas, Jamaica and Cuba in Caribbean.

Tube & Barrel Sponges

YELLOW TUBE SPONGE
Aplysina fistularis
Tube Sponges – Aplysinidae
SIZE: to 120 cm (4 ft.)
ID: Yellow to orange solitary tubes form clusters; soft convoluted surface. In shallow water typically form clusters of shorter tubes often with branchlets; in deep water more frequently solitary tubes without branchlets. Reefs, walls and sand from 15 to 100 ft. Abundant to common Bahamas, Caribbean; occasional Florida.

TUBULATE SPONGE   *Agelas tubulata*
SIZE: to 46 cm (18 in.)   Tube Sponges – Agelasidae
ID: Smooth (occasionally pitted or with grooves) surfaced pink to orange or brown tubes cluster from a common base; tube walls often partially fused; wide openings with rims of lighter color. Usually below 40 ft. Occasional S. Florida, Bahamas, Caribbean.

BROWN TUBE SPONGE
Agelas conifera
Tube Sponges – Agelasidae
SIZE: to 1 m (3 ft.)
ID: Highly variable growth patterns; typically brown, tan, pink, yellow or green clusters of short fused tubes, also form erratic shapes like moose antlers or octopus arms; numerous openings encircled with a lighter shade; occasionally form clusters of independent tubes arising from a single base, or solitary trumpets; surface usually smooth but might be pitted with darker zoanthids. Typically inhabit protected crevices of reefs and walls from 35 to 130 ft. Common to occasional Florida, Bahamas, Caribbean.

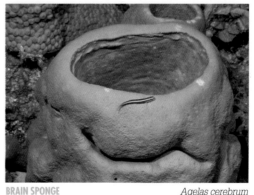

BROWN CLUSTER TUBE SPONGE   *Agelas wiedenmyeri*
SIZE: to 7.5 cm (3 in.)   Tube Sponges – Agelasidae
ID: Cluster of small smooth brown tubes growing from a common mass; tubes often irregular in shape and may appear pinched. Reef tops, often around bases of coral heads to 75 ft. Occasional Florida, Bahamas, Caribbean.

BRAIN SPONGE   *Agelas cerebrum*
SIZE: to 30 cm (12 in.)   Tube Sponges – Agelasidae
ID: Solitary or small clusters of vase-shaped tubes in gray, pink, lavender, green or tan; deep grooves meander throughout the body. Tubulate Sponge [previous page] may also have grooves but only cover portion of tubes. Reefs to 60 ft. Occasional Bahamas, Caribbean.

17

STRAWBERRY VASE SPONGE *Mycale laxissima*
SIZE: to 30 cm (12 in.) Vase Sponges – Mycalidae
ID: Brilliant red to orange cup-shaped sponge with rough exterior; solitary or form small clusters; translucent collar rims openings. Reefs and walls from 35 to 130 ft. Occasional S. Florida, Bahamas, Caribbean.

BRANCHING VASE SPONGE *Callyspongia vaginalis*
SIZE: to 1 m (3 ft.) Vase Sponges – Callyspongiidae
ID: Thin vase-shaped gray to lavender tubes with irregular conical projections; form clusters with a few or as many as 30 tubes; in current prone areas may also grow in fan shapes. Reefs to 65 ft. Common S. Florida, Bahamas, Caribbean.

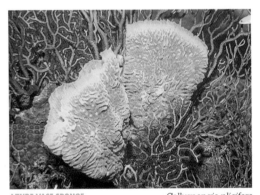

AZURE VASE SPONGE *Callyspongia plicifera*
SIZE: to 45 cm (18 in.) Vase Sponges – Callyspongiidae
ID: Pink to purple or fluorescent blue vase-shaped sponges with rough exterior formed by convoluted ridges and valleys; solitary or small groups. Reefs and walls from 20 to 75 ft. Common to occasional S. Florida, Bahamas, Caribbean.

PINK VASE SPONGE *Niphates digitalis*
SIZE: to 30 cm (12 in.) Vase Sponges – Niphatidae
ID: Pink to blue or gray vases or short tubes with rough exteriors; openings rimmed with spines connected by translucent membrane. Reefs from 25 to 75 ft. Occasional S. Florida, Bahamas, Caribbean.

BROWN BOWL SPONGE
SIZE: to 45 cm (18 in.)
ID: Brown to reddish brown bowls often forming irregular, incomplete shapes; may encrust substrate around base; hard rough texture. Reefs, walls and rubble from 35 to 100 ft. Occasional S. Florida, Bahamas, Caribbean.

Cribrochalina vasculum
Vase Sponges – Niphatidae

GIANT BARREL SPONGE
Xestospongia muta
Barrel Sponges – Petrosiidae
SIZE: to 2 m (6 ft.)

ID: Huge barrel-shaped sponge gray to brown or reddish brown; hard deeply grooved exterior with jagged rims; generally solitary but often with one or two smaller individuals around base. Reef slopes from 50 to 130 ft. Although sturdy, rims can be easily damaged. Three- to four-foot specimens estimated to be 100 to 200 years old; the largest specimens have been estimated to be more than 2000 years old making the species one of the longest-lived animals on Earth. Common to occasional S. Florida, Bahamas, Caribbean.

Barrel Sponges

NETTED BARREL SPONGE   *Verongula gigantea*
SIZE: to 1½ m (5 ft.)   Barrel Sponges – Aplysinidae
ID: Large barrel-shaped sponge with distinct raised netlike texture;
green, yellow-green to greenish brown; smooth light yellow interior
pitted with excurrent pores. Reefs from 35 to 130 ft. Occasional
Bahamas, Caribbean; rare S. Florida.

LEATHERY BARREL SPONGE   *Geodia neptuni*
SIZE: to 75 cm (2½ ft.)   Barrel Sponges – Geodiidae
ID: Squatty barrel or vase-shaped gray to brown sponge; hard
leathery walls covered with large deep pits with rounded edges;
yellowish interior. Reefs from 40 to 100 ft. Common S. Florida,
Bahamas, Caribbean.

TOUCH-ME-NOT SPONGE
Neofibularia nolitangere
Barrel Sponges –
Desmacellidae
SIZE: to 120 cm (4 ft.)
ID: Massive dark brown
thick-walled sponge with
lumpy feltlike surface; grow
in a variety of irregular
shapes; interior has many
variably-sized openings. Often
home to numerous tiny white
Sponge Worms, *Haplosyllis*
cf. *spongicola* and Yellowline
and Shortstripe Gobies in
genus *Gobiosoma*. Contact
with bare skin can cause
stinging rash. Latin name,
nolitangere, means "do-not-
touch." Reefs and slopes
from 10 to 130 ft. Abundant
to common S. Florida,
Bahamas, Caribbean.

BELL SPONGE
Ircinia campana
Barrel Sponge – Irciniidae
SIZE: to 50 cm (20 in.)
ID: Tough fleshy barrel to vase-shaped sponge with convoluted surface covered with conical bumps; thin rims; colors vary from pinkish to purplish brown, reddish brown or brown. Abundant to occasional S. Florida, Caribbean; also Gulf of Mexico

LOGGERHEAD SPONGE
Spheciospongia vesparium
Barrel Sponges – Clionaidae
SIZE: to 150 cm (5 ft.)
ID: Squatty barrels or various irregular-shapes with hard leathery convoluted surfaces and flattened or rounded tops; shallow central depression with numerous excurrent openings; shades of gray to dark brown or charcoal; often covered with sediment. Occasionally eaten by Hawksbill Turtles. Hard inshore bottoms from 15 to 60 ft. Common Florida, Bahamas, Caribbean.

BLACK BALL SPONGE *Ircinia strobilina*
SIZE: to 45 cm (18 in.) Ball Sponges – Irciniidae
ID: Ball or cake-shaped with one or more shallow depressions clustered with excurrent openings; gray to black with rough surface of raised conical bumps often with white tips. Reefs and hard bottoms from 10 to 75 ft. Common Florida, Bahamas, Caribbean.

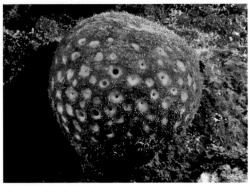

STINKER SPONGE *Ircinia felix*
SIZE: to 30 cm (12 in.) Ball Sponges – Irciniidae
ID: Form domes, encrust or branch; typically with hexagonal surface design; gray to bluish gray with numerous small excurrent openings. Calm shallows, seagrass and patch reefs from 3 to 65 ft. Common Florida, Bahamas, Caribbean.

ORANGE BALL SPONGES *Cinachyrella* spp.
SIZE: to 20 cm (8 in.) Ball Sponges – Tetillidae
ID: Half dozen similar appearing species in genus form small rounded yellow balls; evenly pitted with small yellow excurrent openings; occasionally encrusting. Inshore to deep reefs and hard bottoms from 3 to 180 ft. Common Florida, Bahamas, Caribbean.

DARK VOLCANO SPONGE *Svenzea zeai*
SIZE: to 1 m (3 ft.) Irregular Sponges – Scopalinidae
ID: Reddish brown to gray or black mass with lobes, branched or encrust substrate; smooth surface sometime pitted with flat or raised excurrent openings. Shallow hard bottoms, seagrass and reefs from 2 to 60 ft. Occasional S. Florida, Bahamas, Caribbean.

PITTED SPONGE *Verongula rigida*
SIZE: to 35 cm (14 in.) Irregular Sponges – Aplysinidae
ID: Brown to tan mass of lobes, or clusters of short cones or tubes; pit and ridges form honeycomb texture; excurrent openings often lighter color. Reefs from 30 to 75 ft. Common S. Florida, Bahamas, Caribbean.

ORANGE ELEPHANT EAR SPONGE *Agelas clathrodes*
SIZE: to 2 m (6 ft.) Irregular Sponges – Agelasidae
ID: Orange massive rubbery sponge riddled with rounded and elongate openings (similar Citron Sponge [next] without elongate openings); form huge mounds, fans or encrustations. Reefs and walls from 35 to 135 ft. Occasional S. Florida, Bahamas, Caribbean.

CITRON SPONGE
Agelas citrina
Irregular Sponges – Agelasidae
SIZE: to 2 m (6 ft.)
ID: Soft pink, tan or orange sponge with irregular lobes covered with bumps (similar Orange Elephant Ear Sponge [previous] lacks bumps and have elongate openings). Reefs and walls below 40 ft. Occasional Bahamas, S. and W. Caribbean.

FIRE SPONGE *Tedania ignis*
SIZE: to 30 cm (12 in.) Irregular Sponges – Tedaniidae
ID: Irregular orange to red mass with scattered cone-shaped projections tipped with excurrent openings. Contact causes stinging rash. Lagoons, seagrass, rubble and patch reefs from 1 to 35 ft. Common Florida, Bahamas, Caribbean.

LUMPY OVERGROWING SPONGE *Desmapsamma anchorata*
SIZE: to 40 cm (16 in.) Irregular Sponges – Desmacididae
ID: Soft pink mass often with branches and numerous raised excurrent openings; orange interior. Reefs from 15 to 75 ft. Common Florida, Bahamas, Caribbean.

Rope Sponges

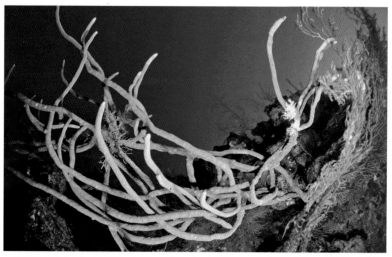

Aplysina cauliformis
Rope Sponges – Aplysinidae
SIZE: to 3 m (10 ft.)
ID: Long smooth ropelike purple, yellow or lavender branches curve upward toward ends; small excurrent openings with slightly raised rims form straight rows (Similar Scattered Pore Rope Sponge [next] openings scattered along branches.) Deep slopes and walls from 40 to 130 ft. Common Bahamas, Caribbean; occasional S. Florida.

SCATTERED PORE ROPE SPONGE   *Aplysina fulva*
SIZE: to 3 m (10 ft.)   Rope Sponges – Aplysinidae
ID: Long ropelike brown, greenish yellow to green or purple branches occasionally forming massive bushlike structures; small scattered excurrent openings. Slopes and walls from 10 to 120 ft. Common Bahamas, Caribbean; occasional S. Florida.

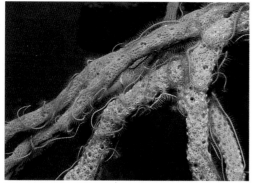

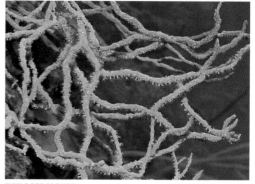

LAVENDER ROPE SPONGE *Niphates erecta*
SIZE: to 120 cm (4 ft.) Rope Sponges – Niphatidae
ID: Long ropelike gray to lavender or pinkish branches either smooth or spiky; flush excurrent openings scattered along branches. Often covered with zoanthids and brittle stars. Reefs and walls from 40 to 100 ft. Occasional S. Florida, Bahamas, Caribbean.

THIN ROPE SPONGE *Clathria juniperina*
SIZE: to 2 m (6 ft.) Rope Sponges – Microcionidae
ID: Long ropelike red to pink tangled masses. Often covered with Golden Zoanthids, *Parazoanthus swiftii.* Reefs and walls from 20 to 100 ft. Occasional S. Florida, Bahamas, Caribbean.

BROWN ENCRUSTING OCTOPUS SPONGE *Ectyoplasia ferox*
SIZE: to 40 cm (16 in.) Rope Sponges – Raspailiidae
ID: Reddish brown to brown with numerous raised excurrent openings encircled with lighter shades; lumpy feltlike surface. Encrust dead areas of reef or forms long arms. Reefs from 40 to 75 ft. Occasional S. Florida, Bahamas, Caribbean.

GREEN FINGER SPONGE *Iotrochota birotulata*
SIZE: to 1 m (3 ft.) Rope Sponge – Iotrochotidae
ID: Green to brownish branches occasionally form bushes; raised conical excurrent openings give rough appearance. Often with Golden Zoanthids, *Parazoanthus swiftii.* Reefs and walls from 15 to 60 ft. Common S. Florida, Bahamas, Caribbean.

ERECT ROPE SPONGE *Amphimedon compressa*
SIZE: to 1 m (3 ft.) Rope Sponges – Niphatidae
ID: Red, burgundy or maroon upright, usually branched, ropelike sponge; scattered excurrent openings without light-colored rims. Reef crests and walls (may not stand erect on walls) from 35 to 70 ft. Common Florida, Bahamas, Caribbean.

WALPER'S BRANCHING SPONGE *Ptilocaulis walpersi*
SIZE: to 30 cm (12 in.)   Rope Sponges – Axinellidae
ID: Red to orange-brown, usually erect but can encrust or form masses, with variable-sized randomly distributed branches; soft and slimy with numerous conical tubercles. Sand and reefs from 2 to 140 ft. Occasional Florida, Bahamas, Caribbean.

RED-ORANGE BRANCHING SPONGES *Ptilocaulis* sp.
SIZE: to 40 cm (16 in.)   Rope Sponges – Axinellidae
ID: Red to orange upright branching sponge with rough surface. Similar-appearing *P. walpersi* [previous] *P. gracilis, P spiculifera,* require microscopic examination to differentiate. Reef and walls from 40 to 80 ft. Uncommon Bahamas, Caribbean; rare Florida.

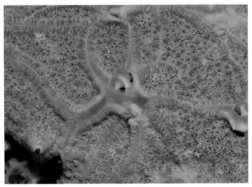

HIGH-VEINED ENCRUSTING SPONGE *Spirastrella hartmani*
SIZE: to 1 m (3 ft.)   Encrusting Sponges – Spirastrellidae
ID: Large thick orange to brown encrusting sponge with wide elevated rootlike canals radiating from raised excurrent openings. Reefs to 40 ft. Occasional Florida, Bahamas, Dominica and Panama in the Caribbean.

PINK & RED ENCRUSTING SPONGE *Spirastrella coccinea*
SIZE: to 1 m (3 ft.)   Encrusting Sponges – Spirastrellidae
ID: Smooth leathery encrusting masses speckled pink and red (occasionally orange); slightly raised excurrent openings. Shaded protected areas of reefs and walls from 30 to 100 ft. Occasional Florida, Bahamas, Caribbean.

RED-ORANGE ENCRUSTING SPONGE *Diplastrella megastellata*
SIZE: to 25 cm (10 in.)   Encrusting Sponges – Spirastrellidae
ID: Thin reddish orange encrusting sponge with rootlike canals radiating from slightly raised excurrent openings. Shaded areas, such as ledge overhangs and caves, on reefs and walls from 25 to 75 ft. Common Caribbean; occasional S. Florida, Bahamas.

ORANGE SIEVE ENCRUSTING SPONGE *Diplastrella* sp.
SIZE: to 45 cm (18 in.)   Encrusting Sponges – Spirastrellidae
ID: Reddish orange encrusting sponge with raised sievelike areas of tiny tightly packed pores surrounded by large protruding excurrent openings. Shaded protected areas of reefs and walls from 20 to 100 ft. Occasional Caribbean.

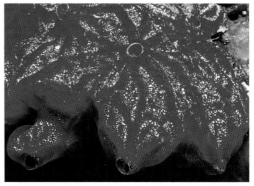

RED SIEVE ENCRUSTING SPONGE *Phorbas amaranthus*
SIZE: to 45 cm (18 in.) Encrusting Sponges – Hymedesmiidae
ID: Brilliant red encrusting sponge with raised circular sievelike areas of tiny incurrent pores surrounding small protruding excurrent openings. Shaded protected areas of reefs and walls from 20 to 100 ft. Occasional Caribbean.

RED ENCRUSTING SPONGE *Monanchora arbuscula*
SIZE: to 25 cm (10 in.) Encrusting Sponges – Crambeidae
ID: Brilliant red encrusting sponge occasionally forms lumps; rootlike canals radiate from raised conical excurrent openings often with white spots between. Reefs from 25 to 75 ft. Common Caribbean; occasional S. Florida, Bahamas.

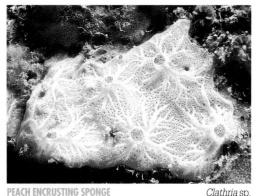

ORANGE-VEINED ENCRUSTING SPONGE *Clathria raraechelae*
SIZE: to 30 cm (12 in.) Encrusting Sponges – Microcionidae
ID: Orange encrusting sponge with numerous rootlike canals radiating from raised excurrent openings; scattering of large incurrent pores. Protected areas of reefs from 25 to 100 ft. Occasional S. Caribbean; also reported from Jamaica.

PEACH ENCRUSTING SPONGE *Clathria sp.*
SIZE: to 25 cm (10 in.) Encrusting Sponges – Microcionidae
ID: Thin peach-colored encrusting sponge with rootlike canals radiating from raised excurrent opening with numerous large incurrent pores. Protected areas of reefs and walls from 25 to 75 ft. Occasional S. Florida, Bahamas, Caribbean.

STAR ENCRUSTING SPONGE *Halisarca caerulea*
SIZE: to 25 cm (10 in.) Encrusting Sponges – Halisarcidae
ID: Thin encrusting red, blue, lavender or gray sponge with star-shaped canals radiating from excurrent openings. (Canals do not overlap like those of similar-appearing species.) Reefs from 25 to 100 ft. Occasional Florida, Bahamas, Caribbean.

Mycale laevis
Encrusting Sponges –
Mycalidae

SIZE: to 45 cm (18 in.)

ID: Porous bright orange encrusting sponge covered with a smooth transparent membrane; rather large raised excurrent openings rimmed with thin raised translucent collars streaked with white lines. Grow beneath and line edges of plate and occasionally boulder-type corals creating a scalloped pattern. **BR-** Specimens in protected areas often remain white. Reefs and hard bottoms from 20 to 100 ft. Abundant to common Florida, Bahamas, Caribbean.

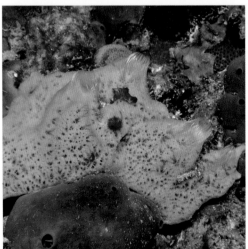

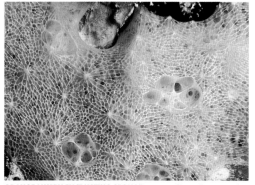

ORANGE LUMPY ENCRUSTING SPONGE *Scopalina ruetzleri*
SIZE: to 30 cm (12 in.) Encrusting Sponges – Scopalinidae
ID: Soft milky orange to yellow sponge with weblike texture; encrusts or forms small lumps; excurrent openings flush or raised with thin translucent collars. Reefs and hard bottoms from 15 to 75 ft. Common Florida, Bahamas, Caribbean.

CONVOLUTED ORANGE SPONGE *Myrmekioderma rea*
SIZE: to 1 m (3 ft.) Encrusting Sponges – Heteroxyidae
ID: Massive orange to yellow sponge with convoluted texture forming mazelike pattern; scattered excurrent openings raised slightly or form cones. Protected areas of reefs and walls from 40 to 130 ft. Can cause stinging rash. Occasional Bahamas, Caribbean.

VISCOUS SPONGE
Plakortis angulospiculatus
Encrusting Sponges –
Plakinidae
SIZE: to 30 cm (12 in.)
ID: Brown to tan encrusting sponge resembles a flow of viscous material; smooth and soft with slightly raised or flush excurrent openings. Undercuts and caves on reefs and walls from 30 to 100 ft. Common Florida, Bahamas, Caribbean.

BROWN VARIABLE SPONGE *Cliona varians*
SIZE: to 45 cm (18 in.) Encrusting Sponges – Clionaidae
ID: Tan to brown sponge that encrust or form lumpy masses; protruding excurrent openings rimmed with a lighter shade. Encrust on deeper areas; forms masses on shallow areas of reefs from 10 to 100 ft. Occasional Florida, Bahamas, Caribbean.

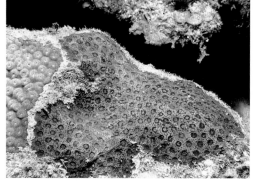

CORAL ENCRUSTING SPONGE *Cliona caribbaea*
SIZE: to 1 m (3 ft.)   Encrusting Sponges – Clionaidae
ID: Thin olive to brown encrusting sponge with numerous tiny excurrent openings. Reefs from 15 to 100 ft. where it overgrows and bores into living coral taking on form and pattern of underlying structure. Occasional Caribbean.

AMBROSIA SPONGE *Axinyssa ambrosia*
SIZE: height to 5 cm (2 in.) Encrusting Sponges – Halichondriidae
ID: Encrusting mass usually covered by sediment with only yellow to orange fingerlike projections visible above surface. Common to uncommon Florida, Bahamas, E. Caribbean.

RED BORING SPONGE *Cliona delitrix*
SIZE: to 30 cm (12 in.)   Boring Sponges – Clionaidae
ID: Bright red to reddish brown or orange; encrust and bore into coral heads; prominent raised excurrent openings with high thin collar often of lighter shade; numerous scattered elevated papillae. Reefs from 15 to 100 ft. Occasional S. Florida, Bahamas, Caribbean.

YELLOW EXCAVATING SPONGE *Siphonodictyon brevitubulatum*
SIZE: height to 5 cm (2 in.)   Boring Sponges – Phloeodictyidae
ID: Much of structure excavates beneath surface of coral with only short (¹/₃ in. tall) yellow protrusions visible; some bearing excurrent openings other incurrent openings. Grow on several coral species on reefs from 30 to 130 ft. Uncommon Caribbean.

WHITE CONE SPONGE *Siphonodictyon xamaycaense*
SIZE: height to 10 cm (4 in.)   Boring Sponges – Phloeodictyidae
ID: Much of structure excavates beneath surface of coral with half-inch irregular white tubes tappering up to less than a quarter inch openings. Usually in clusters on reefs below 100 ft. Uncommon Bahamas; also Jamaica in Caribbean.

VARIABLE BORING SPONGE   *Siphonodictyon coralliphagum*
SIZE: 10 cm (4 in.)   Boring Sponges – Phloeodictyidae
ID: Sulfur to lemon yellow or occasionally white; primarily excavates beneath coral's surface with encrustations or vaselike projections extending above surface. Reef and walls from 30 to 130 ft. Common Bahamas, Caribbean; rare Florida.

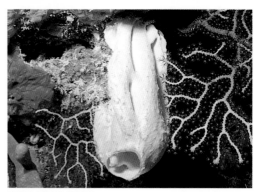

YELLOW CALCAREOUS SPONGE   *Clathrina canariensis*
SIZE: to 10 cm (4 in.)   Calcareous Sponges – Clathrinidae
ID: Bright translucent yellow intertwining tubes with netlike texture; soft and quite fragile. Cave ceilings and undercuts and other dark protected recesses from 25 to 75 ft. Occasional to rare Florida, Bahamas, Caribbean.

WHITE CRYPTIC SPONGE   *Leucandra aspera*
SIZE: to 30 cm (12 in.)   Calcareous Sponges – Grantiidae
ID: Small white deeply grooved vase, solitary tubes or cluster of tubes occasionally with pink, gold or green shading. Cave ceilings and beneath overhangs on deep reefs and walls from 50 to 130 ft. Common Caribbean; rare Florida, Bahamas.

SPINYBALL SPONGE
Leucandra barbata
Calcareous Sponges – Grantiidae
SIZE: to 2 cm (³/₄ in.)

ID: Tiny white spheres with numerous needle-thin spines protruding from surface; solitary excurrent opening; occasionally encrusted with debris. Dark recesses of caves on wall and slopes from 25 to 130 ft. Occasional to rare Caribbean; rare Florida, Bahamas.

31

IDENTIFICATION GROUP 2
Phylum Cnidaria
(Nigh-DARE-ee-uh / L. a nettle)
Hydroids, Jellyfishes & Anemones

Most cnidarians are tiny individual animals that group together, by the thousands, to form colonies, such as, corals and hydroids. These colonies, that vary greatly in size and shape, attach to substrate or living organisms to form most of a coral reef's hard and soft structure. A few species, such as jellyfish and anemones, are not colonial and live as individuals in open water or attached to the substrate by hydrostatic pressure.

Animals in this phylum have a simple structure consisting of a cup-shaped body, a central, single opening that functions both as a **mouth** and **anus,** and a number of **tentacles** that encircle the mouth. When the animal is attached, it is called a **polyp;** if it is unattached and free-swimming, it is called a **medusa.** A unique characteristic shared by all cnidarians is numerous stinging capsules, called **nematocysts,** which is the origin of the phylum's Latin name. These minute capsules, located primarily on the tentacles, are used for both capturing prey and defense.

The stings of most cnidarians have no harmful effect on divers, but a few are quite toxic and should be avoided. In the event of a sting, never rub the affected area or wash with fresh water or soap. Both actions can cause additional nematocysts to discharge. Saturating the area with vinegar will immobilize unspent nematocysts; a sprinkling of meat tenderizer may help to alleviate the symptoms.

The phylum is divided into three classes that include hydroids, jellyfishes, anemones and their relatives. Corals (fire, lace, soft, stony and black) and gorgonians are also classified in this phylum; however, they are identified in a separate volume.

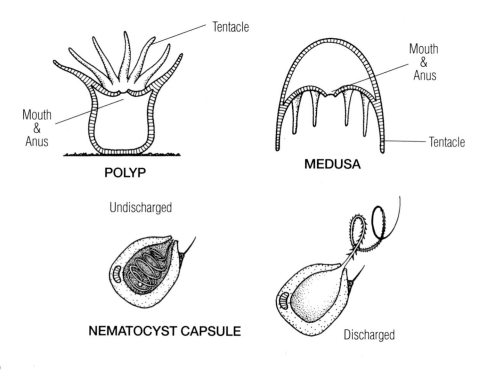

Tentacle

Mouth & Anus

Mouth & Anus

Tentacle

POLYP

MEDUSA

Undischarged

NEMATOCYST CAPSULE

Discharged

GORGONIANS, CORALS, ANEMONES

CLASS: Anthozoa (An-thuh-ZO-uh / L. flowerlike animal)

The class Anthozoa contains many familiar marine invertebrates, including stony and soft corals, black corals and sea anemones. All have only the polyp stage in their life cycles. There are two major sub-classes: Octocorallia, animals with eight tentacles, which include sea fans, sea whips and soft corals (not included in this volume); and Hexacorallia, animals with tentacles in multiples of six, which include stony and black corals (also not included in this volume), sea anemones, zoanthids, corallimorphs and tube-dwelling anemones.

SEA ANEMONES

CLASS: Anthozoa
SUBCLASS: Hexacorallia (Hex-uh-core-AL-ee-uh / Gr. & L. six and coral animal)
ORDER: Actiniaria (Ack-TIN-ee-AIR-ee-uh / L. a ray)

Sea anemones are solitary polyps that attach to the bottom. They lack any hard skeletal parts and are generally quite large compared to the polyps of other cnidarians. Their bodies range from a few inches to over a foot across. The **tentacles,** which vary in length, shape, color and number, are often keys to identification. The pattern of tentacles often appears random, although some species exhibit distinct rings.

Stinging nematocysts on the tentacles rarely affect divers, but are toxic enough to paralyze small fish and invertebrates that stray into their reach. The immobilized prey is drawn by the tentacles into a **slitlike mouth** in the center of the **oral disc.** Living in association with many anemones are certain species of fish, shrimp and crab that are not affected by the nematocysts. Anemones rarely move, but can relocate in a slow, snail-like manner. They prefer secluded areas of the reef where they often lodge in crevices with only their tentacles exposed. If disturbed they can contract their tentacles for protection.

CORALLIMORPHS

CLASS: Anthozoa
SUBCLASS: Hexacorallia
ORDER: Corallimorpharia (Core-AL-uh-more-FAIR-ee-uh / Gr. & L. coral-like)

Corallimorphs are easily confused with anemones. The best visual clue to the order's identity is the arrangement of the tentacles, which form two geometric patterns concurrently. **Tentacles radiate out** from the center of the **oral disc,** like spokes, and form **concentric circles** which progressively increase in diameter from the center. These patterns, however, are often obscure. The tentacles in most species are short and stubby, resembling nubs or warts. Generally, the oral disc is quite flat, and the **mouth protrudes** noticeably. They are occasionally called false corals because their polyps' structure is much like those of hard corals, except they secrete no calcareous skeleton. Corallimorphs may be solitary, but also live in close association, occasionally crowding together so closely that the individual polyps are difficult to distinguish from one another.

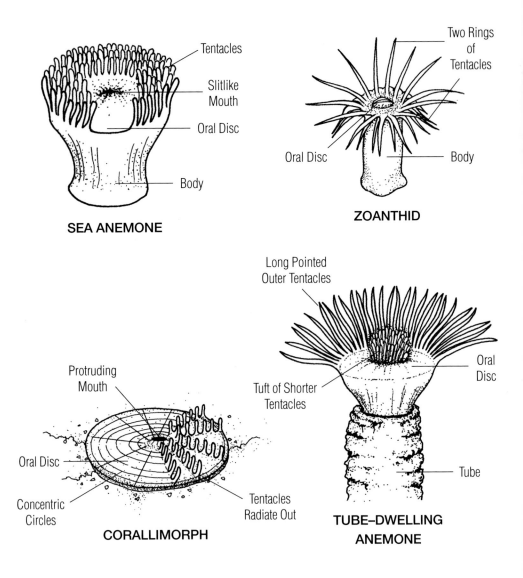

Tentacles

Slitlike Mouth

Oral Disc

Body

SEA ANEMONE

Two Rings of Tentacles

Oral Disc

Body

ZOANTHID

Long Pointed Outer Tentacles

Protruding Mouth

Oral Disc

Concentric Circles

Tuft of Shorter Tentacles

Tentacles Radiate Out

CORALLIMORPH

Oral Disc

Tube

TUBE–DWELLING ANEMONE

TUBE-DWELLING ANEMONES

CLASS: Anthozoa, Subclass Hexacorallia
ORDER: Ceriantharia (Sair-ee-an-THAIR-ee-uh / L. & Gr. wax flower)

These anemones live inside **tubes** buried in mud, sand or fine gravel. Their oral disc and crown of tentacles nearly always remain hidden during the day, only extending at night when the animals feed. They can be distinguished from other anemonelike animals by the arrangement of their tentacles. Several rings of long, **pointed outer tentacles** extend from the edge of the **oral disc**, and at the center is a **tuft of shorter tentacles** that often conceal the mouth.

ZOANTHIDS

CLASS: Anthozoa
SUBCLASS: Hexacorallia
ORDER: Zoanthidea (Zo-an-THID-ee-uh / Gr. animal flower)

Zoanthids appear similar to anemones, but are considerably smaller, usually no larger than a half inch, and are generally colonial or live in close proximity to one another. The **oral disc** is without tentacles except for **two rings of tentacles** around the outer edge, which visually distinguish them from other anemonelike animals. Some species live in association with sponges, hydroids and other invertebrates.

HYDROIDS

CLASS: Hydrozoa (High-druh-ZO-uh / Gr. water animal)
ORDER: Leptothecata Lep-TOE-thee-CATE-uh) / Gr. & L thin + sheath

Hydroids are usually colonial, and have a branched skeleton that generally grows in patterns resembling feathers or ferns. Individual polyps are attached to this structure. The arrangement of the **stalk, branches** and attached **polyps** is usually the key to visual identification. Most species are whitish or neutral shades, ranging from brown to gray or black and rarely display vibrant colors.

Most hydroids have a complex life cycle. The polyps in an adult colony are specialized for either feeding or reproduction. The reproductive polyps give rise to buds that form free-swimming medusae. This stage, often small in size and short-lived, is only occasionally observable by divers. When in these reproductive stages, called **hydromedusae,** they can be distinguished from similar-appearing "true" jellyfish by the margin of their **dome,** which turns inward, forming a "shelf" called a **velum. Radial canals** run from the **mouth** to the margin of the velum. The velum is absent in jellyfish. Varying numbers of **tentacles** with stinging nematocysts hang from the dome's margin. The hydromedusa is the dominant stage in a few species.

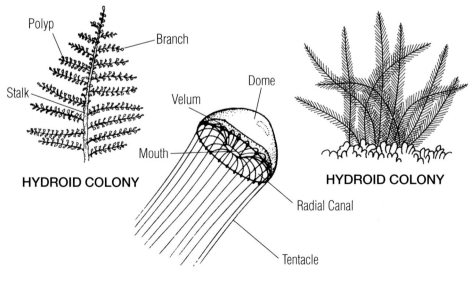

Polyp
Branch
Stalk
Dome
Velum
Mouth
HYDROID COLONY
HYDROID COLONY
Radial Canal
Tentacle
HYDROMEDUSA

BOX JELLIES

CLASS: Cubozoa (Cu-bo-ZO-uh / Gr. cube shaped)
SUBCLASS: Cubomedusae (Cue-BO-muh-due-see / L. cube-shaped medusa)

Box jellies, also commonly called sea wasps, can be identified by their distinctive **cuboidal dome.** One or more nematocyst-bearing **tentacles** hang from each of the four corners of the open end of the cube. Additional tentacles are absent from the remaining margin. The sting of many box jellies can be severe, frequently requiring medical attention.

SIPHONOPHORES

CLASS: Hydrozoa
ORDER: Siphonophora (Sigh-fawn-NOFF-or-uh / Gr. to have hollow tubes)

Siphonophores are a complex form of unattached hydroid colonies that float by means of a **gas-filled float.** Below the float hang numerous nematocyst-bearing **tentacles** that can be contracted close to the float, or relaxed to extend to great lengths. The best known example is the **Portuguese Man-of-war,** which floats on the surface and moves by turning its float to the wind. These unique animals are capable of stinging a diver so severely that medical attention is required. Unlike the Portuguese Man-of-war, most siphonophores float below the surface in open water, controlling their depth by regulating the gas content of the float. They move about by pulsating modified medusae, called **swimming bells,** that are just below the gas float. Their sting is not a threat to divers, but can be felt for a short time.

JELLYFISHES

CLASS: Scyphozoa (Sky-fuh-ZO-uh / Gr. cup-shaped animal)

Jellyfishes are translucent, unattached medusae that swim in open water. All have a prominent **dome,** which varies in shape from a shallow saucer to a deep bell. Hanging from the margin of the dome are **nematocyst-bearing tentacles,** the number and length vary greatly from species to species. Occasionally the margin is scalloped, forming lobes called **lappets.** The mouth is at the end of a **feeding tube** that extends from the center of the dome's underside. In some species, four frilly **oral arms** hang to considerable length from the feeding tube. Both the feeding tube and oral arms carry stinging nematocysts.

Jellyfishes move through the water by pulsating contractions of the dome. Although only a few jellyfish are toxic, caution should be taken with all members of the group.

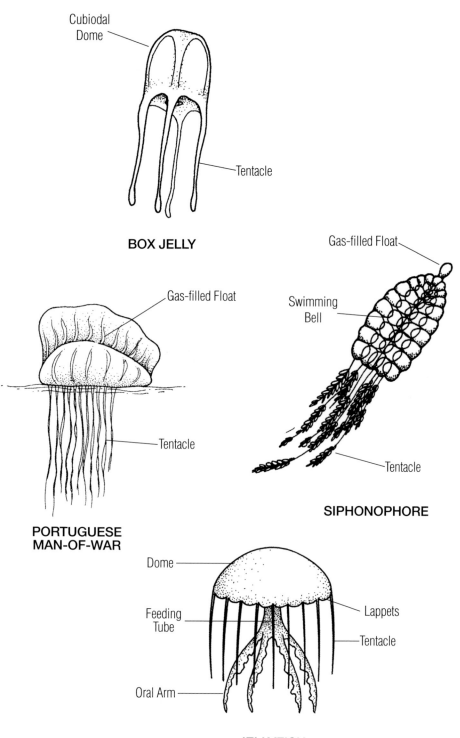

Cubiodal
Dome

Tentacle

BOX JELLY

Gas-filled Float

**PORTUGUESE
MAN-OF-WAR**

Tentacle

Gas-filled Float

Swimming
Bell

Tentacle

SIPHONOPHORE

Dome

Feeding
Tube

Lappets

Tentacle

Oral Arm

JELLYFISH

Anemones

GIANT ANEMONE
Condylactis gigantea
Anemones – Actiniidae
SIZE: to 30 cm (12 in.)

ID: Largest anemone in Tropical Western Atlantic; elongate tentacles white, gray or yellow-green often with swollen tips which can be pinkish to purple; tentacles often have tapered tips; bodies typically hidden in recesses; **BR-** bodies occasionally inflate into balloonlike structure. Reefs, rocky seawalls, seagrass from 15 to 100 ft. Common S. Florida, Bahamas, Caribbean.

CLUB-TIPPED ANEMONE *Telmatactis cricoides*
SIZE: disc to 10 cm (4 in.) Anemones – Isophelliidae
ID: Tentacles with enlarged clublike tips encircle a protruding central oral opening; colors and markings highly variable. Caves and deep recesses from 5 to 40 ft. Common central, E. & S. Caribbean; rare Florida Keys, Bahamas, N.W. Caribbean..

SUN ANEMONE *Stichodactyla helianthus*
SIZE: disc to 15 cm (6 in.) Anemones – Stichodactylidae
ID: Greenish brown flattened disc covered with numerous short thick tentacles with rounded tips; typically form dense clusters that may carpet large areas. Shallow back reefs from 3 to 30 ft. Occasional Bahamas, E. & S. Caribbean; rare N. W. Caribbean.

Anemones

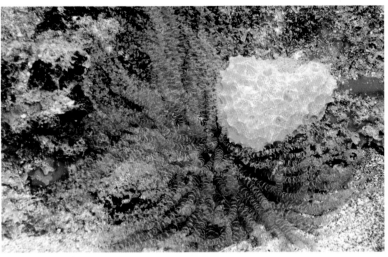

CORKSCREW ANEMONE
Bartholomea annulata
Anemones – Aiptasiidae
SIZE: to 18 cm (7 in.)
ID: Numerous long thin translucent gray or greenish **tentacles with whitish corkscrewlike markings;** bodies usually hidden in small reef recesses or beneath rocks or hard debris from 5 to 130 ft.; mild sting; tentacles retract when disturbed; Red Snapping Shrimp, *Alpheus armatus*, and Pederson Cleaning Shrimp, *Ancylomenes pedersoni*, regularly associate with anemone. Common Florida, Bahamas, Caribbean.

KNOBBY ANEMONE
Ragactis lucida
Anemones – Aiptasiidae
SIZE: to 10 cm (4 in.)
ID: **Nematocyst-bearing knobs line long thin pointed translucent gray or greenish tentacles;** bodies usually hidden in small reef recesses or beneath rocks or hard debris from 5 to 100 ft.; mild sting. Tentacles retract when disturbed. Common to occasional Florida, Bahamas, Caribbean.

PALE ANEMONE   *Aiptasia tagetes*
SIZE: disc to 5 cm (2 in.)   Anemones – Aiptasiidae
ID: Thin pointed transparent tentacles encircle brownish to bluish white oral disc. Solitary or form clusters on exposed surfaces of reefs, wrecks and rocks from 5 to 60 ft.; do not sting. Occasional Florida, Bahamas, Caribbean.

PALE CLUMPING ANEMONE   *Aiptasia* sp.
SIZE: disc to 2.5 cm (1 in.)   Anemones – Aiptasiidae
ID: Pale yellowish green translucent tentacles encircle small olive to white oral disc; form clusters inside shallow recesses on reefs; attach to sponges and gorgonians. Occasional Florida, Bahamas, Caribbean.

RED WARTY ANEMONE
Bunodosoma granuliferum
Anemones – Actiniidae
SIZE: to 9 cm (3½ in.)
ID: Three rows of short red, golden, brown or olive conical tentacles encircle red to reddish brown oral disc; **muscular body column covered with vertical rows of beadlike warts.** Rubble to 30 ft. Occasional Florida, Bahamas, Caribbean.

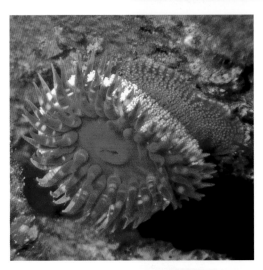

BRANCHING ANEMONE
Lebrunia danae
Anemones – Aliciidae
SIZE: to 30 (12 in.)
ID: Stubby branching pseudotentacles with prominent nematocyst-bearing knobs; shades of brown to gray or blue-green with lighter markings. Bodies inside reef recesses from 5 to 130 ft.; retract pseudotentacles if disturbed; long unbranched true tentacles only extended at night; can cause moderate sting. Common to occasional Florida, Bahamas, Caribbean.

Anemones

HIDDEN ANEMONE *Lebrunia coralligens*
SIZE: tentacles to 6.5 cm (2½ in.)   Anemones – Aliciidae
ID: Stout pseudotentacles with enlarged tips; whitish with brown to olive or blue-green tips often striped. **Tentacles extend in a single row from fissures in living or dead corals;** mild sting. Occasional Bahamas, Caribbean; rare S. Florida.

BERRIED ANEMONE
Alicia mirabilis
Anemones – Aliciidae
SIZE: extend to 35 cm (14 in.)
ID: When closed during day appear as knobby yellowish tan to brown fist-sized mass; body extends at night unfurling mass of long thin translucent tentacles. Sand, rocky outcroppings, wrecks, mooring lines and reefs from 20 to 130 ft.; moderate sting. Rare Florida, Bahamas, Caribbean.

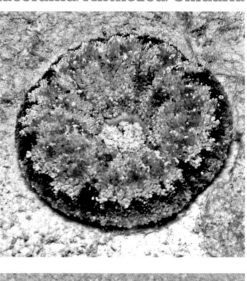

ELEGANT ANEMONE *Actinoporus elegans*
SIZE: to 23 cm (9 in.) Anemones – Aurelianidae
ID: Body column buried in sand exposing only flattened oral disc covered with numerous short tentacles; when retracted oral disc appears as spotted donut; colors highly variable. Nocturnal; sand and rubble from 10 to 60 ft. Uncommon Jamaica, S. & E. Caribbean.

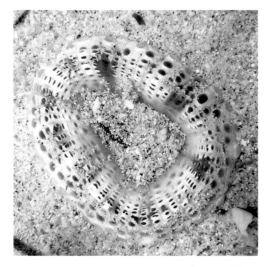

BEADED ANEMONE *Phymanthus crucifer*
SIZE: disc to 15 cm (6 in.) Anemones – Phymanthidae
ID: Rows of beadlike warts radiate from mouth to encircling border of 200 short striped or banded tentacles; colors highly variable, often green. Bury in sand or cracks between rubble to 30 ft.; retract when disturbed. Occasional Bahamas, Caribbean.

Anemones

HITCHHIKING ANEMONE   *Calliactis tricolor*
SIZE: to 7.5 cm (3 in.)   Anemones – Hormathiidae
ID: Smooth brown to red or olive oral disc encircled with several
rows of translucent, occasionally banded, tentacles. Most
commonly attached to shells inhabited by hermit crabs; close
tightly when disturbed. Occasional Florida, Bahamas, Caribbean.

TURTLE GRASS ANEMONE   *Viatrix globulifera*
SIZE: disc to 2 cm (¾ in.)   Anemones – Boloceroididae
ID: Small body flat and obscure when deflated; when inflated
large and lumpy; translucent tentacles most commonly extended
at night. Attach to seagrass blades, occasionally gorgonians to
20 ft.; moderate sting. Occasional Florida, Bahamas, Caribbean.

BLISTERED GRASS ANEMONE   *Bunodeopsis antilliensis*
SIZE: to 3.5 cm (1½ in.)   Anemones – Boloceroididae
ID: Flattened elongated brown to black body with white to
orange spherical nodules "blisters" on surface; long translucent
tentacles extended at night from central oral opening. Turtle
Grass blades to 25 ft. Occasional Florida, Bahamas, Caribbean.

LIGHT BULB ANEMONE   Undetermined
SIZE: to 7.5 cm (3 in.)   Anemones – Undetermined
ID: Distinctive translucent bulb-shaped tentacles, tipped with thin elongate curling tips; banded in shades of green, tan and white. Reefs, wrecks and rocky outcroppings to 130 ft. Known from N. Gulf of Mexico.

SPONGE ANEMONE   Undetermined
SIZE: to 3 cm (1¼ in.)   Anemones – Undetermined
ID: Long translucent brownish tentacles with bands and speckles; occasionally with white around oral opening. Extend from folds in surfaces of sponges from 25 to 130 ft. Occasional Caribbean.

BLUE-SPOTTED ANEMONE   Undetermined
SIZE: disc to 4 cm (1½ in.)   Anemones – Undetermined
ID: Oral disc ringed with wide green, brown and grayish white bands; blue spots form spokes on disc; long pointed translucent tentacles with whitish spots. Known from central & E. Caribbean.

FLAMING ANEMONE   Undetermined
SIZE: disc to 4 cm (1½ in.)   Anemones – Undetermined
ID: Yellow oral disc with radiating reddish brown markings encircled with numerous short inflated reddish brown tentacles. Recesses in reefs to 40 ft. Known from Bonaire.

WHISPY-Y ANEMONE   Undetermined
SIZE: disc to 2.5 cm (1 in.)   Anemones – Undetermined
ID: Long pointed reddish translucent tentacles encircle oral disc; reddish brown spokes radiate from mouth split into "Y" at base of tentacles. Rubble to 40 ft. Known from Los Frailes Islets, Venezuela.

ORANGE-BLISTERED ANEMONE   Undetermined
SIZE: disc to 2 cm (¾ in.)   Anemones – Undetermined
ID: Flat grayish body covered with inflated yellow to orange nodules; brown translucent tentacles extend from central oral opening. Associate with and attach to sea cucumbers. Known from Dominica.

Corallimorphs

FLORIDA CORALLIMORPH
Ricordea florida
Corallimorphs –
Ricordeidae
SIZE: disc to 5 cm (2 in.)
ID: Knoblike tentacles forming radial spokelike rows extend from protruding mouth to edge; band of more elongate tentacles encircle outer edge; green, often with mixed shades of blue, yellow, orange and brown. Typically form matlike communities on reefs from 15 to 100 ft. Occasional Florida, Bahamas, Caribbean.

WARTY CORALLIMORPH   *Rhodactis osculifera*
SIZE: to 9 cm (3½ in.)   Corallimorphs – Discosomatidae
ID: Flat disc with inflated tentacles that **open into forked extensions;** short tentacles around greenish translucent edge of disc; tentacles greenish blue, yellow, orange, red. Solitary or clusters on reefs to 75 ft. Occasional Florida, Bahamas, Caribbean.

FORKED TENTACLE CORALLIMORPH   *Discosoma carlgreni*
SIZE: disc to 6.5 cm (2½ in.)   Corallimorphs – Discosomatidae
ID: Tiny, widely spaced, forked tentacles cover disc; green, brown and gray splotches; occasionally translucent. Solitary or small clusters on protected reef areas from 10 to 60 ft. Uncommon Caribbean; rare S. Florida.

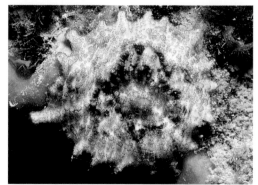

UMBRELLA CORALLIMORPH   *Discosoma neglecta*
SIZE: disc to 6.5 cm (2½ in.)   Corallimorphs – Discosomatidae
ID: Flattened oral disc; short square-tipped tentacles encircle edge; light green to olive or dark brown, usually streaked or splotched. Typically solitary in protected areas of reef from 30 to 90 ft. Rare Florida, Bahamas, Caribbean.

ORANGEBALL CORALLIMORPH
Corynactis caribbeorum
Corallimorphs –
Corallimorphidae
SIZE: disc to 5 cm (2 in.)
ID: Orange ball-like tips on long translucent tentacles extend from disc face and edge; body and disc typically shades of orange to brown, occasionally yellow, green or blue. Nocturnal; protected areas of reefs, wrecks and rock structures from 20 to 80 ft.; retract when exposed to direct beam of hand light. Occasional Bahamas, Caribbean.

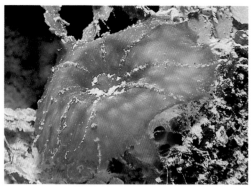

PARACHUTE CORALLIMORPH — Undetermined
SIZE: disc to 6.5 cm (2½ in.)   Corallimorphs – Undetermined
ID: Umbrella-shaped oral disc; tiny pointed tentacles encircle edge; widely spaced rows of tiny white tentacles radiate from protruding mouth; shades of green and somewhat translucent. Reefs from 15 to 100 ft. Known from Jamaica.

DISC CORALLIMORPH — Undetermined
SIZE: to 5 cm (2 in.)   Corallimorphs – Undetermined
ID: Flat disc; numerous rows of tiny tentacles radiate from protruding mouth; fringe of tiny tentacles encircle edge; light green mouth and border, brownish green disc. Solitary on reefs from 15 to 100 ft. Known from Roatan.

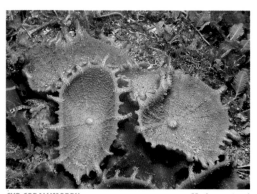

CUP CORALLIMORPH — Undetermined
SIZE: disc to 7.5 cm (3 in.)   Corallimorphs – Undetermined
ID: Shallow cuplike oral disc with flat blunt tentacles of varying lengths encircling edge; numerous rows of tiny knoblike tentacles radiate from protruding mouth; shades of brown to green. Reefs from 15 to 100 ft. Occasional E. & S. Caribbean.

FRINGED CORALLIMORPH — Undetermined
SIZE: disc to 7.5 cm (3 in.)   Corallimorphs – Undetermined
ID: Flat oral disc; fringe of long thin pointed tentacles encircle edge; thin widely spaced tentacles and rows of bluish white spots radiate from protruding mouth. Protected areas of reef from 15 to 100 ft. Known from Grand Cayman.

Zoanthids

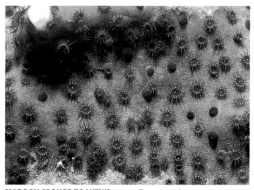

SPONGE ZOANTHID *Parazoanthus parasiticus*
SIZE: to 6 mm (¹/₄ in.)   Zoanthids – Parazoanthidae
ID: Color highly variable including brown, yellow-brown and shades of green; oral disc somewhat darker. Large numbers colonize surface of several species of sponges to 100 ft. Common Florida, Bahamas, Caribbean.

MAROON SPONGE ZOANTHID *Parazoanthus puertoricense*
SIZE: to 6 mm (¹/₄ in.)   Zoanthids – Parazoanthidae
ID: Maroon, burgundy or purple polyps; tiny white spots between tentacles. Large numbers colonize surface of several species of sponges; most common sponge zoanthid below 80 ft. Common Caribbean.

GOLDEN ZOANTHID *Parazoanthus swiftii*
SIZE: to 6 mm (¹/₄ in.)   Zoanthids – Parazoanthidae
ID: Gold to yellow polyps; colonies form meandering rows; large numbers colonize surface of several species of sponges from 40 to 100 ft.; most common on rope-type sponges. Common Bahamas, Caribbean.

HYDROID ZOANTHID *Parazoanthus tunicans*
SIZE: to 6 mm (¹/₄ in.)   Zoanthids – Parazoanthidae
ID: Polyps vary from pale yellow to brown or dark green; tentacles occasionally different shades. Colonies encrust Feather Bush Hydroids, *Dentitheca dendritica*, from 30 to 130 ft. Occasional Florida, Bahamas, Caribbean.

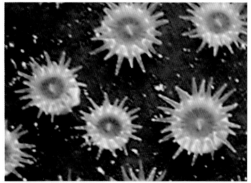

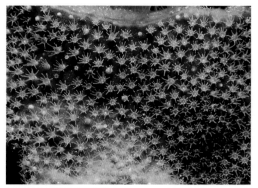

BROWN SPONGE ZOANTHID *Parazoanthus catenularis*
SIZE: to 6 mm (¹/₄ in.)   Zoanthids – Parazoanthidae
ID: Twenty light brown to yellowish brown tentacles ring slightly darker oral disc; white body stalk. Colonize surface of several species of deep dwelling sponges below 60 ft. Occasional Caribbean.

YELLOW SPONGE ZOANTHID *Epizoanthus cutressi*
SIZE: to 6 mm (¹/₄ in.)   Zoanthids – Epizoanthidae
ID: Twenty bright yellow tentacles ring darker yellow polyps. Colonize surface of several species of deep dwelling sponges below 60 ft. Occasional Caribbean.

MAT ZOANTHID *Zoanthus pulchellus*
SIZE: disc to 1.2 cm (¹/₂ in.) Zoanthids – Zoanthidae
ID: Discs ringed with tiny tentacles mottled in greens and earth tones. Grow in dense mats of individual polyps to 60 ft.; often packed so tightly discs form polygons; at depths often fluoresce orange. Common Bahamas, Caribbean; occasional S. Florida.

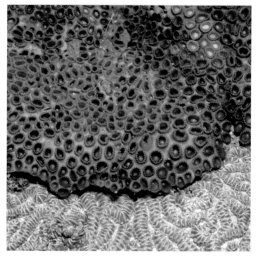

ENCRUSTING ZOANTHID *Palythoa caribaeorum*
SIZE: disc to 1.2 cm (¹/₂ in.) Zoanthids – Sphenopidae
ID: Brown to white discs ringed with tiny tentacles grow as connected colonies. Form thick mats that overgrow reefs with water movement from 10 to 40 ft.; may overgrow and kill stony corals. Abundant S. Florida; occasional Bahamas, Caribbean.

SUN ZOANTHID *Palythoa grandis*
SIZE: disc to 3 cm (1¹/₄ in.) Zoanthids – Sphenopidae
ID: One of largest zoanthids; flat brown or greenish disc often mottled with white; spokelike design radiates from mouth; tiny tentacles ring edge. Solitary or small overlapping clusters on reefs from 40 to 130 ft. Occasional S. Florida, Caribbean.

BROWN ZOANTHID Undetermined
SIZE: disc to 1.2 cm (¹/₂ in.) Zoanthids – Undetermined
ID: Flat bluish green disc ringed with long thin tentacles; white center; spokelike pattern and wide ring of darker shades toward edge of disc. Form clusters in protected areas of reefs from 20 to 60 ft. Occasional Caribbean; rare S. Florida.

Tube-dwelling Anemones

BANDED TUBE-DWELLING ANEMONE
Isarachnanthus nocturnus
Tube-dwelling Anemones –
Arachnactidae
SIZE: to 15 cm (6 in.)
ID: Long wispy translucent tentacles extend from edge of oral disc; green spokes radiating from cluster of short central tentacles. Nocturnal; bury in sand from 10 to 80 ft.; body tube extends from sand at night; retract when exposed to direct beam of hand light. Identification tentative. Occasional Florida, Bahamas, Caribbean.

GIANT TUBE-DWELLING ANEMONE
Ceriantheomorphe brasiliensis
Tube-dwelling Anemones –
Cerianthidae
SIZE: disc to 15 cm (6 in.)
ID: Two rows of long wispy tentacles encircle central tuft of short tentacles; shades of gray to lavender. Nocturnal; sand and rubble from 15 to 80 ft.; retract when exposed to direct beam of hand light. Identification tentative. Uncommon Florida, Bahamas, Caribbean.

WIDEBAND TUBE-DWELLING ANEMONE
Undetermined

Tube-dwelling Anemones – Undetermined

SIZE: to 13 cm (5 in.)

ID: Similar to Banded Tube-dwelling Anemone [previous page], but lacks banding and central tentacles pinkish rather than green. Body tube extends from sand at night; retract when exposed to direct beam of hand light. Known from Cayman.

TRANSPARENT TUBE-DWELLING ANEMONE   Undetermined

SIZE: to 13 cm (5 in.)   Tube-dwelling Anemones – Undetermined

ID: Numerous long wispy translucent tentacles extend to edge of disc; central tuft of short pink and white tentacles. Sand and rubble from 15 to 60 ft. Known from N. Gulf of Mexico.

LAVENDER TUBE-DWELLING ANEMONE   Undetermined

SIZE: to 5 cm (2 in.)   Tube-dwelling Anemones – Undetermined

ID: Numerous long white tentacles encircle edge of oral disc; tuft of short lavender tentacles on central disc. Sand to 60 ft. Known from Venezuela.

LINED TUBE-DWELLING ANEMONE   Undetermined

SIZE: to 7.5 cm (3 in.)   Tube-dwelling Anemones – Undetermined

ID: Pair of lines, formed by dashes, extend length of translucent tentacles; two bands of tentacles on oral disc surround central tuft of short tentacles. Sand from 15 to 60 ft. Known from Venezuela.

WISPY TUBE-DWELLING ANEMONE   Undetermined

SIZE: to 10 cm (4 in.)   Tube-dwelling Anemones – Undetermined

ID: Three bands of long wispy translucent to lavender tentacles surround central tuft of whitish tentacles. Sand to 50 ft. Known from Venezuela.

Hydroids

BRANCHING HYDROID
Sertularella diaphana
Hydroids – Sertulariidae
SIZE: to 14 cm (5¹/₂ in.)
ID: Branches extend alternately on single plane from stout brownish stalk; white polyps attach alternately to the top and bottom of branches. Solitary or in small clusters on reefs from 30 to 100 ft. Common Florida, Bahamas, Caribbean.

ALGAE HYDROID
Thyroscyphus ramosus
Hydroids – Sertulariidae
SIZE: to 13 cm (5 in.)
ID: Scattered branches extend alternately on a single plane from a stout reddish brown central stalk; polyps attach alternately to branches and central stalk. Form clumps often covered with algae. Common to occasional Florida, Bahamas, Caribbean.

UNBRANCHED HYDROID   *Thyroscyphus marginatus*
SIZE: to 9 cm (3¹/₂ in.)   Hydroids – Sertulariidae
ID: Stout gray branchless stalk with alternating polyps extending from opposite sides. Usually grow in clusters on reefs from 5 to 130 ft.; often partially covered with algae. Common to occasional Florida, Bahamas, Caribbean.

CHRISTMAS TREE HYDROID   *Pennaria disticha*
SIZE: to 9 cm (3¹/₂ in.)   Hydroids – Pennariidae
ID: Branches extend alternately on single plane from stout brown central stalk; single polyp at tip of each branch and stalk, additional polyps along branches; usually grow in clusters. Common to occasional Florida, Bahamas, Caribbean.

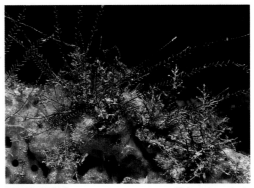

WHISPY HYDROID *Monostaechas sp.*
SIZE: to 5 cm (2 in.) Hydroids – Halopterididae
ID: Clusters of thin central stalks with evenly spaced branches extend from one side; evenly spaced polyps on one side of each branch. Shallow seagrass and algae. Occasional Caribbean.

THREAD HYDROID *Halopteris carinata*
SIZE: to 15 cm (6 in.) Hydroids – Halopterididae
ID: Long thin central stalk lined with short alternating polyp-bearing branches. Grow in clumps on reefs from 20 to 100 ft.; painful sting. Common to occasional Florida, Bahamas, Caribbean.

WHITE STINGER
Macrorhynchia philippina
Hydroids – Aglaopheniidae
SIZE: to 15 cm (6 in.)
ID: Robust, often curved, brown stalk with short alternating white branches in a single plane; each branch tipped with single polyp. Grow in clumps on reefs from 20 to 100 ft.; painful sting. Common to occasional Florida, Bahamas, Caribbean.

STINGING HYDROID
Macrorhynchia allmani
Hydroids – Aglaopheniidae
SIZE: to 7.5 cm (3 in.)
ID: Stalks support a few primary branches of similar size; thin, tightly spaced polyp-bearing secondary branches extend from stalk and primary branches in a single plane. Reefs from 30 to 100 ft.; painful sting. Occasional Florida, Bahamas, Caribbean.

Hydroids

STINGING BUSH HYDROID
Macrorhynchia clarkei
Hydroids – Aglaopheniidae
SIZE: to 30 cm (12 in.)
ID: Dark stalks with numerous primary branches and sub-branches lined with fine, tightly spaced, polyp-bearing secondary branches. Typically cluster on reefs from 20 to 100 ft.; painful sting. Occasional S.E. Florida, Bahamas, Caribbean.

FEATHER PLUME HYDROID   *Aglaophenia latecarinata*
SIZE: to 7.5 cm (3 in.)   Hydroids – Aglaopheniidae
ID: Stout brownish central stalks with alternating branches in a single plane; white polyps attach alternately to top and bottom of branches. Solitary or often in clusters on reefs to 120 ft.; also inhabit Sargassum floats. Occasional central to N. Florida.

SLENDER FEATHER HYDROID   *Gymnangium speciosum*
SIZE: to 30 cm (12 in.)   Hydroids – Aglaopheniidae
ID: Dark stalks with alternating thin, tightly spaced, whitish branches lined with white polyps grow in single plane; shorter branches than Feather Plume Hydroid [previous]. Clusters to 100 ft.; painful sting. Occasional Florida, Bahamas, Caribbean.

FEATHER HYDROID
Gymnangium longicaudum
Hydroids – Aglaopheniidae
SIZE: to 30 cm (12 in.)
ID: Thin tightly spaced whitish branches extend alternately in a single plane from a brown central stalk. Usually grow in clusters on reef tops from 25 to 100 ft.; painful sting. Common to occasional Caribbean.

FEATHER BUSH HYDROID
Dentitheca dendritica
Hydroids – Plumulariidae
SIZE: to 30 cm (12 in.)
ID: Bushlike colonies of stout stalks with angular branches and sub-branches all lined with fine, tightly spaced, polyp-bearing branches. Reefs from 30 to 130 ft.; painful sting. Hydroid Zoanthids, *Parazoanthus tunicans*, often grow on branches. Common Florida, Bahamas, Caribbean.

SEAFAN HYDROID *Solanderia gracilis*
SIZE: to 46 cm (18 in.) Hydroids – Solanderiidae
ID: Heavily branched **reddish to purple stalks** lined with thin short whitish secondary branches bearing white polyps in a single plane. Reefs in areas of surge or current from 15 to 80 ft. Uncommon Florida, Bahamas, Caribbean.

SOLITARY GORGONIAN HYDROID *Ralpharia gorgoniae*
SIZE: to 2.5 cm (1 in.) Hydroids – Tubulariidae
ID: Large solitary white polyps with **long thin translucent tentacles that often curl at tips;** Attach to tips of gorgonian branches, especially sea plumes, from 15 to 65 ft.; painful sting. Occasional to uncommon Bahamas, Caribbean.

SOLITARY SPONGE HYDROID *Zyzzyzus warreni*
SIZE: to 2.5 cm (1 in.) Hydroids – Tubulariidae
ID: Large solitary pinkish polyps with long thin translucent tentacles that do not curl at tips. Attach to sponges from 20 to 100 ft.; painful sting. Occasional Florida, Bahamas, Caribbean.

Hydromedusae & Siphonophores

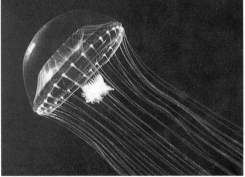

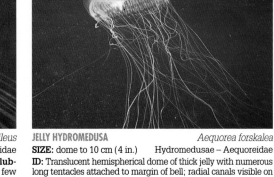

CLUB HYDROMEDUSA *Orchistoma pileus*
SIZE: dome to 2.5 cm (1 in.) Hydromedusae – Orchistomatidae
ID: Transparent hemispherical dome **with distinctive club-shaped organ where tentacles attaches to margin of bell;** few radial canals visible on velum. Float near surface, often in large aggregations. Occasional Florida, Bahamas, Caribbean.

JELLY HYDROMEDUSA *Aequorea forskalea*
SIZE: dome to 10 cm (4 in.) Hydromedusae – Aequoreidae
ID: Translucent hemispherical dome of thick jelly with numerous long tentacles attached to margin of bell; radial canals visible on velum. Float near surface. Occasional to uncommon Florida, Bahamas, Caribbean.

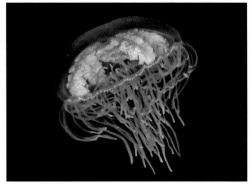

BANDED HYDROMEDUSA *Aequorea sp.*
SIZE: dome to 7.5 cm (3 in.) Hydromedusae – Aequoreidae
ID: Translucent low hemispherical dome with widely spaced long tentacles attached to margin of bell; numerous wide white radial canals on velum give banded appearance. Float near surface. Uncommon Florida, Bahamas, Caribbean.

DELICATE HYDROMEDUSA *Olindias tenuis*
SIZE: dome 4 cm (1½ in.) Hydromedusae – Olindiidae
ID: Translucent dome with four radial canals; gonads with numerous pink papillae; tiny white marginal tentacles fringe dome; numerous short primary tentacles. Nocturnal; open water from 10 to 25 ft. Uncommon Florida, Bahamas, Caribbean.

TWOTENTACLE HYDROMEDUSA *Larsonia pterophylla*
SIZE: dome to 5 cm (2 in.) Hydromedusae – Pandeidae
ID: Small transparent cone-shaped dome trailing two long tentacles; yellowish-brown mass below dome is an extended mouth surrounded by gonads. Pelagic; occasionally over reefs. Uncommon Florida, Bahamas, Caribbean.

BLUE BUTTON *Porpita porpita*
SIZE: to 7.5 cm (3 in.) Chondrophores – Porpitidae
ID: Central brownish disk-shaped gas-filled **float ringed with bright blue, turquoise to green or yellow tentaclelike hydroid colony.** Pelagic, occasionally float over reefs and shallow sand areas; slight sting. Uncommon Florida, Bahamas, Caribbean.

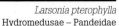

PORTUGUESE MAN-OF-WAR
Physalia physalis
Siphonophores – Physaliidae
SIZE: dome to 30 cm (12 in.)
ID: Translucent pink to purple gas-filled float with numerous long nearly invisible retractable tentacles that can extend to 160 ft. Float on surface propelled by wind; a colonial organism consisting of tiny specialized individuals known as zooids. Extremely painful sting. Following contact remove remaining tentacles, flush with salt water (never fresh water), immerse area in hot water (to 112°F) for 20 minutes to denature toxin (do not use vinegar). Occasional Florida, Bahamas, Caribbean.

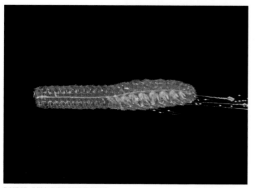

PAIRED-BELL SIPHONOPHORE
Agalma okeni
SIZE: to 6.5 cm (2½ in.)   Siphonophores – Agalmatidae
ID: Translucent; series of paired swimming bells below a tiny gas float followed by rigid angular structure (siphosome) trailing numerous tentacles to 12 in. Open water from surface to 100 ft.; painful sting. Occasional S. Florida, Bahamas, Caribbean.

FLOATING SIPHONOPHORES
Rhizophysa spp.
SIZE: to 5 cm (2 in.)   Siphonophores – Rhizophysidae
ID: Translucent; multiple projections below small gas float bear numerous highly contractible tentacles that can extend to 30 ft. Tentacles contracted in pictured specimen. Open water from surface to 130 ft.; painful sting. Occasional Caribbean.

RED-SPOTTED SIPHONOPHORE
Forskalia edwardsi
Siphonophores – Forskaliidae
SIZE: to 6.5 cm (2½ in.)
ID: Translucent; numerous swimming bells below small gas float extend in multiple directions with **numerous appendages lined with red dots** and tentacles attached. Open water from surface to 130 ft.; painful sting. Occasional to uncommon S. Florida, Bahamas, Caribbean.

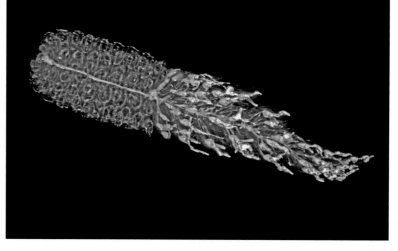

Box Jellies & Jellyfishes

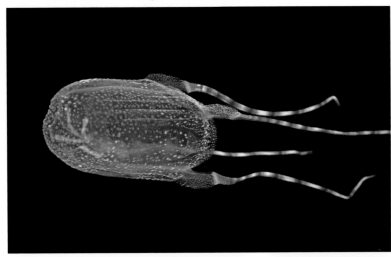

BANDED BOX JELLY
Tamoya ohboya
Box Jellies – Tamoyidae
SIZE: dome length to 5 cm
(2 ½ in.)
ID: Elongate translucent rectangular dome with a tentacle extending from each of the four corners; **distinctly patterned tentacles reddish brown and white banded.** Swim horizontally near surface to 10 ft.; severe and dangerous sting. Rinse affected area with vinegar and/or liquid lidocaine to repress unfired stinging nematocyst; apply papain or bromelain to denature venom. (Do not use meat tenderizer.) Rare Caribbean; most frequently sighted in Bonaire, but also encountered in E. Caribbean, Cozumel, Mexico and Utila, Honduras.

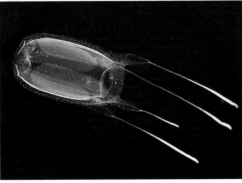

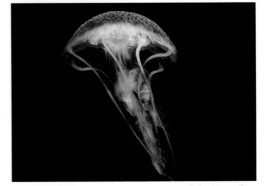

SEA WASP   *Alatina alata*
SIZE: dome length to 25 cm (10 in.)   Box Jellies – Alatinidae
ID: Elongate translucent rectangular dome with pinkish tentacle hanging from each of the four corners. Open water to 20 ft.; painful sting. First aid: [see above]. Tend to occur at night 7/8 day after full moon. Uncommon Florida, Bahamas, Caribbean; circumtropical.

WARTY JELLYFISH   *Pelagia noctiluca*
SIZE: dome to 10 cm (4 in.)   Jellyfishes – Pelagiidae
ID: Translucent with red, mauve or yellow highlights; nematocyst-bearing warts scattered across the dome; 8 contractible marginal tentacles; 4 long frilly oral arms; painful sting. Open water to 10 ft. Occasional Florida, Bahamas, Caribbean.

ATLANTIC SEA NETTLE
Chrysaora quinquecirrha
Jellyfishes – Pelagiidae
SIZE: dome to 25 cm (10 in.)
ID: Whitish to yellow with **16 reddish brown radiating bands near dome margin;** four ruffled oral arms; numerous long tentacles ring margin. Open water near surface; moderate sting. Occasional Florida; also Gulf of Mexico.

MOON JELLY
Aurelia aurita
Jellyfishes – Ulmaridae
SIZE: dome to 40 cm (16 in.)
ID: Translucent whitish, pinkish or bluish dome with numerous short encircling tentacles; **four clover leaf-shaped reproductive organs visible through translucent dome;** four short frilly oral arms. Open water from surface to 20 ft.; often occur in large numbers in inshore waters; mild to moderate sting. Common Florida, Bahamas, Caribbean

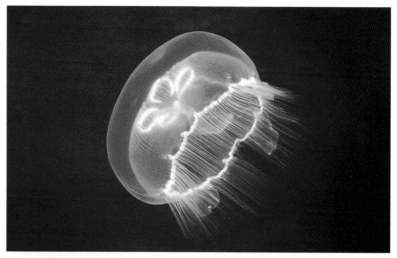

PINK MEANIE
SIZE: to 1 m (3 ft.)
Drymonema larsoni
Jellyfishes – Drymonematidae
ID: Smooth saucer-shaped dome with lappets; numerous tentacles; four large cauliflowerlike lip lobes extend from feeding tube; whitish, pink to purple, occasionally orange. Coastal pelagic; painful sting; Occasional Florida, Bahamas, Caribbean.

SEA THIMBLE
Linuche unguiculata
Jellyfishes – Linuchidae
SIZE: dome to 2 cm (³/₄ in.)
ID: Small brown thimble-shaped dome with a few short tentacles around margin. Surface waters. Contact may produce a mild sting and redness. Blooms can blanket upper layer of water column during late spring especially along east coast of Florida and Bahamas. Tiny larvae, which seem to accompany swarms of adults, can cause an irritating week-long rash to sensitive skin, known as "swimmers itch." Occasional Florida, Bahamas, Caribbean; also circumtropical.

Jellyfishes

CANNONBALL JELLY
Stomolophus meleagris
Jellyfishes – Stomolophidae
SIZE: dome to 25 cm (10 in.)
ID: Bulb-shaped dome white to brown often with colors and markings especially around margin of dome; short forked oral arms encircle stout protruding feeding tube; no marginal tentacles. Open water from surface to 10 ft.; slight sting. Occasional Florida, Caribbean.

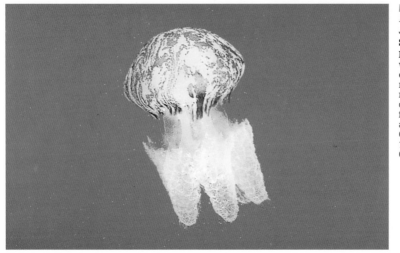

MARBLED JELLY
Lychnorhiza lucerna
Jellyfishes – Lychnorhizidae
SIZE: dome to 15 cm (6 in.)
ID: Marbled markings on whitish dome with lappets encircling margin; oral arms resembling grape clusters nearly equal to in length to diameter of dome; numerous filaments extend from oral arms. Identification tentative. Open water from surface to 15 ft.; painful sting. Rare Caribbean.

WHITE-SPOTTED JELLYFISH
Phyllorhiza punctata
Jellyfishes – Mastigiidae
SIZE: dome to 25 cm (10 in.)
ID: Shades of blue to blue-green or brown with **numerous white spots on thick dome** with slightly lumpy surface; oral arms with clublike appendages; no marginal tentacles. Open water near surface; mild sting. Invasive species. Occasional to uncommon Florida, Bahamas, Caribbean.

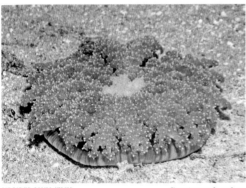

UPSIDEDOWN JELLY   *Cassiopea frondosa*
SIZE: dome to 25 cm (10 in.)   Jellyfishes – Cassiopeidae
ID: Flattened dome with **short branching oral arms** in grapelike clusters; yellowish green; rest on bottom with arms up to sustain symbiotic algae; can swim short distances. Shallow coastal waters; mild sting. Common Florida, Bahamas, Caribbean.

MANGROVE UPSIDEDOWN JELLY   *Cassiopea xamachana*
SIZE: dome to 30 cm (12 in.)   Jellyfishes – Cassiopeidae
ID: Flattened dome with branching oral arms in grapelike clusters; numerous **long leaflike appendages;** grayish, often with blue, red, green; rest on bottom with arms up to sustain symbiotic algae. Coastal waters; mild sting. Common Florida, Bahamas, Caribbean.

IDENTIFICATION GROUP 3
Phylum Ctenophora
(Tee-NOFF-for-uh / L. to bear combs)
Comb Jellies

Ctenophores make up a small phylum of mostly transparent, free-floating marine organisms that can be easily mistaken for jellyfishes. However, there are a few distinct features that easily distinguish the groups. Comb jellies are usually small, no more than one to two inches across, and have either two thin, trailing **tentacles** or lack them altogether. Their delicate bodies, which, for most species, break apart easily when touched, often tend to be oval or pear-shaped rather than having an open dome like jellyfish. Stinging nematocysts are absent in the phylum.

The group's most important visual characteristic is the presence of eight rows or bands of hair-cilia, called **ciliated combs**. Beating of the cilia in coordinated waves, which provides mobility, also sends waves of iridescent light along the comb rows. Comb jellies often appear in large numbers, called blooms, just beneath the surface where they prey on tiny planktonic animals.

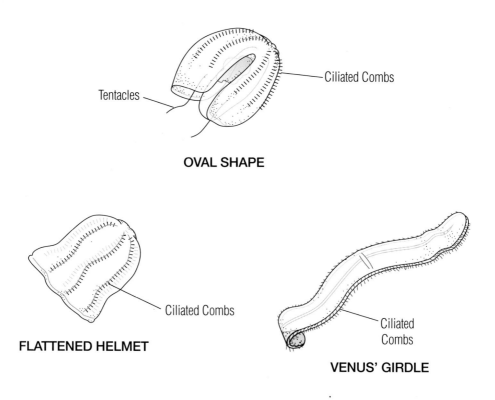

Tentacles

Ciliated Combs

OVAL SHAPE

Ciliated Combs

FLATTENED HELMET

Ciliated Combs

VENUS' GIRDLE

SEA WALNUT
Mnemiopsis mccradyi

Comb Jellies – Bolinopsidae

SIZE: to 10 cm (4 in.)

ID: Walnut or occasionally pear-shaped with large oral lobes and some lateral compression; often speckled with numerous small warts; opalescent or translucent; frequently with greenish amber cast. Open water from surface to 15 ft. Often appear in large aggregations over reefs, in bays and harbors, especially in summer months. Bioluminescent; if disturbed at night produce a greenish blue light. Common Florida, Bahamas, Caribbean.

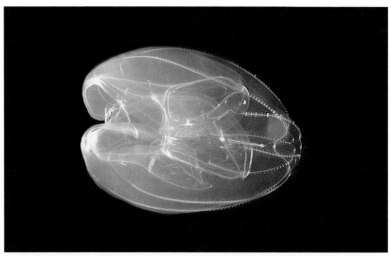

WARTY COMB JELLY
Leucothea multicornis

Comb Jellies – Leucotheidae

SIZE: to 20 cm (8 in.)

ID: Largest comb jelly; numerous long conical papillae; transparent to translucent occasionally with yellowish markings; oral lobes tinted brown; two short tentacles. Open water; surface to 130 ft. During calm weather often float near surface. May appear in large aggregations over reefs in late spring and summer. Bioluminescent; if disturbed at night produce a greenfish blue light. Occasional Florida, Bahamas, Caribbean.

WINGED COMB JELLY *Ocyropsis maculata immaculata*

SIZE: to 9 cm (3½ in.) Comb Jellies – Ocyropsidae

ID: Two large oral lobes and compressed body form hourglass shape; transparent to translucent; occasionally have milky warts. Open water; surface to 15 ft. Occasional Florida, Bahamas, Caribbean.

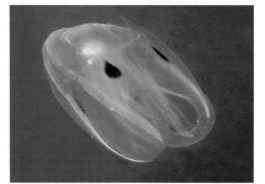

SPOT-WINGED COMB JELLY *Ocyropsis* sp.

SIZE: to 10 cm (4 in.) Comb Jellies – Ocyropsidae

ID: Two large oral lobes and compressed body form hourglass shape; transparent to translucent; **four conspicuous brown spots** on large oral lobes. Open water; surface to 15 ft. Occasional Florida, Bahamas, Caribbean; also circumtropical.

Comb Jellies

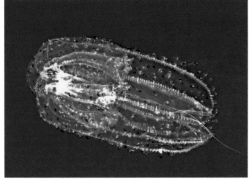

BROWN-SPOTTED COMB JELLY   *Leucothea pulchra*
SIZE: to 25 cm (10 in.)   Comb Jellies – Leucotheidae
ID: Brownish orange wartlike papillae on body; large oral lobes (not spread); two long secondary tentacles extend from mouth. **TR**-Juvenile: In process of developing lobes. Open water; near surface when calm. Uncommon Florida, Bahamas, Caribbean.

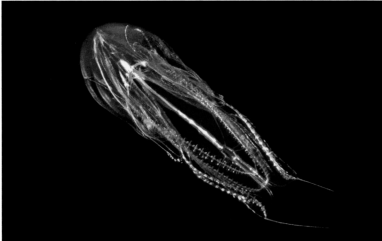

REDSPOT COMB JELLY
Eurhamphaea vexilligera
Comb Jellies – Eurhamphaeidae
SIZE: to 9 cm (3½ in.)

ID: Narrow transparent elongated body with small oral lobes (about one-quarter of body length). Pores in the combs of cilia contain a red, oily, dye-like substance that makes the combs appear as rows of brilliant red dots. If disturbed emit red dye into water as a fluorescing cloud. Bioluminescent; if disturbed at night produce a greenish blue light. Extremely fragile. Occasional Florida, Caribbean, Bahamas.

SEA GOOSEBERRY
Euplokamis sp.
Comb Jellies – Euplokamidae
SIZE: to 2 cm (¾ in.)

ID: Egg-shaped narrowing at. oral end; comb rows extend from three-quarters body length; two tentacles with branching side filaments; when contracted, filaments coil tightly into tear-drop shape. Transparent to translucent with slight reddish pigmentation along edges of comb rows. Propelled by ciliated combs which can reverse spreading tentacles in a corkscrew pattern. Open water; near surface. Occasional Caribbean.

VENUS'S GIRDLE
Cestum veneris

Comb Jellies – Cestidae

SIZE: to 150 cm (5 ft.)

ID: Long ribbon-shaped body. Young transparent becoming violet with age; often display greenish blue fluorescence; edge of body curves out from central axis. A similar, but smaller species, Small Venus's Girdle, *Velamen parallelum*, [next], has straight edge extending from central axis. Although can reach 5 ft., rarely more than 2 ft. Open water; often near surface. Occasional Florida, Bahamas, Caribbean.

SMALL VENUS'S GIRDLE
Velamen parallelum

Comb Jellies – Cestidae

SIZE: to 15 cm (6 in.)

ID: Transparent ribbon-shaped body often with blue to violet fluorescence; edge of body straight from central axis. Similar, larger species, Venus's Girdle, *Cestum veneris*, [previous], has curving edge extending from central axis. Swim with undulating motion. Oceanic; occasionally over deep reefs. Occasional Florida, Bahamas, Caribbean.

FLATTENED HELMET COMB JELLY
Beroe ovata

Comb Jellies – Beroidae

SIZE: to 15 cm (6 in.)

ID: Translucent flat helmet-shape; often bluish but can appear milky; internal canals often pink to reddish brown; young spotted. Range from shallows of mangrove bays to oceanic waters. Primarily consume other comb jellies. Occasional Florida, Bahamas, Caribbean.

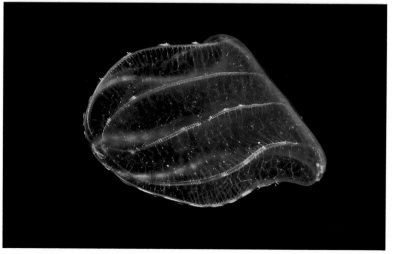

Phylum Platyhelminthes

(Plat-ee-hell-MIN-theez / Gr. broad flat worm)

Flatworms

Flatworms, Order Polycladida, are the most primitive animals with bilateral symmetry, a definite front and rear section, and a dorsal and ventral surface. The primitive beginnings of specialized body organs, a complex nervous system, and three tissue layers are present. Like the cnidarians, they have a single body opening on their ventral surface, which serves as both **mouth and anus.** Most reef species have rudimentary sensory organs in the form of **pseudotentacles** on their heads, although a few species have evolved actual tentacles. **Eye spots** that function simply in the detection of light are developed in many species.

Flatworms are flat, elongate ovals that range in length from one to five inches. The only animals on the reef that they can be confused with are the thick-bodied nudibranches (sea slugs), which are also brightly colored and have an oval shape. Although not particularly uncommon, flatworms are not frequently sighted because they spend the majority of their time under rocks and in dark recesses, scavenging for small invertebrates and the remains of dead animals. Their slow, gliding movement over the bottom is accomplished primarily by the beating of cilia on their ventral surface. In larger species, muscular waves, or ripples, running the length of the body, assist in movement. On rare occasions they swim in open water using an undulating motion.

Acoel Flatworms

Traditionally acoel flatworms are classified in Platyhelminthes. However, recent studies using molecular phylogenetic analysis suggest that acoels are not members of Platyhelminthes, but are rather extant members of the earliest diverging Bilateria. It has been suggested they be placed in Phylum Acoelomorpha. Nonetheless, we include them in this chapter until classification status is clearly established.

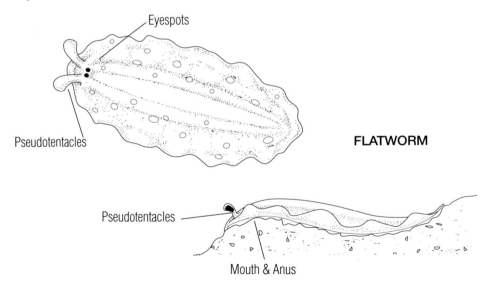

Eyespots

Pseudotentacles

FLATWORM

Pseudotentacles

Mouth & Anus

ACOEL FLATWORMS
Acoela Flatworms –
Convolutidae
SIZE: to 6 mm (¹/₄ in.)
ID: Typically small flat and disc-shaped; no eyespots; often in great numbers on sponges and corals. There are conflicting data on where Acoela belong on the tree of life. Traditionally the group has been considered as flatworms.

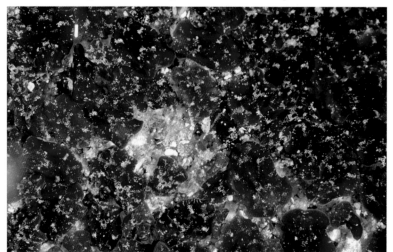

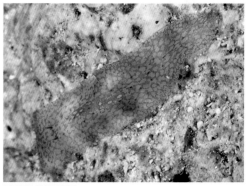

LATTICED FLATWORM   *Styloplanocera fasciata*
SIZE: to 4 cm (1¹/₂ in.) Polyclad Flatworms – Gnesiocerotidae
ID: Tan with brown netlike pattern; scattering of brown spots; dense covering of tiny tubercles; pair of short thin tentacles set back from front of head. Beneath rocks in shallows, including tide pools. Uncommon Florida, W. Caribbean.

RUSTY FLATWORM   *Melloplana ferruginea*
SIZE: to 4 cm (1¹/₂ in.)   Polyclad Flatworms – Pleioplanidae
ID: Translucent white; internal organs form opaque white mid-dorsal streak (occasionally organs rusty brown); two small clusters of light sensitive spots on head. Beneath rocks and on algae. Uncommon Florida, Bahamas, Caribbean.

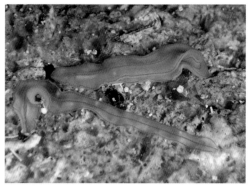

REDBAND FLATWORM   *Cestoplana rubrocincta*
SIZE: to 7.5 cm (3 in.)   Polyclad Flatworms – Cestoplanidae
ID: Reddish yellow ribbonlike body with three thin red to orange stripes; front of head and belly white. Beneath rocks in shallows. Eastern Atlantic species; known from Grand Cayman.

STIPPLED FLATWORM   *Idioplana atlantica*
SIZE: to 2.5 cm (1 in.) Polyclad Flatworms – Pseudostylochidae
ID: Salmon; stippled with brownish orange oval spots that decrease in number toward head and become smaller along margin of body; pair of widely spaced tentacles set back on head. Seagrass and reefs to 20 ft. Rare Florida, W. Caribbean.

Polyclad Flatworms

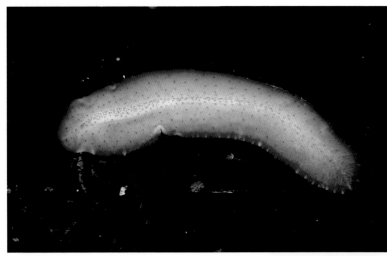

FRECKLED FLATWORM
Enchiridium periommatum
Polyclad Flatworms –
Prosthiostomidae
SIZE: to 4.5 cm (1³/₄ in.)
ID: Elongate; translucent white with dense brown to orange speckling along midbody becoming sparse toward margin of skirt. Reefs and hard bottoms to 40 ft. Common to uncommon Florida, Caribbean.

POPE'S FLATWORM *Diposthus popeae*
SIZE: to 1.4 cm (¹/₂ in.) Polyclad Flatworms – Diposthidae
ID: Translucent wedge-shape body; visible internal organs appear pinkish. Coral reefs and rubble. Uncommon Caribbean.

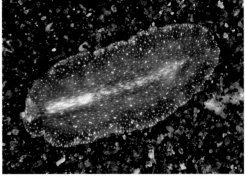

ARCEYE FLATWORM *Cycloporus sp.*
SIZE: to 4 cm (1¹/₂ in.) Polyclad Flatworms – Euryleptidae
ID: Translucent brown to gray with white spots and speckles; internal organs appear as white midbody streak; pair of close-set folded pseudotentacles; **parallel arcs of black cerebral eyespots behind tentacles.** Rubble to 30 ft. Known from St. Vincent.

PINKSTREAK FLATWORM *Eurylepta aurantiaca*
SIZE: to 2.5 cm (1 in.) Polyclad Flatworms – Euryleptidae
ID: Yellowish to reddish translucent with small white and reddish brown spots; pink to reddish, often raised, midsection with **crossbar of white toward rear;** two dark eyespots. Often beneath rocks to 20 ft. Uncommon Florida, Caribbean.

LINED FLATWORM
Maritigrella crozieri
Polyclad Flatworms –
Euryleptidae
SIZE: to 5 cm (2 in.)
ID: Reddish brown, yellowish or white with **network of dark crisscrossing lines;** thin white margin; occasionally dark submargin; close-set folded pseudotentacles. Rocks, rubble, reefs and mangroves to 35 ft.; occasionally swim. Occasional Florida, Bahamas, Caribbean.

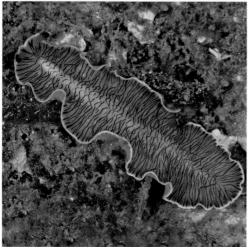

Polyclad Flatworms

NEWMAN'S FLATWORM *Maritigrella newmanae*
SIZE: to 2.5 cm (1 in.)   Polyclad Flatworms – Euryleptidae
ID: White with **thin gold margin;** tightly reticulated network of brownish lines; usually 3 to 5 transverse dark bands; folded pseudotentacles white with dark tips. Rubble from shoreline to 15 ft. Common to occasional Florida, Caribbean.

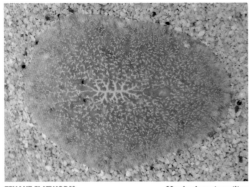

TENANT FLATWORM *Hoploplana inquilina*
SIZE: to 8 mm (³/₈ in.)   Polyclad Flatworms – Hoploplanidae
ID: Translucent bluish or gray with dense reticulated markings over body; **branching white internal organs;** pair of short dark tentacles in front. Beneath rubble, but most frequent inside mantle cavities of oyster-drilling snails. Rare Florida, Bahamas.

GOLDLINE FLATWORM *Maritigrella aureolineata*
SIZE: to 4.5 cm (1³/₄ in.) Polyclad Flatworms – Pseudocerotidae
ID: Broad reddish brown central area with white speckled dark lobes projecting into white, green and yellow margin. Sand, rubble and seagrass to 35 ft. Uncommon Florida, Bahamas, Caribbean.

YELLOW-LINED FLATWORM
Pseudobiceros sp.
Polyclad Flatworms –
Pseudocerotidae
SIZE: to 5 cm (2 in.)
ID: Black with bright yellow central line and branching lines extending to yellow margin; wavy skirt. Algae-covered shallows to 20 ft. Uncommon Caribbean.

LEOPARD FLATWORM
Pseudobiceros pardalis
Polyclad Flatworms –
Pseudocerotidae
SIZE: to 13 cm (5 in.)
ID: Reddish purple to brown with numerous black-ringed orange to yellow spots. Reef and rubble to 75 ft. **MR-** Strong swimmers. **ML-** Juvenile. Visually identical to similar *Pseudoceros pardalis*. Occasional S. Florida, Bahamas, Caribbean.

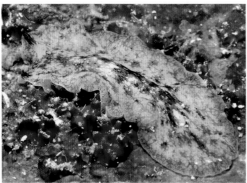

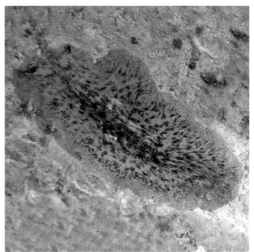

SHARPEYE FLATWORM   *Pericelis cata*
SIZE: to 6.5 cm (2½ in.)   Polyclad Flatworms – Pericelidae
ID: Gray to light brown with dark and occasionally white blotches; widely separated folded pseudotentacles with dark edges and numerous tiny dark eyespots. Beneath rocks to 20 ft. Occasional Caribbean.

Polyclad Flatworms

CARIBBEAN FLATWORM *Pseudobiceros caribbensis*
SIZE: to 2.5 cm (1 in.) Polyclad Flatworms – Pseudocerotidae
ID: Transparent brown with scattering of dark brown spots and a few larger white spots down midbody; occasionally a thin central stripe; folded pseudotentacles white tipped with brown submargin. Rubble to 15 ft. Uncommon Caribbean.

BLACK VELVET FLATWORM *Pseudoceros bolool*
SIZE: to 5 cm (2 in.) Polyclad Flatworms – Pseudocerotidae
ID: Velvety black; light gray underside darkening near margin; cluster of eyespots inside clear area. Reefs to 35 ft. Indo-Pacific species; rare Bahamas, Caribbean.

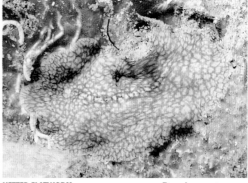

SPLENDID FLATWORM *Pseudobiceros splendidus*
SIZE: to 5 cm (2 in.) Polyclad Flatworms – Pseudocerotidae
ID: Navy blue to dark purple with wavy skirt; thin purple margin and orange to gold submargin. Reef and rubble, often beneath rocks to 75 ft.; good swimmers. Indo-Pacific species; rare Florida, Bahamas, Caribbean.

NETTED FLATWORM *Pseudoceros texanus*
SIZE: to 5 cm (2 in.) Polyclad Flatworms – Pseudocerotidae
ID: White to light gray with tan to brown netlike pattern; short folded pseudotentacles. Reef and rubble, often beneath rocks to 35 ft.; good swimmers. Indo-Pacific species; rare Florida, Bahamas, Caribbean.

BICOLORED FLATWORM *Pseudoceros bicolor*
SIZE: to 4.5 cm (1³/₄ in.) Polyclad Flatworms – Pseudocerotidae
ID: Black to light brown with white radial lines or blotches extending inward from margin; occasionally with white specks; occasionally yellowish green margin. Shallow patch reefs and rubble to 35 ft. Uncommon Florida, Bahamas, Caribbean.

MARGINED-BICOLORED FLATWORM *Pseudoceros bicolor marcusorum*
SIZE: to 4.5 cm (1³/₄ in.) Polyclad Flatworms – Pseudocerotidae
ID: Brown to brownish black with white speckles and spots; occasionally central stripe formed by midbody spots; broad white margin with dark blotches; white-tipped pseudotentacles. Patch reefs, sand and rubble to 35 ft. Uncommon Florida, Caribbean.

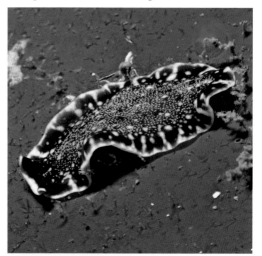

RAWLINSON'S FLATWORM *Pseudoceros rawlinsonae*
SIZE: to 2.5 cm (1 in.) Polyclad Flatworms – Pseudocerotidae
ID: Black to reddish or light brown; occasionally with white speckles and spots; white margin with radial stripes or blotches. **MR-** Brown form has small white branches. Patch reefs, rubble and seagrass to 35 ft. Rare Florida, Bahamas, Caribbean.

RETICULATED FLATWORM
Phrikoceros mopsus
Polyclad Flatworms –
Pseudocerotidae
SIZE: to 1.8 cm (³/₄ in.)

ID: Tan to yellowish with reticulated brown pattern; usually with a black and white midbody stripe; often white speckles and black spots; wavy skirt with thin black margin. Sand, rubble to 20 ft. Uncommon Florida, Caribbean.

WHITECROSS FLATWORM *Thysanozoon brocchii*
SIZE: to 1.2 cm (½ in.) Polyclad Flatworms – Pseudocerotidae
ID: Brown with numerous bulbous tubercles with pointed tips; white midbody stripe with **white crossing band just behind midbody;** white spots around margin. Shallow sand and rubble. Uncommon Florida, Caribbean.

BULBOUS FLATWORM *Thysanozoon* sp.
SIZE: to 1.2 cm (½ in.) Polyclad Flatworms – Pseudocerotidae
ID: Solid back to dark reddish brown with numerous bulbous tubercles; occasional white spotting and white spots around margin. Occasional Florida.

IDENTIFICATION GROUP 5

Phylum Annelida

(Aah-NELL-id-uh / L. little rings)

Segmented Worms

Common earthworms, as well as many marine worms, are members of this phylum. Their distinguishing characteristic is the repetitive segments which divide the worm's body. Marine worms that inhabit reefs belong to the class Polychaeta, and are commonly referred to as polychaetes or polychaete worms.

Feather Duster Worms

CLASS: Polychaeta (Polly-KEY-tuh / Gr. many hairs)
ORDER: Sabellida (Suh-BELL-ih-da / L. sand)
FAMILY: Sabellidae (Suh-BELL-ih-dee / L. sand)

Feather dusters, also known as fan worms, do not appear to be worms at all, because their bodies are hidden inside **parchmentlike tubes** attached to the reef. The flexible tube is constructed of fine sand held together with glue that is secreted by collar glands just below the head. Feather dusters have a highly modified head with a crown of featherlike appendages called **radioles** that are normally extended from the tube. These work as both gills, and for capturing plankton, which is moved to its mouth at the center of the feathery crown. The dramatic colors and patterns of the radioles are often the keys to visual identification. Feather duster worms are very sensitive to nearby movement and changes in light intensity and, if disturbed, instantly retract the crown.

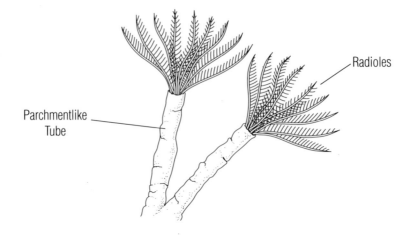

Radioles

Parchmentlike
Tube

FEATHER DUSTER WORMS

Calcareous Tube Worms

CLASS: Polychaeta
ORDER: Sabellida
FAMILY: Serpulidae (Sir-PYULE-ih-dee / L. to creep)

Serpulids build hard, **calcareous tubes** which are often hidden in or on rock, coral, or, occasionally, sponge. Their extended crown of colorful **radioles** form spirals and whorls. Like feather duster worms, the radioles are used to catch food, and will instantly retract when disturbed. A hardened structure, called an **operculum**, covers the tube opening when the worm withdraws. **Hornlike growths** that often extend from the operculum are useful in species identification.

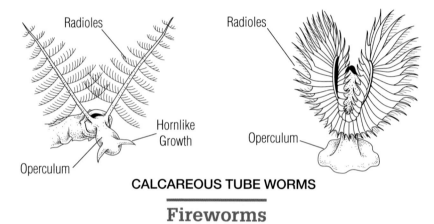

CALCAREOUS TUBE WORMS

Fireworms

CLASS: Polychaeta
ORDER: Amphinomida (Am-fin-NOME-ih-da / L. moving round about)
FAMILY: Amphinomidae (Am-fin-NOME-ih-dee / L. moving round about)

For defense, free-living fireworms have developed the sensory hairs on each segment into bundles of tiny, white, sharp, detachable **bristles**. Also, extending from the segments are clusters of reddish, irregular-branching **gill filaments**, part of their circulatory system. Located on the head is a fleshy plate, called a **caruncle**; its size and shape is often a clue for species identification. These somewhat flattened worms can grow to 12 inches in length. They prefer the cover of rocks during the day, but occasionally can be found crawling about the reef, where they feed on branched corals and gorgonians. When disturbed, fire worms flare their sharp, detachable bristles. These bristles can easily penetrate the skin and break off, causing a painful, irritation.

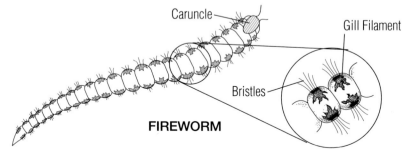

FIREWORM

Scale Worms

CLASS: Polychaeta
ORDER: Phyllodocida (Fill-uh-do-SEE-duh)
FAMILY: Polynoidae (Polly-NOY-dee / L. to creep)

These typically flattened worms have two rows of rounded plates **(scales)** that cover their segments. **Swollen tubercles** often rise from the scales, and some species have small bundles of **bristles** extending from the bottom of segments. Many species of scale worms are commensal with other marine invertebrates including sea stars, sea cucumbers and soft corals, while others are free living or inhabit tubes they construct.

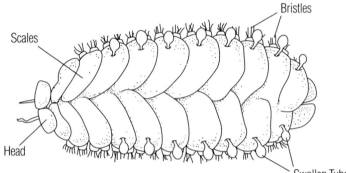

SCALE WORM

Phylum Nemertea

(Neh-MER-tee-uh / G. sea nymph)

Ribbon Worms

CLASS: Anopla (AN-uh-pluh)
SUBCLASS: Heteronemertea (HEH-te-ro-neh-MER-tee-uh)

Ribbon worms are long, slender, elastic and somewhat flattened. Most species occurring on tropical reefs are brightly colored and striped. Their anatomical features are quite similar to flatworms, but are more highly organized having a digestive system that includes both a **mouth** and **anus**. Although fairly common they are rarely observed spending most of their lives under rocks, beneath algae or inside deep recesses where they prey on small invertebrates.

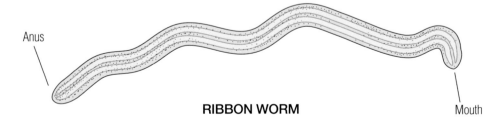

RIBBON WORM

Phylum Phoronida

(For-RON-ah-duh / L. character in Greek mythology)

Horseshoe Worms

FAMILY: Phoronidae (For-RON-ee-dee)

Horseshoe worms, often called phoronids, are a small group of marine animals consisting of only two genera that include about 12 species. They are small, wormlike animals that secrete a leathery or chitinous tube within which the body moves freely, but never leaves. Only the feeding head and anus are extended from the tube. The tube may be anchored to rocks, pilings or buried in sand or mud. The feeding head of several species extend out of the tube as a pair of rolled spirals bearing numerous slender ciliated tentacles composed of two parallel ridges curved into the shape of a horseshoe. If disturbed, the head can be completely withdrawn into the tube.

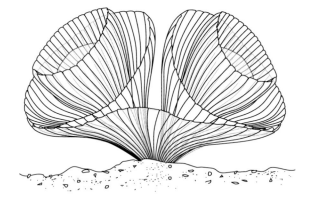

FEEDING HEAD OF HORSESHOE WORM

Feather Duster Worms

SIZE: crown to 15 cm (6 in.)

ID: Largest Caribbean feather duster; radioles arranged in a double circular pattern; banded in shades of brown, reddish brown, tan, gold and reddish purple; parchmentlike tubes often buried. Reefs and sand, often grow from coral heads and inside sponges from 10 to 60 ft. Common to uncommon Florida, Bahamas, Caribbean.

SOCIAL FEATHER DUSTER *Bispira brunnea*

SIZE: crown to 3 cm (1¼ in.)   Feather Duster Worms – Sabellidae

ID: Grow in clusters; crowns extend from exposed parchmentlike tubes; circular crowns white, tan, brown or purple; often two-toned with darker centers; occasional banding. Reefs with some water movement from 15 to 60 ft. Common Bahamas, Caribbean.

VARIEGATED FEATHER DUSTER
Bispira variegata
Feather Duster Worms –
Sabellidae
SIZE: crown to 3 cm (1¼ in.)
ID: Crowns can be a solid color, variegated or banded with brown, maroon or violet; parchmentlike tubes usually hidden; dark eyespots often visible on stems of radioles. Reefs, rubble or sand from 20 to 75 ft.; typically in small groups. Occasional Florida, Bahamas, Caribbean.

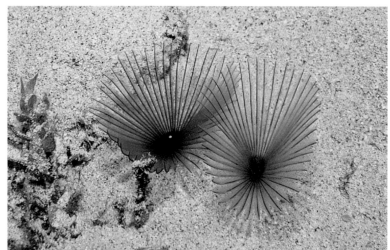

YELLOW FANWORM   *Notaulax occidentalis*
SIZE: crown to 3 cm (1¼ in.)   Feather Duster Worms – Sabellidae
ID: Yellow crown occasionally spotted or thinly banded with purple; occasionally white, red or purple; parchmentlike tubes usually hidden. Protected areas of older reefs without living coral from 10 to 70 ft. Occasional Florida, Bahamas, Caribbean.

BROWN FANWORM   *Notaulax nudicollis*
SIZE: crown to 3 cm (1¼ in.)   Feather Duster Worms – Sabellidae
ID: Crown spotted and banded in white, brown or purple; parchmentlke tubes usually hidden. Protected areas of older reefs without living coral from 10 to 70 ft. Common to occasional Florida, Bahamas, Caribbean.

79

Feather Duster Worms

SPLITCROWN FEATHER DUSTER   *Anamobaea oerstedi*

SIZE: crown to 5 cm (2 in.)   Feather Duster Worms – Sabellidae

ID: **Crowns oval with longitudinal split creating mirrored halves;** brown, orangish, maroon and violet, often with white spots and bands; tubes usually hidden. Solitary or small groups on reefs from 15 to 75 ft. Common Florida, Bahamas, Caribbean.

GHOST FEATHER DUSTER *Anamobaea* sp.
SIZE: crown 2 cm (¾ in.)   Feather Duster Worms – Sabellidae
ID: Circular crown of radioles nearly colorless to white with three very faint maroon bands; darker ring just above mouth. Cluster in large groups; parchmentlike tube visible. Sand near reefs from 15 to 60 ft. Common Florida, Bahamas, Caribbean.

RUFFLED FEATHER DUSTER *Hypsicomus* sp.
SIZE: crown 2 cm (¾ in.)   Feather Duster Worms – Sabellidae
ID: Crown has **pleated structure**; yellowish brown with narrow white ring encircling outer edge and wider white band near mouth; short parchmentlike tube usually visible. Protected areas of reefs and walls from 25 to 75 ft. Occasional

SHY FEATHER DUSTER
Megalomma sp.

Feather Duster Worms –
Sabellidae

SIZE: crown to 2.5 cm (1 in.)
ID: Circular crown with distinctive V-shaped fold on one side; **two inner radioles of fold long and tipped with ball-like eyespots;** lavender or brown with banding and spotting; parchmentlike tube usually hidden inside tight crevices. Eye-spots on tips of radioles cause worm to be unusually sensitive to movement. Reefs from 6 to 75 ft. Occasional S. Florida, Bahamas, Caribbean.

Feather Duster & Calcareous Tube Worms

BLACK-SPOTTED FEATHER DUSTER
Branchiomma nigromaculata
Feather Duster Worms – Sabellidae

SIZE: crown to 2.5 cm (1 in.)
ID: Distinctive **horseshoe-shaped crown;** brownish with white banding; parchmentlike tube usually hidden. Reefs from 6 to 75 ft.; tubes usually extend from tight crevices or sponges. Common S. Florida, Bahamas, Caribbean.

REDCOLLAR TUBE WORM   *Filogranella* sp.
SIZE: crown 2 cm (³/₄ in.) Calcareous Tube Worms – Serpulidae
ID: Grow in clusters with red feathery crowns extending from long white calcareous tubes with **red collars below tube openings.** Sand and rubble. Known from St. Vincent in E. Caribbean.

RED FANWORM   *Pyrgopolon ctenactis*
SIZE: crown to 2.5 cm (1 in.) Calcareous Tube Worms – Serpulidae
ID: Horseshoe-shaped crown with extended calcareous operculum; typically sponge, algae or other serpulids attached to end of operculum; white collar with 20 rounded red knobs encircle operculum mouth. Reefs to 40 ft. Uncommon Caribbean.

STAR HORSESHOE WORM
Pomatostegus stellatus
Calcareous Tube Worms –
Sepulidae
SIZE: crown to 4 cm (1½ in.)
ID: Double fold of radioles
form U-shaped crown; red,
yellow or brown with
highlights of contrasting
colors; long operculum has
rounded tip without spikes
or horns; fine spines form
star-shaped pattern at center
of operculum; calcareous tube
usually hidden. Reefs from
10 to 100 ft. Common Florida,
Bahamas, Caribbean.

RED-SPOTTED HORSESHOE WORM *Protula tubularia*
SIZE: crown to 4 cm (1½ in.)Calcareous Tube Worms – Serpulidae
ID: Double fold of white radioles with red spots form a deep
rounded U-shaped crown; tube has trumpetlike flair. Sheltered
areas of reefs from 15 to 60 ft. Common Caribbean.

TOUCH-ME-NOT FANWORM *Hydroides spongicola*
SIZE: crown to 2.5 cm (1 in.) Calcareous Tube Worms – Serpulidae
ID: Fan-shaped crown translucent with white markings; circular
operculum on long stalk; tubes hidden. Live in association with
Touch-me-not Sponges, *Neofibularia nolitangere*. Occasional
Florida, Bahamas, Caribbean.

Calcareous Tube Worms

CHRISTMAS TREE WORM
Spirobranchus giganteus
Calcareous Tube Worms –
Serpulidae

SIZE: crown to 4 cm (1½ in.)

ID: Two spiraling crowns of radioles; double-horned operculum extends from between radioles; calcareous tube with large spikelike protrusion; highly variable colors and markings.**MR** Spawning. **BR & BL-** Worms highly sensitive to movement retract crowns and close operculum; after a moment radioles emerge slowly; note two pinkish horns extending from operculum. Reefs from 10 to 100 ft.; tubes usually encased in living coral. Abundant Florida, Bahamas, Caribbean; also circumtropical.

SEA FROST
Salmacina huxleyi
Calcareous Tube Worms –
Serpulidae
SIZE: tubes to 15 cm (6 in.)
ID: Tangles of thin white intertwining tubes; often encrust but may grow in small disordered clumps; tiny red crowns of radioles at times extend from ends of tubes. Sheltered areas of reefs and rubble from 20 to 130 ft., often encrust bases of rope and tube sponges beneath overhangs. Common Florida, Bahamas, Caribbean.

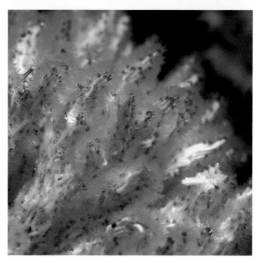

BLUSHING STAR CORAL FANWORM
Vermiliopsis sp.
Calcareous Tube Worms –
Serpulidae
SIZE: crown to 6 mm (¹/₄ in.)
ID: Tiny reddish fans grow on surface of Blushing Star Coral, *Stephanocoenia intersepta;* tubes encased within coral structure. Pictured specimens were collected and visual identification of genus determined by microscopic examination. Little is known about this worm, and it is probably an undescribed species. Occasional S. Florida, Bahamas, Caribbean.

Fireworms

BEARDED FIREWORM   *Hermodice carunculata*
SIZE: to 30 cm (12 in.)   Fireworms – Amphinomidae
ID: Fleshy beardlike appendage on head (caruncle); short tufts
of white bristles and red gill filaments line body; red, green,
yellow or brown. **BR-** Juvenile. Multiple habitats to 130 ft.; bristles
cause painful wound. Common Florida, Bahamas, Caribbean.

BLACKLINE FIREWORM
Chloeia viridis
Fireworms – Amphinomidae
SIZE: to 15 cm (6 in.)
ID: Dark central stripe on back formed by a **black elongated marking on each segment encircled in white;** caruncle on head a ribbed longitudinal arch; light red with white or brownish, yellowish or tan bristles; tufts of gill filaments line each side of center line. Sand and rubble, occasionally on reefs from shallow to 130 ft.; bristles cause painful wound. Common to occasional Florida, Bahamas, Caribbean.

WHITE-SPOTTED FIREWORM   *Chloeia* sp.
SIZE: to 15 cm (6 in.)   Fireworms – Amphinomidae
ID: Two stripes down center of back formed by series of white spots;** light red to tan or brown with heavy covering of red and white bristles. Sand and rubble from shallow to 130 ft.; bristles cause painful wound. Occasional Florida, Bahamas, Caribbean.

Scale & Large Elongated Worms

ORNATE SCALE WORM
Undetermined
Scale Worms – Polynoidae
SIZE: to 6.5 cm (2½ in.)

ID: There are seven families of scale worms in Order Phyllodocida and Suborder Aphroditiformia that can be recognized by two rows of overlapping protective plates, known as elytra, usually 18 pairs, which may be ornamented with papillae, tubercles or hairs. Many species live symbiotically with corals, sponges, sea stars or sea cucumbers; typically secretive often beneath rocks and debris, some species burrow into sand.

FRINGED SCALE WORM *Harmothoe areolata*
SIZE: to 5 cm (2 in.) Scale Worms – Polynoidae
ID: Two rows of overlapping tan, brown or gray plates with **numerous tiny dark papillae scattered over surface and fringe of papillae lining edge;** fringe of tentacles extend from rear. Sand and rubble. Uncommon Florida, Bahamas, Caribbean.

YELLOW-RIMMED SCALE WORM *Acoetes* sp.
SIZE: to 5 cm (2 in.) Scale Worms – Acoetidae
ID: Overlapping protective plates brown to tan rimmed with narrow yellow border. Sand and rubble. Known from St. Vincent in E. Caribbean.

VARIEGATED SCALE WORM *Malmgreniella variegata*
SIZE: to 2.5 cm (1 in.) Scale Worms – Polynoidae
ID: Two rows of overlapping white to tan plates; **dark crescent-shaped marking on inner half of each rounded plate** with thin dark margin; head region narrows to point. Occasional Caribbean.

BOBBIT WORMS *Eunice* spp.
SIZE: to 2 m (6 ft.)   Large Elongated Worms – Eunicidae
ID: Typically large muscular segmented worms living in concealed habitats such as inside reef interiors, sand burrows or beneath rocks. **TR-** Distinguished by a large retractable jaw complex consisting of two pairs of scissorlike serrated plates, one above the other; usually 5 prominent beaded and banded antennaelike structures extend from head. Comblike branched gills extend from each mid-body segment. Most family members in genus *Eunice* with more than 200 species worldwide. Length varies from two inches to many feet. Pictured specimen measured approximately 5 ft. in length and an inch in width.

ATLANTIC PALOLO *Eunice fucata*
SIZE: to 60 cm (2 ft.)   Large Elongated Worms – Eunicidae
ID: Long thin reddish tan with iridescent sheen; faint transverse band on each of first 40 segments. Beneath rocks. Identification tentative. Occasional Florida, Bahamas, Caribbean.

GREENHEAD EUNICE *Eunice violaceomaculata*
SIZE: to 30 cm (12 in.)   Large Elongated Worms – Eunicidae
ID: Five banded antennae; first five body segments iridescent greenish blue; 6th segment has white band; remaining segments greenish blue and tan; banded legs. Identification tentative. Uncommon Florida, Caribbean; also Gulf of Mexico.

LONG-BRISTLED EUNICE *Eunice longisetis*
SIZE: to 40 cm (16 in.)   Large Elongated Worms – Eunicidae
ID: Tan to brown with reddish forebody followed by white band; beaded antennae. Juvenile pictured. Identification tentative. Uncommon Florida, Caribbean.

Segmented Worms

TUBE-DWELLING WORMS
Tube-building Worms –
Onuphidae
SIZE: to 6 cm (2¼ in.)
ID: Family members
construct thin parchmentlike
tubes of mucus and sand,
which can be stationary or
transported. Five tentacles
extend from the head;
segments 2-8 bear parapodia
use for crawling or digging.

BLUE AND ORANGE ONUPHID *Onuphis* sp.
SIZE: to 5 cm (2 in.)   Tube-building Worms – Onuphidae
ID: Dark iridescent blue with white banding; three elongate
antennae with wide orange bases and purplish tips; segments
2-8 bear orange and white branched parapodia. Known from St.
Vincent in E. Caribbean.

PAINTED BRISTLE WORM *Hesione picta*
SIZE: to 5 cm (2 in.)   Hesionoid Worms – Hesionidae
ID: Fifteen white bands on gray to dark gray robust elongate
body; prominent white parapodia with tufts of short bristlelike
projections, known as setae, extend from sides of body segments.
Often beneath rocks. Uncommon Florida, Caribbean.

DARK-LINED BRISTLE WORM
Hesione intertexta
Hesionoid Worms –
Hesionidae
SIZE: to 5.5 cm (2¼ in.)
ID: Light tan with numerous
short brown to black
longitudinal striations; series
of white medial spots and
dashes form a vague central
stripe. Sand and rubble.
Occasional Florida, Bahamas,
Caribbean; also circumtropical.

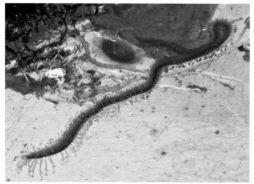

RAGWORMS & CLAM WORMS
SIZE: to 7.5 cm (3 in.)   Ragworms & Clam Worms – Nereididae
ID: The polychaete worm family Nereididae includes nearly 500 primarily marine species. Identification to species requires a close examination in a laboratory setting. Photo from Grand Cayman.

ORANGE ZEBRA SYLLID WORM
Trypanosyllis zebra
SIZE: to 5.5 cm (2¼ in.)   Syllid Worms – Syllidae
ID: Orange with a dark line between segments; numerous long translucent-white cirri curling at tips extend from sides of each segment; two eyespots, three tentacles and two palps on head. Uncommon Florida, Bahamas, Caribbean; also circumtropical.

YELLOWFLAP SYLLID WORM
Proceraea janetae
Syllid Worms – Syllidae
SIZE: to 4.5 cm (1¾ in.)

ID: Long slender whitish worm with series of yellow flaplike cirri running length of back; short dark bands and spots. Often found in association with Great Star Coral, *Montastraea cavernosa.* Occasional Caribbean.

ROBUST SYLLID WORM
Amblyosyllis sp.
Syllid Worms – Syllidae
SIZE: to 4.5 cm (1¾ in.)

ID: Nine dark bulbous body segments with long thin white cirri; head white with bold dark spotting. Probably an undescribed species. Known from San Andres, Colombia.

Segmented Worms

SPONGE WORM
Haplosyllis gula
SIZE: to 4 mm (1/8 in.)
Syllid Worms – Syllidae
ID: Thousands of tiny translucent white worms on inner walls of sponges, most commonly on Touch-me-not Sponge, *Neofibularia nolitangere* from 10 to 130 ft. Occasional Florida, Bahamas, Caribbean.

SPAGHETTI WORMS
Spaghetti Worms – Terebellidae
SIZE: body to 15 cm (6 in.)
tentacles to 1 m (3 ft.)

ID: Long elastic translucent to white feeding tentacles extend from coral, rocks or rubble; body encased inside tube constructed of sand and "cement" secreted from glands. Retractable tentacles lined with fine hairlike cilia extend from the mouth spreading across sea floor in search of food; tentacles quickly retract when disturbed. Common Florida, Bahamas, Caribbean.

CHAETOPTERID WORMS *Mesochaetopterus* sp.
SIZE: palp to 15 cm (6 in.) Chaetopterid Worms – Chaetopteridae
ID: Worms construct mucus tubes just beneath surface; extend two antennalike structures, known as palps, at night to feed. Identification to species requires laboratory examination of specimen. Occasional Florida, Caribbean.

SOUTHERN LUGWORM
Arenicola cristata
Lugworms – Arenicolidae
SIZE: to 15 cm (6 in.)
ID: Volcanic cone-shaped mounds in sand; resident worms live in U-shaped burrows below sand and never appear above surface. Sand and seagrass from 3 to 60 ft; the deposit feeders ingest sand removing organic material before expelling remains from burrows with water pressure forming conical mounds. Common Florida, Bahamas, Caribbean.

WORM ROCK *Phragmatopoma caudata*
SIZE: to 4 cm (1½ in.) Worm Rock – Sabellariidae
ID: Intertwining rows of fluted holes cover surface of hard cementlike structures created over many generations by marine worms; may eventually form shallow-water reefs, known as worm reefs. Common coastal S.E. Florida.

ACORN WORMS
SIZE: to 20 cm (8 in.) Acorn Worms – Class Enteropneusta
ID: Burrowing deposit feeding worms live in U-shaped burrows beneath sand; ingest sand removing organic material before expelling remains that form coiling cast. In phylum Hemichordata. Occasional Florida, Bahamas, Caribbean.

Ribbon, Spoon & Peanut Worms

RIBBON WORMS
Ribbon Worms –
Phylum Nemertea

ID: Elongate and elastic, typically flat, nonsegmented worms. Cryptic and not regularly sighted; tend to be nocturnal; many species are quite colorful. Numerous ribbon worms use tiny ciliated hairs on their bodies to crawl slowly forward on a trail of mucus secreted by the worms. Reliable visual identification yet to be established for most species; many remain scientifically undescribed.

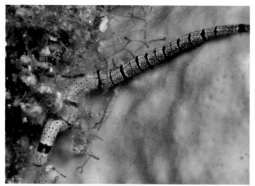

BLACK-BANDED RIBBON WORM *Tubulanus rhabdotus*
SIZE: to 15 cm (6 in.)   Ribbon Worms – Tubulanidae
ID: Gray body with dark banding; single wide band just behind mouth. **TR-** Worm consuming radioles of feather duster worm. Shallow oyster beds, coral reefs and dock pilings. Uncommon Florida, Bahamas, Caribbean.

WHITE-STRIPED RIBBON WORM
Micrura sp.
Ribbon Worms – Lineidae
SIZE: to 10 cm (4 in.)
ID: Long flattened white body with red dorsal surface split by **distinctive white central stripe** running length of back. Occasional W. Caribbean.

RED-BLISTERED SPOON WORM *Ochetostoma erythrogrammon*
SIZE: to 15 cm (6 in.)   Spoon Worms – Phylum Echiura
ID: Pinkish with **several reddish stripes formed by rounded, slightly raised, blisterlike structures;** thin rolled feeding proboscis extends from head. Uncommon Florida, Bahamas, Caribbean.

PEANUT WORMS
SIZE: to 7.5 cm (3 in.)   Peanut Worms – Phylum Sipuncula
ID: Robust translucent unsegmented worms with numerous thin, slightly raised, stripes extending length of bodies, which narrow anteriorly; numerous tiny ciliated tentacles encircling mouths. Burrow beneath sand. Uncommon Florida, Bahamas, Caribbean.

Horseshoe Worms

SIZE: to 2.5 cm (1 in.)

ID: Twin spiraling crowns with two and a half to three whorls; colors highly variable from translucent to pink, peach, dark reddish or black. Clusters extend from sand around the bases of tube-dwelling anemones. Uncommon Florida, Bahamas, Caribbean; circumtropical.

UNDETERMINED
Phoronopsis sp.
Horseshoe Worms –
Phylum Phoronida

SIZE: to 2.5 cm (1 in.)

ID: Twin spiraling crowns with four whorls; white to pink or greenish. Solitary; extend from tubes buried in sand. Photo from St. Vincent in E. Caribbean.

CALIFORNIA HORSESHOE WORM
Phoronopsis californica
Horseshoe Worms –
Phylum Phoronida
SIZE: to 4 cm (1½ in.)
ID: Long pair of spiraling crowns with 4 to 12 whorls bearing more than 1,500 tentacles that vary from orange to brown or red, often with white highlights. A solitary species; only a small portion of buried white-speckled tube extends above sand. Occasional Florida, Bahamas, Caribbean; also Pacific and Eastern Atlantic.

UNDETERMINED

Horseshoe Worms –
Phylum Phoronida
SIZE: to 4 cm (1½ in.)
ID: Twin tightly spiraling crowns; orange with purple highlights with white speckling. Known from S.E. Florida.

Phylum Arthropoda

(Are-THROP-uh-duh / Gr. jointed leg)

Subphylum Crustacea

(Krus-STAY-shuh / L. covered by a hard shell)

Shrimp, Lobsters, Crabs, Barnacles

Including insects, spiders, and many marine creatures, arthropods make up the largest phylum in the Animal Kingdom with about two million described species. The phylum members' most distinguishing features are jointed legs and an exoskeleton. A cuticular material, forming the often elaborate exoskeletons, is secreted to form an array of plates and tubes connected by flexible membranes to allow movement. While the exoskeleton provides excellent protection, it has the drawback of restricting growth. To remedy this problem, all arthropods periodically molt – shedding their old covering and replacing it with a new enlarged version. Because the animal is vulnerable to predators during this process, molting usually takes place in secluded recesses.

Marine arthropods are members of the Subphylum Crustacea; and most reef-dwelling species, including shrimps, crabs, and lobsters reside in Class Malacostraca, which have three distinct body parts, head, thorax and abdomen. The head and thorax are fused and covered by a dorsal shell called a carapace. Members of the largest group of crustaceans, Order Decapoda, are distinguished by having five pairs of legs. The first pair, or sometimes the second, pair of legs of most decapods have evolved claws for feeding and defense leaving four pairs of walking legs.

Shrimp

ORDER: Decapoda (Deck-ah-POE-duh / Gr. ten legs)
INFRAORDER: Caridea and Stenopodidea (Ka-RID-ee-uh)

Shrimp can easily be distinguished by their **long, hairlike antennae** and laterally compressed bodies with long muscular abdomens bearing fringed swimmerets, known as **pereopods.** Antennae are used for locating food as well as recognizing other individuals and their sexual status. Regular grooming of the antennae, by shrimp and other decapods, keeps receptor sites clean. A few species, known as cleaner shrimp, feed by removing parasites, dead tissue and bacterial debris from fishes. Quite a few shrimp are symbiotic, living exclusively in association with host invertebrates, such as anemones, sea urchins and feather stars. Although normally secretive, most venture out into the open to feed at night.

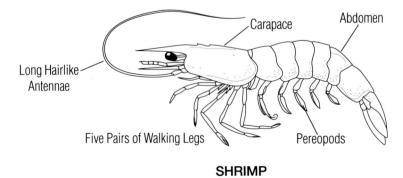

SHRIMP

Lobsters

ORDER: Decapoda
INFRAORDER: Achelata and Astacidea (A-key-LAH-tuh)

Lobsters can be distinguished by their heavy, muscular abdomens and wide, flattened tails. Many have long antennae, except the slipper lobsters whose antenna have evolved into **flattened plates.** Lobsters are nocturnal bottom-dwellers that take refuge during the day under shallow ledge overhangs. They use well-developed legs to walk, but when danger threatens, they can swim backward with darting speed, using powerful strokes of the abdomen and tail.

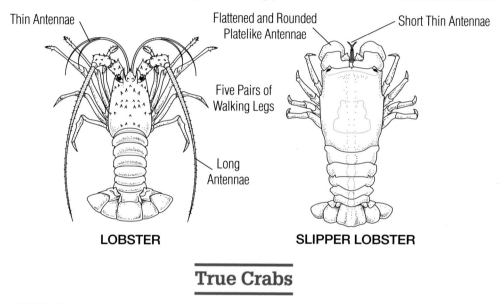

Thin Antennae

Flattened and Rounded Platelike Antennae

Short Thin Antennae

Five Pairs of Walking Legs

Long Antennae

LOBSTER   **SLIPPER LOBSTER**

True Crabs

ORDER: Decapoda
SECTION: Brachyura (Brack-ee-YOUR-uh / Gr. short tail)

True crabs have greatly reduced abdomens and tails, which are kept folded back under their large, rounded and often flattened carapace. They are quickly distinguished from porcelain crabs by having four pairs of visible walking legs. Most do not have noticeable antennae, or at most they are quite thin and short. Many crabs, especially smaller species, are reclusive during the day, appearing at night to feed.

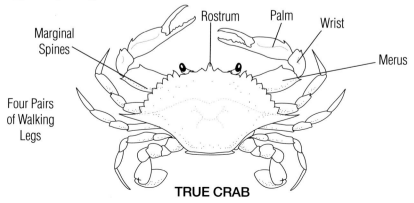

Rostrum   Palm   Wrist

Marginal Spines

Merus

Four Pairs of Walking Legs

TRUE CRAB

Porcelain Crabs

ORDER: Decapoda
SECTION: Anomura (An-oh-MURE-uh / Gr. irregular tail)

Porcelain Crabs appear much like true crabs, but are distinguished by appearing to have only three pairs of walking legs. Their last pair of legs is greatly reduced and hidden beneath the carapace. Their flexible, crablike abdomen is not as compact as those of true crabs but is also kept tucked under the body. Also, unlike true crabs, they have a long pair of antennae. Many species live within the tight confines of branching corals, and on anemones and soft corals where they capture planktonic food by repeatedly extending fanlike mouth parts called setae.

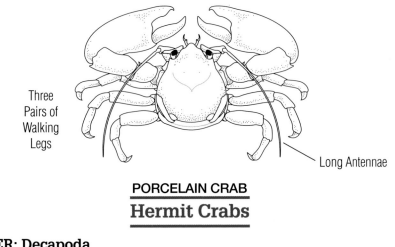

Three Pairs of Walking Legs

Long Antennae

PORCELAIN CRAB

Hermit Crabs

ORDER: Decapoda
SECTION: Anomura

Hermit Crabs use empty seashells as mobile protective retreats, however a few non-mobile species live in small holes in corals and occasionally sponges. They occupy the shell by wrapping their long, modified abdomen around the internal spirals of the shell with only head, antennae and legs extending from the opening. If threatened, they withdraw completely inside the shell for protection. When they outgrow their homes, they simply move into a larger shell.

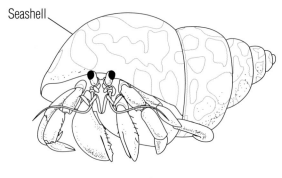

Seashell

HERMIT CRAB

Squat Lobster

ORDER: Decapoda
SECTION: Anomura

Squat Lobsters are not lobsters at all and are more closely related to porcelain crabs and hermit crabs. They are easily distinguished by their flattened bodies and very long claws and arms, which they tend to hold nearly straight forward. Like true crabs their abdomen is typically folded under itself. They appear to have only three pairs of walking legs because the last pair is greatly reduced and kept folded beneath the abdomen.

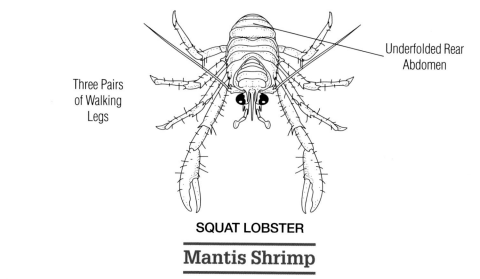

Three Pairs of Walking Legs

Underfolded Rear Abdomen

SQUAT LOBSTER

Mantis Shrimp

ORDER: Decapoda
ORDER: Stomatopoda (Stow-ma-duh-POE-duh / Gr. mouth + foot)

Mantis Shrimp, which look much like praying mantis insects, are not actually shrimp. Stomatapods can be easily distinguished by their large stalked eyes and by having only three pairs of walking legs. They have large powerful claw arms, which are normally held in folded position, poised to strike. There are two basic groups of mantis depending on their type of claw arms: smashers, which have blunt raptorial appendages for breaking shells for food; and spearers that have long back-folding raptorial appendages for grasping prey. Many spearers hunt from the entrance of their burrows, while smashers often prowl in the open during the day.

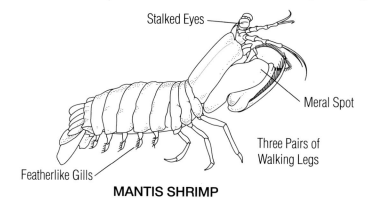

Stalked Eyes

Meral Spot

Three Pairs of Walking Legs

Featherlike Gills

MANTIS SHRIMP

Snapping Shrimp

RED SNAPPING SHRIMP
Alpheus armatus
Snapping Shrimp –
Alpheidae
SIZE: to 5 cm (2 in.)
ID: Dark red to orange body; white blotches on lower abdomen and black spots above; red and purplish legs and uropods (tail); claws red with whitish blotches and red tubercles; red and white banded antennae; **row of iridescent, greenish gold spots on major claw,** also greenish-gold spots at the base of the antennules and along the dorsal midline of the abdomen. Act as cleaner. Live in male/female pairs within Corkscrew Anemone, *Bartholomea annulata,* to 40 ft. Common Caribbean; also Gulf of Mexico.

MANYSPOT SNAPPING SHRIMP
Alpheus polystictus
Snapping Shrimp –
Alpheidae
SIZE: to 5 cm (2 in.)
ID: Dark red to orange body with white spots on lower abdomen and vague black markings above; red and purplish legs and uropods (tail); red and white banded antennae; **thick scattering of gold spots cover both claw arms and antennal scales,** also gold spots on base of antennae. The last abdominal segment is bluish on juveniles. Act as cleaners. Live in male/female pairs within Corkscrew Anemone, *Bartholomea annulata.* Occasional S. Caribbean; rare N. Caribbean.

SPOTLESS SNAPPING SHRIMP
Alpheus immaculatus
Snapping Shrimp –
Alpheidae
SIZE: to 4 cm (1¹/₂ in.)
ID: Body dark red to orange with white spots on lower abdomen and black markings above; red and purplish legs and uropods (tail); red and white banded antennae (not banded on juveniles); both claw arms red to orange with a few large white blotches and small red tubercles; **white spots on claws with no gold markings.** Act as cleaners. Live in male/female pairs within Corkscrew Anemone, *Bartholomea annulata.* Occasionally shallow, most often below 40 ft. Caribbean.

STRIPED SNAPPING SHRIMP   *Alpheus formosus*
SIZE: to 3 cm (1¹/₄ in.)   Snapping Shrimp – Alpheidae
ID: Elongate reddish to purplish brown with broad, unmarked tan dorsal stripe from head to tail and tan lower body; elongate brown claw arms. Sand, rubble, and seagrass, often under rocks and debris to 20 ft. Common Florida, Bahamas, Caribbean.

ORANGE-STRIPED SNAPPING SHRIMP   *Alpheus paraformosus*
SIZE: to 1.9 cm (³/₄ in.)   Snapping Shrimp – Alpheidae
ID: Elongate purplish brown with broad, tan dorsal stripe from head to tail **marked with orange center stripe;** elongate brown claw arms. Sand, rubble, and seagrass, often under rocks and debris to 20 ft. Rare Caribbean from Bonaire, Panama and Utila.

103

Snapping Shrimp

SAND SNAPPING SHRIMP
Alpheus cf. *floridanus*
Snapping Shrimp –
Alpheidae
SIZE: to 5 cm (2 in.)
ID: Build extensive burrows shared with single or pair of gobies. Whitish tan (similar to sand color) occasionally with vague banding or dash markings running length of back; long claw arms. Primarily **symbiotic with Orangespotted Goby, *Nes longus,*** that act as sentinels while shrimp emerge from opening. Wary; dart into cover when approached, but usually reappear. Inhabit areas of fine sand, often in canals, harbors or mangroves from shallows to 120 ft. Occasional Florida, Bahamas, Caribbean.

REDBAND SNAPPING SHRIMP *Alpheus packardii*
SIZE: to 3 cm (1¼ in.)   Snapping Shrimp – Alpheidae
ID: Elongate translucent gray to green body with brown mottling and red to yellow bands on abdomen; **two pale bands on large claws.** Inhabit holes in rubble from 20 to 100 ft. Common Florida, Bahamas, Caribbean.

FLOWER GARDEN YELLOW SNAPPING SHRIMP *Alpheus amarillo*
SIZE: to 2 cm (¾ in.)   Snapping Shrimp – Alpheidae
ID: Robust yellow body with vague markings; major claw with three longitudinal ridges and pinkish tip. Inhabit rubble from shallows to depths. Rare Texas Flower Garden Banks in Gulf of Mexico, S. Caribbean from Bonaire to St. Vincent.

SMOOTHCLAW SNAPPING SHRIMP *Alpheus* cf. *paracrinitus*
SIZE: to 2 cm (¾ in.)   Snapping Shrimp – Alpheidae
ID: Elongate translucent body with some brown areas and 8 narrow reddish brown body bands; large smooth major claw. Often in pairs. Inhabit variety of habitats from tidepools to 30 ft. Common Florida, Bahamas, Caribbean.

CLUBCLAW SNAPPING SHRIMP *Alpheus* spp.
SIZE: to 4 cm (1½ in.)   Snapping Shrimp – Alpheidae
ID: Translucent with reddish internal organs visible; clublike major claw with yellow and purple highlights. Member of *Alpheus edwardsii* complex with 10 similar-appearing species in Western Atlantic. Rubble to 20 ft. Known from Bonaire.

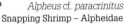

HUMMELINCK SNAPPING SHRIMP *Parabetaeus hummelincki*
SIZE: to 2.5 cm (1 in.)   Snapping Shrimp – Alpheidae
ID: Translucent with six reddish body bands at joints of body segments (sometimes indistinct); pink-tipped claws; blue eyes. Inhabit crevices and beneath rocks from intertidal to 50 ft. Uncommon Florida, Bahamas, Caribbean.

THREE-RIDGED SNAPPING SHRIMP *Alpheopsis trigonus*
SIZE: to 7.5 cm (3 in.)   Snapping Shrimp – Alpheidae
ID: Three ridges run length of carapace; equal-size claws; translucent body with wide bands of red or orange. Beneath rocks and debris in sand and rubble to 40 ft. Rare Bahamas, Caribbean.

GLASSY SNAPPING SHRIMP *Automate sp.*
SIZE: to 1.2 cm (½ in.)   Snapping Shrimp – Alpheidae
ID: Smooth cylindrical, transparent body with internal organs evident (red eggs inside abdomen); unequal-size claws. One of four similar-appearing genus members in Western Atlantic. Beneath rocks and grass beds. Known from Key Largo, Florida.

STIPPLED SNAPPING SHRIMP *Synalpheus* cf. *hemphilli*
SIZE: to 2.5 cm (1 in.)   Snapping Shrimp – Alpheidae
ID: Stout bluish gray body with turquoise patches on back; smooth swollen large claw and slender walking legs. Reclusive; pairs inhabit sponges to 170 ft. Identification tentative. Uncommon Florida, Bahamas, Caribbean.

LARGECLAW SNAPPING SHRIMP *Synalpheus sp.*
SIZE: to 2 cm (¾ in.)   Snapping Shrimp – Alpheidae
ID: Thirty genus members difficult to identify to species without specimen. Stout body with large smooth cylindrical snapping claw and smaller second claw. Inhabit sponges and crevices to 170 ft. Uncommon Florida, Bahamas, Caribbean.

Commensal Shrimp

SIZE: to 2.5 cm (1 in.)

ID: Transparent body with purple spotting; two pairs of long white antennae; white claws and legs with purple bands. Live in association with a variety of anemones, primarily Corkscrew Anemone, *Bartholomea annulata*, Branching Anemone, *Lebrunia danae*, the Giant Anemone, *Condylactis gigantea,* and Knobby Anemone, *Ragactis lucida.* Cleaning shrimp that perch at the edge of host anemone and sway their bodies and wave antennae to attract client fish. Reefs from 10 to 60 feet. Common S. Florida, Bahamas, Caribbean.

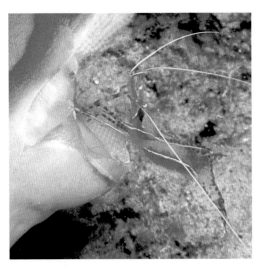

TWOCLAW SHRIMP   *Brachycarpus biunguiculatus*
SIZE: to 5 cm (2 in.)   Commensal Shrimp – Palaemonidae
ID: Reddish brown to transparent body with long slender claw arms; banding on abdomen and legs. Reclusive and nocturnal; a wide variety of habitats to 130 ft. Common Florida, Bahamas, Caribbean.

BROWN GRASS SHRIMP
Leander tenuicornis
Commensal Shrimp – Palaemonidae
SIZE: to 2.5 cm (2 in.)
ID: Robust body; **conspicuous abdominal hump;** pronounced serrated rostrum; typically two oscillated spots on lower side; thin claw arms and banded legs; acquire a variety of colors and markings to match surroundings. Shallow seagrass, dock pilings and *Sargassum*. Occasional Florida, Bahamas, Caribbean.

SEA PLUME SHRIMP   *Neopontonides chacei*
SIZE: to 7 mm (¹/₄ in.)   Commensal Shrimp – Palaemonidae
ID: Robust smooth roundish body; transparent with color highlights matching host sea plume; white eyes. Identification tentative. Uncommon S. Florida, N.W. Caribbean; also Gulf of Mexico.

PINKEYE GORGONIAN SHRIMP   *Neopontonides* sp.
SIZE: to 8 mm (³/₈ in.)   Commensal Shrimp – Palaemonidae
ID: Flat smooth body with rounded abdominal segments; stalked pink eyes; transparent with purple to reddish spotting. Possibly *N. beaufortensis* or undescribed species. Inhabit gorgonians to 30 ft. Known from St. Vincent.

Commensal Shrimp

Periclimenes yucatanicus
Commensal Shrimp –
Palaemonidae
SIZE: to 2.5 cm (1 in.)
ID: Transparent with three to four tan and white saddle markings on back and white spots along sides; legs and claw arms banded white with purple, lavender, or red (usually at night). Long banded antennae. Associate with anemones including Corkscrew Anemone, *Bartholomea annulata*, Branching Anemone, *Lebrunia danae*, and Giant Anemone, *Condylactis gigantea*, to 60 ft. Act as cleaners. Common S. Florida, Bahamas, Caribbean.

SUN ANEMONE SHRIMP
Periclimenes rathbunae
Commensal Shrimp –
Palaemonidae
SIZE: to 2.5 cm (1 in.)
ID: Translucent body with numerous brown, white and occasionally red spots; bands and various other markings, including intricate design on carapace and abdominal segments. Live in association with a number of anemones, but most commonly Sun Anemone, *Stichodactyla helianthus*, from 3 to 60 ft. Occasional Florida, Bahamas, Caribbean.

GOLDEN CRINOID SHRIMP
Periclimenes crinoidalis
Commensal Shrimp –
Palaemonidae
SIZE: to 2 cm (³/₄ in.)
ID: Translucent yellow to orangish with abdominal hump; stalked eyes. **Live exclusively on Golden Crinoid, *Davidaster rubiginosa*.** Reefs from 30 to 130 ft. Range not well established, probably exist wherever host crinoid commonly found. Occasional E. and S. Caribbean.

BROWN CRINOID SHRIMP
Periclimenes meyeri
SIZE: to 2 cm (³/₄ in.)   Broken-back Shrimp – Palaemonidae
ID: Variable reddish brown to dark brown often with translucent elongate patch on side and white upper abdomen and tail. **Live exclusively on Black & White Crinoid, *Nemaster grandis*,** from 30 to 130 ft. Occasional S. Caribbean.

RED AND WHITE CRINOID SHRIMP
Periclimenes cf. meyeri
Commensal Shrimp –
Palaemonidae
SIZE: to 2 cm (³/₄ in.)
ID: Similar in basic size and shape to Brown Crinoid Shrimp [previous] but distinct in color and its association with the Swimming Crinoid, *Analcidometra armata*. Known from Bay Islands in W. Caribbean.

Commensal Shrimp

BLACK CORAL SHRIMP
Periclimenes antipathophilus
Commensal Shrimp –
Palaemonidae
SIZE: to 1.2 cm (½ in.)
ID: Transparent with bright red highlights and a pale yellow spot dorsally on the 4th and 5th abdominal segments. Often in groups; associate with at least three species of black corals of the genus *Antipathes*, including *A. gracilis* and *A. pennacea*, at depths of 50 to 150 ft. Belongs to the *Periclimenes iridescens* species complex [above]. Occasional S. Bahamas, Caribbean.

BASKET STAR SHRIMP
Periclimenes perryae
Commensal Shrimp –
Palaemonidae
SIZE: to 1.2 cm (¹/₂ in.)
ID: Robust flattened body usually reddish to gold with white or dark highlights; banded legs; stalked eyes; wide blunt antennal scales; wide dark band on white tail. **Live with Giant Basket Star,** *Astrophyton muricatum,* which uncurls arms to feed on plankton at night exposing shrimp. Basket stars will close when illuminated with light beam concealing shrimp. Reefs from 15 to 90 ft. S. Florida, S. Caribbean; also Gulf of Mexico.

WHITEFOOT SHRIMP
Periclimenes harringtoni
Commensal Shrimp –
Palaemonidae
SIZE: to 1.2 cm (¹/₂ in.)
ID: Translucent reddish brown with a scattering of white spots over body and appendages; legs slender; claw arms differ in size; prominent white blotch on claws. Associate with Touch-me-not Sponge, *Neofibularia nolitangere,* from 20 to several hundred feet. Live inside large excurrent openings. Blend in well with sponge walls and tiny Sponge Worm, *Haplosyllis spongicola,* which inhabit sponge walls by the thousands. Known from scattered locations including Cayman, Bonaire, Dry Tortugas, St. Vincent.

Commensal Shrimp

YELLOWBAND SHRIMP
Periclimenes sp. 1
Commensal Shrimp –
Palaemonidae
SIZE: to 2.5 cm (1 in.)
ID: Smooth translucent orange body covered with a scattering of fine white specks; red, white and yellow banded legs and claw arms; three irregular ocellated white patches on lower side of abdomen. Live in association with Upsidedown Jelly, *Cassiopea frondosa*. Rare; known only from this photographed specimen from Dominica.

JELLYFISH SHRIMP   *Periclimenes* sp. 2
SIZE: to 2 cm (³/₄ in.)   Commensal Shrimp – Palaemonidae
ID: Elongate translucent body with reddish brown mottling; long pointed rostrum. Known from several specimens observed on domes of unidentified jellyfish near surface waters off Jacksonville, Florida.

GORGONIAN SHRIMP   *Pseudocoutierea antillensis*
SIZE: to 1.2 cm (¹/₂ in.) Commensal Shrimp – Palaemonidae
ID: Tiny robust ventrally compressed body; white eyes. Associate with gorgonians acquiring color of host. Uncommon Turks and Caicos Islands, Caribbean.

BLACK URCHIN SHRIMP
Tuleariocaris neglecta
Commensal Shrimp –
Palaemonidae
SIZE: to 1.5 cm (⁵/₈ in.)
ID: Black to purple elongate body tapering toward front and rear; often with broad white stripe on sides; short translucent legs. Live on spines of Long-spined Urchin, *Diadema antillarum*, and Magnificent Urchin, *Astropyga magnifica*, to 25 ft. Perch on spines with head pointed towards base of urchin. Occasional Florida, E. and S. Caribbean.

WIRE CORAL SHRIMP
Pseudopontonides principis

Commensal Shrimp – Palaemonidae

SIZE: to 1.2 cm (¹/₂ in.)

ID: Long tapering carapace with flat rostrum and long slender claw arms; highly variable from olive to brown to dark gray, white, tan and orange to match host; body occasionally speckled or banded. Associate with Wire Coral, *Cirrhipathes leutkeni,* Feather Black Coral, *Antipathes pennacea,* and possibly other Antipatharians, from 45 to 225 ft. Occasional Caribbean; also Gulf of Mexico.

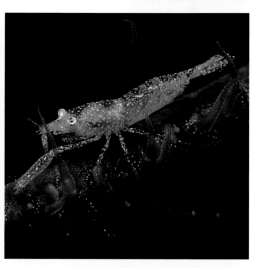

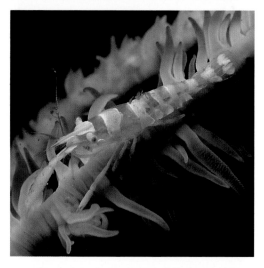

CARIBBEAN PEN SHRIMP   *Pontonia mexicana*

SIZE: to 2.5 cm (1 in.)   Commensal Shrimp – Palaemonidae

ID: Smooth cylindrical body; white reticulated pattern on large claw arms of unequal size; female [right] **BL-** Male: Translucent orange. Living pen shells, *Pinna carnea* and *Atrina rigida,* to 30 ft. Uncommon Florida, Bahamas Caribbean.

Broken-back Shrimp

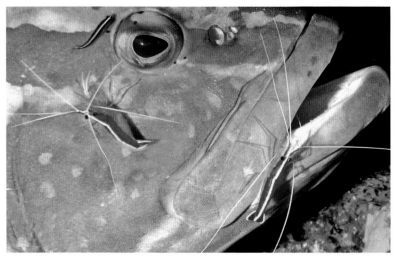

SCARLET-STRIPED CLEANER SHRIMP
Lysmata grabhami
Broken-back Shrimp – Hippolytidae
SIZE: to 5 cm (2 in.)
ID: Two broad red stripes with a narrow white center stripe extending down back to tail; pale cream to yellow body and legs. Long white hairlike antennae. Active cleaning shrimp. Reef crevices from 3 to 90 ft; perch near entrance waving antennae to attract client fish. If a bare hand is slowly extended toward the shrimp may leave retreat and attempt to clean fingers. Occasional Florida, Bahamas, Caribbean.

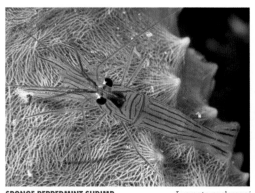

ANKER'S PEPPERMINT SHRIMP   *Lysmata ankeri*
SIZE: to 4.5 cm (1³/₄ in.) Broken-back Shrimp – Hippolytidae
ID: Semi-translucent reddish orange with thin dark reddish stripes; **a distinct curved band crosses the 3rd segment of the abdomen at the point where it slopes toward the tail.** Reefs and rocky shores to 80 ft. S.E. Florida, Haiti, S. Caribbean.

SPONGE PEPPERMINT SHRIMP   *Lysmata pederseni*
SIZE: to 4.5 cm (1³/₄ in.) Broken-back Shrimp – Hippolytidae
ID: Translucent body with dark red stripes; **two bands on carapace (2nd at start of abdomen) curved slightly in opposite directions.** Tube sponges from 10 to 80 ft. Common S. Florida, Bahamas, E. Caribbean to Venezuela.

FLORIDA PEPPERMINT SHRIMP   *Lysmata boggessi*
SIZE: to 4.5 cm (1³/₄ in.) Broken-back Shrimp – Hippolytidae
ID: Reddish brown semi-translucent with thin indistinct stripes; **wider U-shaped band on carapace points toward head;** dark areas on tail. Seagrass, hard bottom, beneath ledges from 30 to 50 ft. Uncommon Key West, W. Florida, possibly Caribbean.

PEPPERMINT SHRIMP   *Lysmata wurdemanni*
SIZE: to 4.5 cm (1³/₄ in.) Broken-back Shrimp – Hippolytidae
ID: Whitish translucent with thin stripes and wide dark bands across abdomen; **connected double band on carapace.** Hard bottom of inlets, jetties, buoys, pilings from 3 to 90 ft. Uncommon S.E. Florida, possibly N. Caribbean; Gulf of Mexico.

SLENDER SARGASSUM SHRIMP *Latreutes fucorum*
SIZE: to 2 cm (³/₄ in.) Broken-back Shrimp – Hippolytidae
ID: Highly variable color either solid, striped or barred; often blue markings; **upturned bladelike rostrum flanked by spine on side;** short claw arms of unequal size. *Sargassum* and seagrass. Occasional Florida, Bahamas, central and E. Caribbean.

UNARMED CRYPTIC SHRIMP *Latreutes* cf. *inermis*
SIZE: to 2 cm (³/₄ in.) Broken-back Shrimp – Hippolytidae
ID: Green with wide white mid-dorsal stripe and blue dots; elongate spineless bladelike rostrum. Identification tentative; similar to *L. inermis* from Lesser Antilles. Known from S.E. Florida at 10 ft. on Green Feather Algae, *Caulerpa sertularioides*.

SHORT SARGASSUM SHRIMP *Latreutes parvulus*
SIZE: to 1.2 cm (¹/₂ in.) Broken-back Shrimp – Hippolytidae
ID: Short and stocky with dots and blotches; green legs; spiny rear tapers to point; row of short spines along crest of carapace. Encrusted with debris. Reefs and rubble to 150 ft; but not *Sargassum*. Rare Florida, Puerto Rico, S. Caribbean; Gulf of

MANNING GRASS SHRIMP *Thor manningi*
SIZE: to 1 cm (³/₈ in.) Broken-back Shrimp – Hippolytidae
ID: Tiny stocky translucent body with green and white or brown and white highlights; banded legs. Seagrass and sand; often associate with anemones. Abundant to occasional Caribbean; also Gulf of Mexico.

SQUAT ANEMONE SHRIMP
Thor amboinensis
Broken-back Shrimp –
Hippolytidae
SIZE: to 1.2 cm (¹/₂ in.)
ID: Stocky reddish brown body with bold white saddle and spot markings rimmed with blue; often hold tail aloft. Live near or within a variety of anemones from 10 to 60 ft; generally in groups. Identification tentative; genus recently split into three groups based on microscopic anatomical differences. Common S. Florida, Bahamas, Caribbean.

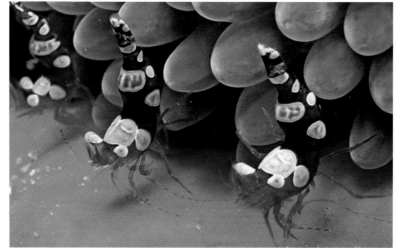

Broken-back Shrimp

ARROW SHRIMP
Tozeuma carolinense
Broken-back Shrimp –
Hippolytidae
SIZE: to 4 cm (1½ in.)
ID: Slender elongate body with long serrated snout and **pointed abdominal hump;** highly variable colors from translucent to tan, gray, purple or green. Associate with sea plumes and seagrass to 50 ft.; mimic color of host. Occasional Florida, Bahamas, Caribbean.

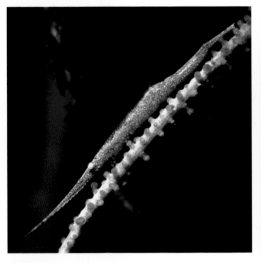

SERRATE ARROW SHRIMP
Tozeuma serratum
Broken-back Shrimp –
Hippolytidae
SIZE: to 6 cm (2¼ in.)
ID: Slender elongate reddish and translucent body with white markings; long red-and-white banded snout serrated both top and bottom; high smoothly **rounded abdominal hump;** regularly associated with hydroids from 10 to 420 ft. Rare N.W. Florida, S. Caribbean.

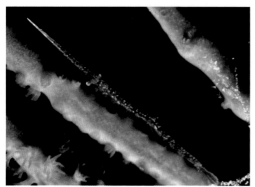

GORGONIAN TOOTHPICK SHRIMP *Tozeuma cornutum*
SIZE: to 3 cm (1¼ in.)   Broken-back Shrimp – Hippolytidae
ID: More slender and elongate than other genus members; translucent with red, white and golden speckling; long serrated white-tipped snout and slight abdominal hump; associate with sea plumes from 15 to 55 ft. Rare Florida, Caribbean.

NICHOLSON'S SHRIMP *Hippolyte nicholsoni*
SIZE: to 2.5 cm (1 in.)   Broken-back Shrimp – Hippolytidae
ID: Translucent with whitish carapace and belly; two narrow whitish bars encircle abdomen joining whitish belly; white eyes on short stocks. Associate with gorgonians from 6 to 100 ft. Uncommon Florida, Bahamas, Caribbean.

ROUGHBACK SHRIMP
Trachycaris rugosa
Broken-back Shrimp –
Hippolytidae
SIZE: to 3 cm (1¼ in.)
ID: Bulbous forebody with elevated abdomen and tail; short blunt upturned rostrum; forward curved spines on crest of carapace; red, brown, green and multicolored with vague line markings and blotches; vertical light colored patch below eye. Nocturnal; inhabit a variety of habitats. Uncommon E. Florida, Bahamas, Caribbean; also Gulf of Mexico.

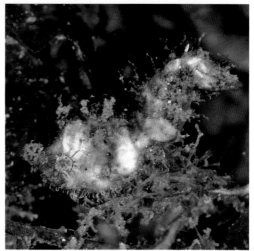

Cave Shrimp, Bumblebee & Hinge-beak Shrimp

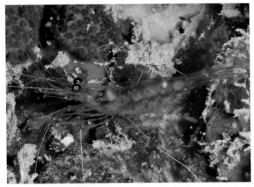

ANTIGUAN CAVE SHRIMP *Janicea antiguensis*
SIZE: to 10 cm (4 in.) Cave Shrimp – Barbouriidae
ID: Translucent tan to pale reddish with some darker banding at the edge of each abdominal segment; spindly white legs. Nocturnal; inhabit crevices and caves along algae-covered rocky shorelines. Common Bahamas, Caribbean.

STERRER'S CAVE SHRIMP *Parhippolyte sterreri*
SIZE: to 6.5 cm (2½ in.) Cave Shrimp – Barbouriidae
ID: Translucent white with six red bands on abdomen, the third forming a rear-facing point; long wispy antennae. Similar *Janicea antiguensis* [previous] has larger eyes. Caves to 60 ft. Rare; known from Bahamas, Bonaire.

CIRCLED BUMBLEBEE SHRIMP
Gnathophyllum circellum
Bumblebee Shrimp –
Gnathophyllidae
SIZE: to 1.2 cm (½ in.)
ID: Barrel-shaped, smooth golden-brown body with distinct pattern of **large ocellated yellow spots bordered with dark brown rings**; short rostrum, equal-sized claw arms; legs, tail and antennae translucent white. Cryptic; known to 40 ft. Rare; known from Florida, Bahamas, Bonaire, but probably has more extensive range.

ELEGANT BUMBLEBEE SHRIMP *Gnathophyllum elegans*
SIZE: to 2 cm (¾ in.) Bumblebee Shrimp – Gnathophyllidae
ID: Stocky brown cylindrical body tapering toward tail with **numerous yellow spots**; larger claw arms of equal size; banded legs. **BR-** Juvenile: Fewer larger spots. Coral and sponges to 90 ft. Rare; known from E. Florida.

STRIPED BUMBLEBEE SHRIMP
Gnathophyllum americanum
Bumblebee Shrimp – Gnathophyllidae
SIZE: to 1.2 cm (½ in.)
ID: Small stocky body with alternating black and white banding; white claw arms almost as long as body. **ML-Juvenile:** Typically in pairs, regularly associate with sea cucumbers, sea urchins and other echinoderms. Dine on their hosts' tiny tube feet. Common E. Caribbean; occasional to rare balance of Caribbean, Florida and Bahamas; also circumtropical.

URCHIN BUMBLEBEE SHRIMP   *Gnathophylloides mineri*
SIZE: to 2 cm (¾ in.) Bumblebee Shrimp – Gnathophyllidae
ID: Stocky with **gray-lined stripe on back bordered by white bands,** dark brown below. Associate with Variegated Urchin, *Lytechinus variegatus*, West Indian Sea Egg, *Tripneustes ventricosus,* to 10 ft. Uncommon S. Florida, Bahamas, Caribbean.

RED NIGHT SHRIMP   *Cinetorhynchus manningi*
SIZE: to 5 cm (2 in.) Hinge-beak Shrimp – Rhynchocinetidae
ID: Red with pale to bright white abdominal bands; carapace often light red to white or golden with white spots. Nocturnal; coral reef recesses and sea walls to 90 ft. Shy; eyes glow in light beam. Common S. Florida, Bahamas, Caribbean.

Night, Glass Sponge, Boxer & Rock Shrimp

NIGHT SHRIMP COMPLEX

Night Shrimp – Processidae
SIZE: to 2.5 cm (1 in.)
ID: Family Processidae is made up of several genera including *Ambidexter*, *Nikoides*, and *Processa*, containing nine Tropical Western Atlantic species. All have smooth translucent or whitish bodies with red highlights and large eyes; thin translucent claw arms, the left shorter and more robust than the right. Identification of species requires examination of an in-hand specimen. Nocturnal; usually on shallow sand or mud. Become disoriented in beam of light causing the animal to spin. Occasional Florida, Bahamas, Caribbean.

CRIMSON CORAL SHRIMP   *Microprosthema semilaeve*
SIZE: to 2.5 cm (1 in.)   Glass Sponge Shrimp – Spongicolidae
ID: Compact lobsterlike red body that flexes sharply upward; large white-tipped claw arms. Hide under rocks in shallow sand and rubble. Known from scattered location in S. Florida, Bahamas, Caribbean.

TAWNY CONCH SHRIMP   *Microprosthema manningi*
SIZE: to 2 cm (3/4 in.)   Glass Sponge Shrimp – Spongicolidae
ID: Compact lobsterlike translucent body with tan and white highlights; numerous short spines on carapace; long folded claw arms with robust claws. Inhabit abandoned conch shells and dead coral to 10 ft. Uncommon S. Florida, Caribbean.

BANDED CORAL SHRIMP
Stenopus hispidus

Boxer Shrimp –
Stenopodidae

SIZE: to 5 cm (2 in.)

ID: Red and white banded body and claws with bands occasionally bordered in purple; two pairs of long, white hairlike antennae (often only part visible when animal is concealed); long equal-sized claw arms held at 45-degree angle. If claw arms break they regenerate, as a result claw arms may differ in size. Also commonly known as "Barber Pole Shrimp." Nocturnal; reef and sponge pockets to 130 ft.; act as cleaners attracting client fishes by waving long antennae. Common Florida, Bahamas, Caribbean.

GOLDEN CORAL SHRIMP
Stenopus scutellatus

Boxer Shrimp –
Stenopodidae

SIZE: to 3 cm (1¼ in.)

ID: Translucent yellow body and legs with red and occasionally white bands on abdomen and claws; two pairs of long white hairlike antennae; long equal-sized claw arms carried at 45-degree angle. If claw arms break they regenerate, as a result claw arms may differ in size. Reclusive; often under debris or inside recesses from 10 to 130 ft. Occasional Florida, Bahamas, Caribbean.

WHITECLAW CORAL SHRIMP
Odontozona sp.

SIZE: to 2 cm (¾ in.)   Boxer Shrimp – Stenopodidae

ID: Translucent with thin orange bands across abdominal segments; thin walking legs; **long claw arms with white scissorlike claws.** An undescribed species. Rare; photographed inside deep crevice at 40 ft. in Bonaire.

SAWTOOTH ROCK SHRIMP
Sicyonia parri

SIZE: to 2 cm (¾ in.)   Rock Shrimp – Sicyoniidae

ID: Stocky body with red carapace and white blotches on abdomen and tail; scattered bristles on carapace and abdomen; spines on crest of carapace and along top of rostrum. Nocturnal. Uncommon Florida, Bahamas, Caribbean.

Prawns, Ghost, Lobster & Mud Shrimp

BROWN SHRIMP *Farfantepenaeus aztecus*
SIZE: to 23 cm (9 in.)   Prawns – Penaeidae
ID: Elongate translucent body with brown, red or greenish speckled banding along abdominal segments. Commercially harvested. Nocturnal; often bury in sand and mud to 540 ft. Common E. Florida, Yucatan; also Gulf of Mexico.

PINK-SPOTTED SHRIMP *Farfantepenaeus brasiliensis*
SIZE: to 26 cm (10 in.)   Prawns – Penaeidae
ID: Elongate brownish red (at times yellow or brown) with white spot at mid-side of abdomen; occasionally with white banding. Commercially harvested. Nocturnal; often bury in sand or mud with vegetation to 900 ft. Occasional E. Florida, Bahamas, Caribbean.

CARIBBEAN WHITE SHRIMP *Farfantepenaeus notialis*
SIZE: to 19 cm (7½ in.)   Prawns – Penaeidae
ID: Elongate body in a variety of colors but most often translucent yellow with reddish blotches and highlights on tail; yellowish legs with white tips. Nocturnal; often bury in sand to 50 ft. Occasional Caribbean.

VELVET SHRIMP *Metapenaeopsis goodei*
SIZE: to 2 cm (¾ in.)   Prawns – Penaeidae
ID: Elongate transparent body with vague reddish markings; large bluish eyes. Nocturnal; sand and seagrass beds to 900 ft.; often bury. Occasional Florida, Bahamas, Caribbean.

RED-ORANGE GHOST SHRIMP *Corallianassa longiventris*
SIZE: to 10 cm (4 in.)   Ghost Shrimp – Callianassidae
ID: Orangish brown with red highlights; large claws unequal in size and shape. Inhabit smooth circular burrows in sand near grass beds to 30 ft. Shy; can be baited part way out of burrow with grass or algae. Occasional S. Florida, Caribbean.

LOBSTER SHRIMP COMPLEX

SIZE: to 7.5 cm (3 in.)   Lobster Shrimp – Axiidae

ID: A little known family of burrowing lobster (lobster shrimp) with 20 described species in the Western Atlantic. All have thick calcified carapaces and large claw arms. Cryptic; most live within burrows or crevices, occasionally in open at night.

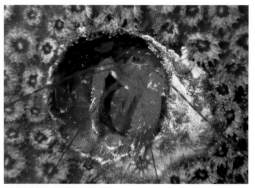

SERRATED LOBSTER SHRIMP   *Axiopsis serratifrons*

SIZE: to 6.5 cm (2½ in.)   Lobster Shrimp – Axiidae

ID: Males brown to black; females tan to olive green. Unequal-size claws with bristles and brown tips. Pairs inhabit burrows inside crevices to 20 ft. Remain in burrow during day, may emerge at night. Baited out with shrimp for photograph. Florida, Belize.

NODULOSE LOBSTER SHRIMP   *Coralaxius nodulosus*

SIZE: to 1.2 cm (½ in.)   Lobster Shrimp – Axiidae

ID: Dark red body; legs, antennae, and antennules red-and-white banded; large claws of unequal size and shape covered with nodules. Inhabit holes in rocks and living *Porites* coral from 20 to 760 ft. Rare; known from Cuba, Curacao, St. Vincent.

SCARLET LOBSTER SHRIMP   *Neaxiopsis gundlachi*

SIZE: to 7.5 cm (3 in.)   Lobster Shrimp – Strahlaxiidae

ID: Elongate crimson body and rounded rostrum; tufts of brown bristles on lower sides of abdomen; unequal-size crimson claw arms; pink walking legs. Burrow in sand and mud to 30 ft. Rare; known from Cuba, Curacao, St. Vincent.

OPERCULATE MUD SHRIMP   *Pomatogebia* cf. *operculata*

SIZE: to 2.5 cm (1 in.)   Mud Shrimp – Upogebiidae

ID: Smooth elongate shiny pinkish cream body; front of carapace flattened; tiny black eyes. Mated pairs live in coral crevices and burrows from 5 to 85 ft. Uncommon N.W. Florida, Bahamas, Central and South American coasts.

Lobsters

CARIBBEAN SPINY LOBSTER   *Panulirus argus*
SIZE: to 60 cm (2 ft.)   Spiny Lobsters – Palinuridae
ID: Tan, black and white with large white spots on abdomen; two black and white horns between eyes. **TR & ML** - Juvenile: Banded legs; broad stripe on back. Nocturnal; hide under ledges from 3 to 200 ft.; often in groups. Florida, Bahamas, Caribbean.

SPOTTED SPINY LOBSTER   *Panulirus guttatus*
SIZE: to 46 cm (18 in.)   Spiny Lobsters – Palinuridae
ID: Tan to dark purple body and legs covered with numerous black-ringed white spots. Nocturnal; during day hide under reef ledges and among rock structures from 6 to 75 ft.; often in groups. Occasional Florida, Bahamas, Caribbean.

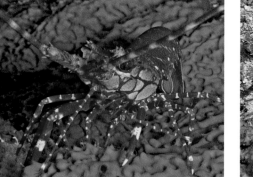

RED-BANDED LOBSTER   *Justitia longimanus*
SIZE: to 20 cm (8 in.)   Spiny Lobsters – Palinuridae
ID: Body red with large gold areas outlined with red on side of carapace; red and gold banded antennae; legs red with white banding. Nocturnal; inhabit deeper reef ledges from 40 to 130 ft.; usually solitary. Uncommon S. Florida, Bahamas, Caribbean.

COPPER LOBSTER   *Palinurellus gundlachi*
SIZE: to 20 cm (8 in.)   Spiny Lobsters – Palinuridae
ID: Red to yellowish orange without obvious markings; no spines; hairy in appearance; short conical antennae. Shy; seldom appear in open; inhabit pockets in deeper reefs from 60 to 130 ft. Uncommon S. Florida, Bahamas, Caribbean.

FLAMING REEF LOBSTER *Enoplometopus antillensis*
SIZE: to 12 cm (4½ in.)   Reef Lobsters – Enoplometopidae
ID: Red with white bulls-eye on side of carapace; legs and wide, flattened equal-sized claws banded; white spots on abdomen. Shy; hide inside reef ledges from 30 to 600 ft. Uncommon Florida, Bahamas, Caribbean.

SPANISH SLIPPER LOBSTER *Scyllarides aequinoctialis*
SIZE: to 30 cm (12 in.)   Slipper Lobsters – Scyllaridae
ID: Body and legs tan to dark brown with orange; 4 to 5 purplish spots on first segment of abdomen; platelike antennae edge smooth, second set squared. Nocturnal; various habitats from 10 to 130 ft. Occasional S. Florida, Bahamas, Caribbean.

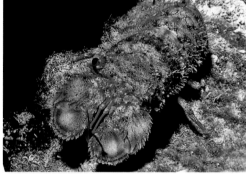

SCULPTURED SLIPPER LOBSTER *Parribacus antarcticus*
SIZE: to 30 cm (12 in.)   Slipper Lobsters – Scyllaridae
ID: Carapace and antennae mottled tan to yellow-brown with cobblestonelike texture; spines and bristles edge platelike antennae. Inhabit reefs and rocky structures from 20 to 75 ft. Occasional Bahamas, Caribbean; uncommon S. Florida.

REGAL SLIPPER LOBSTER *Arctides guineensis*
SIZE: to 18 cm (7 in.)   Slipper Lobsters – Scyllaridae
ID: Tan with red and blue highlights; carapace relatively smooth; deep sculpturing on abdomen; bristles on body more prominent toward lower side. Nocturnal; inhabit reefs, sand and seagrass from 25 to 60 ft. Uncommon Bahamas, Caribbean.

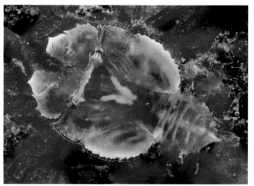

RIDGED SLIPPER LOBSTER *Scyllarides nodifer*
SIZE: to 20 cm (8 in.)   Slipper Lobster – Scyllaridae
ID: Mottled red and tan carapace and abdomen covered with granules; red and white banded legs; platelike antennae with granules and smooth edges. Inhabit sand, rubble and seagrass from 6 to 190 ft. Uncommon Florida, Bahamas, Caribbean.

JUVENILE SLIPPER LOBSTER Unidentified
SIZE: to 2.5 cm (1 in.)   Slipper Lobster – Scyllaridae
ID: Flattened body translucent with white tinting. Possibly Sculptured Slipper Lobster [above], but identification uncertain. Rare to uncommon Florida, Bahamas, Caribbean.

Rubble & Coral Crabs

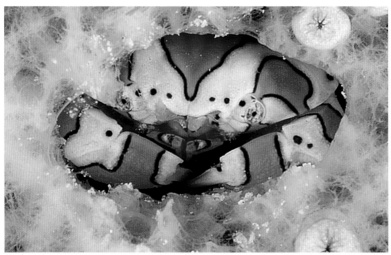

GAUDY CLOWN CRAB
Platypodiella spectabilis
Rubble Crabs – Xanthidae
SIZE: to 2 cm (³/₄ in.)
ID: Rounded, somewhat bumpy, dome-shaped carapace colorfully patterned (variable among individuals) in red, orange, yellow and black; broad flattened claw arms with longitudinal ridges. Nocturnal, cryptic and wary; variety of habitats from rubble to reefs and pier pilings. Occasional Florida, Bahamas, Caribbean.

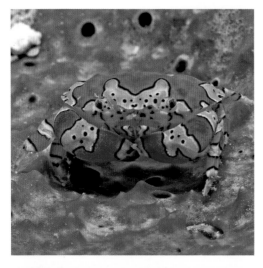

NODOSE RUBBLE CRAB   *Paractaea rufopunctata*
SIZE: to 2.5 cm (1 in.)   Rubble Crabs – Xanthidae
ID: Rounded, dome-shaped yellowish carapace and claw arms covered with nodules, often of contrasting colors; legs and carapace edged with short bristles. Inhabit sand and rubble to 600 ft. Occasional Florida, Bahamas, Caribbean.

ERODED MUD CRAB
Glyptoxanthus erosus
Rubble Crabs – Xanthidae
SIZE: to 5 cm (2 in.)
ID: Dome-shaped red, tan and white carapace, robust claw arms and legs with dense covering of irregular nodules; bristles on claw arms and yellow-tipped walking legs. Nocturnal; inhabit rocky rubble from shallows to 45 ft. Occasional Florida, Bahamas, Caribbean.

BRISTLED RUBBLE CRAB *Platyactaea setigera*
SIZE: to 2.5 cm (1 in.) Rubble Crabs – Xanthidae
ID: Flattened reddish orange oval carapace indented toward rear; parallel white line markings on back; short hairs on body, legs and claw arms; black claws. Rubble and seagrass to 20 ft. Occasional S. Florida, Bahamas, Caribbean.

DENTICULATE RUBBLE CRAB *Xanthodius denticulatus*
SIZE: to 3 cm (1¼ in.) Rubble Crabs – Xanthidae
ID: Oval flattened carapace from salmon to gray with dark brown broken line markings; 9-10 blunt teeth on lateral margins; claw arms dimpled with purplish mottling. Rock and rubble from shallows to 70 ft. S. Florida, Bahamas, Caribbean.

ELKHORN CORAL CRAB *Domecia acanthophora*
SIZE: to 2 cm (¾ in.) Coral Crabs – Domeciidae
ID: Flattened carapace, legs and claw arms reddish with numerous white spots; black mask rims front and sides of carapace. **BR-** Juvenile: tan with orange. Elkhorn and fire coral from shallows to 50 ft. Occasional Florida, Caribbean.

Swimming Crabs

Achelous ordwayi
Swimming Crabs –
Portunidae
SIZE: to 5 cm (2 in.)
ID: Typical of all swimming crabs: flat carapace wider than long with two prominent lateral spines; rear legs end with paddlelike swimming appendages. Red to yellowish brown; a series of about seven forward-pointed spines on edge of carapace between eye and longest lateral spine; three large spines on first section of claw arms; claw tips reddish brown with white bands. **MR**- Juvenile: white with broad reddish band from between eyes to back of carapace. Sand and algal bottoms less than 20 ft. Florida, Bahamas, Caribbean.

SARGASSUM SWIMMING CRAB   *Portunus sayi*
SIZE: to 6.5 cm (2½ in.)   Swimming Crabs – Portunidae
ID: Carapace and appendages reddish brown with scattering of white markings and yellowish edging on legs and claws. **BR**-Juvenile: Inhabit floats of *Sargassum*. Adults inhabit from shallows to 60 ft. Common Florida, Bahamas, Caribbean.

DELICATE SWIMMING CRAB *Portunus anceps*
SIZE: to 2.5 cm (1 in.) Swimming Crabs – Portunidae
ID: Carapace and appendages gray to brown with white and black mottled pattern; orange highlights at leg joints and white banded claw arms. Inhabit shallow sandy shorelines. Occasional Florida, Bahamas, Caribbean.

FLATFACE SWIMMING CRAB *Achelous depressifrons*
SIZE: to 3.5 cm (1½ in.) Swimming Crabs – Portunidae
ID: Carapace flattened in front, light to dark gray with blue highlights; claw arms have light blue inner surface; legs blue. Shallow sand inside bays and inlets to 96 ft. Juv. inhabit floats of *Sargassum*. Uncommon Florida, Bahamas, Caribbean.

IRIDESCENT SWIMMING CRAB *Achelous gibbesii*
SIZE: to 7.5 cm (3 in.) Swimming Crabs – Portunidae
ID: Carapace brownish red with dark red ridges; walking legs and swimming paddles purple; black line beneath spines along front of upper claw arms. Inhabit shallow bays and creek bottoms, and rock jetties. Occasional Florida, E. Caribbean.

FLORIDA SWIMMING CRAB *Achelous floridanus*
SIZE: to 5 cm (2 in.) Swimming Crabs – Portunidae
ID: Carapace brownish orange with reddish ridges; appendages brown with purplish wash; long, slender curved dark claws. Hard, sandy or mud bottoms from 30 ft. to considerable depths. Uncommon Florida, Caribbean.

BLOTCHED SWIMMING CRAB *Achelous spinimanus*
SIZE: to 11 cm (4¼ in.) Swimming Crabs – Portunidae
ID: Gray, brown or bluish carapace with dark horizontal line markings; often purple highlights; lateral spines short; five long spines on first segment of claw arms; legs often banded. Harbors and bays to 60 ft. Common Florida, Bahamas, Caribbean.

OCELLATE SWIMMING CRAB *Achelous sebae*
SIZE: to 9 cm (3½ in.) Swimming Crabs – Portunidae
ID: Reddish brown carapace and appendages with **prominent ocellated spot on either side of rear carapace**; black claws. Sand near reefs and seagrass beds from 15 to 90 ft. Nocturnal; wary and pugnacious. Occasional Florida, Bahamas, Caribbean.

Swimming, Elbow & Hairy Crabs

BLUE CRAB
Callinectes sapidus
Swimming Crabs –
Portunidae
SIZE: to 20 cm (8 in.)
ID: Wide carapace with long spike on each side; greenish brown to olive with light speckling; claw arms and legs partially blue; females have orange claws ; front and side edges of carapace lined with spines, back edge smooth. **Four spines between eyes** (similar appearing Ornate Blue Crab [next] have six). **ML-** Male. Inhabit sand and mud from low tide to 120 ft. Occasional E. Florida, Bahamas and the Antilles. Can be locally abundant.

ORNATE BLUE CRAB　　　　　　　*Callinectes ornatus*
SIZE: to 12 cm (4¾ in.)　　　Swimming Crabs – Portunidae
ID: Wide, light olive to brown, carapace with long white-tipped spine on each side (spine maroon to white on Blue Crab [previous]); **six spines between eyes.** Occasional E. and S.W. Florida, Bahamas, Antilles to South American coast.

BLACKPOINT SCULLING CRAB　　　　　*Cronius ruber*
SIZE: to 9 cm (3½ in.)　　　Swimming Crabs – Portunidae
ID: Carapace and appendages brown to brick red with some mottling; walking legs banded and striped; claws dark red to black with light banding. Inhabit sand and shell debris from shallows to 200 ft. Occasional Florida, Bahamas, Caribbean.

BLADETOOTH ELBOW CRAB
Platylambrus granulata
Elbow Crabs –
Parthenopidae
SIZE: carapace to 2.5 cm (1 in.)
ID: Pinkish gray with some reddish tubercles and scattering of small blackish spots; light purplish claw arms flattened and long (about 3 times as long as carapace) with many large, sharp, triangular, outwardly-projecting, slightly curved spines along outer edges; more numerous smaller spines along inner edges. Sand and mud from 30 to 180 ft. Uncommon Florida, Bahamas, Caribbean.

ROUGH ELBOW CRAB   *Spinolambrus fraterculus*
SIZE: carapace to 1.8 cm (³/₄ in.) Elbow Crabs – Parthenopidae
ID: Triangular carapace (red when not encrusted with sponge) has prominent indentations and numerous teeth along margins; rostrum triangular, blunt, and angled downwards. Shell and coral rubble from 20 to 540 ft. Uncommon Florida, Caribbean.

PLUMED HAIRY CRAB   *Pilumnus floridanus*
SIZE: to 1.8 cm (³/₄ in.)   Hairy Crabs – Pilumnidae
ID: Reddish orange carapace with yellowish mottling sparsely covered with long bristles; walking legs and stout claw arms heavily bristled; small white-tipped spines on pincers. Reefs and rubble to 450 ft. Common Florida, Bahamas, Caribbean.

SHORT-SPINED HAIRY CRAB   *Pilumnus dasypodus*
SIZE: carapace to 6 mm (¹/₄ in.)   Hairy Crabs – Pilumnidae
ID: Brownish red to orange; front two-thirds of carapace, legs and claw arms covered with long, thin bristles; unequal-sized claw arms have short brown-tipped spines. Sand bottoms and man-made structures to 100 ft. Uncommon Florida, Caribbean.

SPINEBACK HAIRY CRAB   *Pilumnus sayi*
SIZE: carapace to 2.5 cm (1 in.)   Hairy Crabs – Pilumnidae
ID: Reddish brown with white blotches and bristles; unequal-sized claw arms and legs bristled with blue highlights; claws dark with three rows of conical spines; red eyes. Shell rubble and pilings in shallows. Uncommon Florida, Bahamas, Caribbean.

Purse & Commensal Pea Crabs

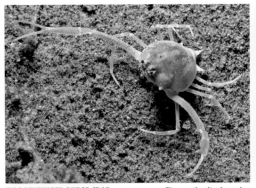

SHOULDERED PURSE CRAB *Iliacantha sparsa*
SIZE: carapace to 1.8 cm (³/₄ in.) Purse Crabs – Leucosiidae
ID: Tan to purplish dome-shaped carapace with tiny orange tubercles; **three blunt triangular spines at rear;** front raised triangular area broad with blunt spine on each side. Sand and rubble from 75 to 240 ft. Uncommon Caribbean, Dry Tortugas.

SMOOTHFINGER PURSE CRAB *Iliacantha liodactylus*
SIZE: carapace to 2.5 cm (1 in.)   Purse Crabs – Leucosiidae
ID: Tan, finely granulate, dome-shaped carapace with **three sharp up-curved spines at rear, side spines two-thirds length of center spine;** fringe of bristles on walking legs. Nocturnal; sand and mud from 25 to 400 ft. Uncommon W. Florida, Caribbean.

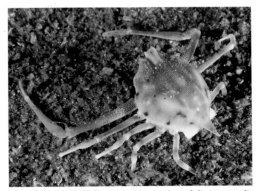

GRANULOSE PURSE CRAB *Acanthilia intermedia*
SIZE: carapace to 2.5 cm (1 in.)   Purse Crabs – Leucosiidae
ID: Tan to pinkish dome-shaped carapace with red blotches toward sides and heavily granulated toward front; **long, up-turned rear spine flanked by broad, blunt triangular spines.** Sand from 30 to 130 ft. Uncommon W. Florida, Caribbean.

MOTTLED PURSE CRAB *Persephona mediterranea*
SIZE: carapace to 5 cm (2 in.)   Purse Crabs – Leucosiidae
ID: Tan carapace and appendages covered with **pattern of red granules;** three up-curved rear spines, center spine slightly longer. Uncommon Florida, Gulf of Mexico to Campeche, Lesser Antilles to Brazil.

THINARM CLUTCH CRAB *Ebalia stimpsonii*
SIZE: carapace to 9 mm (³/₈ in.)   Purse Crabs – Leucosiidae
ID: Bumpy hexagonal carapace and appendages white with pattern of red granules; claw arms thick and nearly cylindrical with white-tipped claws. Sand and shell bottoms from 25 to 600 ft. Uncommon W. Florida, Bahamas, E. Caribbean.

TWOHOLE CLUTCH CRAB *Speloeophorus nodosus*
SIZE: carapace to 8 mm (³/₈ in.)   Purse Crabs – Leucosiidae
ID: Bumpy white hexagonal carapace densely covered with rounded nodules; claw arms short, stout and rough; legs with red blotches. Easily mistaken for dead chunk of coral. Coral reefs from 10 to 60 ft. Uncommon S. Florida, Caribbean.

HEART URCHIN PEA CRAB
Dissodactylus primitivus
Commensal Pea Crabs –
Pinnotheridae
SIZE: to 1.2 cm (½ in.)
ID: Smooth white carapace and appendages edged with fringe of short bristles. Found commensally on underside of Red Heart Urchin, *Meoma ventricosa ventricosa*. Sand flats from 3 to 130 ft. Occasional Florida, Bahamas, Caribbean.

SAND DOLLAR PEA CRAB   *Dissodactylus mellitae*
SIZE: to 6 mm (¼ in.) Commensal Pea Crabs – Pinnotheridae
ID: Pale whitish carapace and appendages with reddish brown mottling. Commensal with sand dollars in family Mellitidae to 400 ft. Occasional to uncommon Florida; also N. Gulf of Mexico.

WRINKLED PEA CRAB   *Clypeasterophilus rugatus*
SIZE: to 1 cm (⅜ in.) Commensal Pea Crabs – Pinnotheridae
ID: Carapace white with short wavy ridges of unequal length; white walking legs with brown banding. Commensal with inflated Sea Biscuit, *Clypeaster rugatus*, Red Heart Urchin *Meoma ventricosa ventricosa*. Florida, Bahamas, Caribbean.

ELLEN'S PEA CRAB   Undetermined
SIZE: to 6 mm (¼ in.) Commensal Pea Crabs – Pinnotheridae
ID: Smooth, shiny oval carapace and appendages white with orange blotching; walking legs primarily orange. Examination of in-hand specimen required for positive identification. Rare; known from Bonaire.

Shore, Mud, Coral & Stone Crabs

MOTTLED SHORE CRAB   *Pachygrapsus transversus*
SIZE: carapace to 1.5 cm (⁵/₈ in.)   Shore Crabs – Grapsidae
ID: Smooth shiny rectangular carapace with transverse ridges; color highly variable with irregular mottling; walking legs dark with gray spotting. Rocky tide lines and shallow pilings. Uncommon S. Florida, E. Caribbean; also Gulf of Mexico.

LOBEFOOT MUD CRAB   *Hexapanopeus lobipes*
SIZE: carapace to 2.5 cm (1 in.)   Mud Crabs – Panopeidae
ID: Vermilion except for orange wash on outer claw arms; finely granulate bumpy carapace; claw arms short and stout with rows of rounded tubercles; walking legs heavily bristled. Sand and rubble to 225 ft. Uncommon S. Florida, Bahamas.

BATWING CORAL CRAB
Carpilius corallinus
Coral Crabs – Carpiliidae
SIZE: to 11 cm (4¹/₄ in.)
ID: Large smooth carapace and appendages vary from red to brown with white to yellowish spotting; upper walking legs and ventral surface of carapace and claw arms whitish; stout claw arms with dark claws. **BL-** Juvenile: White rounded carapace with dark reddish spots and pink highlights. **BR-** Postlarval crab in float of *Sargassum.* Common Bahamas, Caribbean. Can be uncommon to rare in many locations due to overharvesting.

FLORIDA STONE CRAB
Menippe mercenaria
Stone Crabs – Menippidae
SIZE: to 13 cm (5 in.)

ID: Smooth yellowish tan to purplish brown carapace and appendages; stout claw arms flattened with black claws of unequal size. **MR-**Juvenile: Yellow-outlined spots on carapace and upper claw arms turn purple then gray and tan with maturity. Adults often inhabit rock jetties; live inside burrows in soft sediment, usually shallow, but can be to 60 ft. Commercially important; claws are highly prized as food. Legally, only the claws may be taken, which regenerate. Common to uncommon Florida, Bahamas, S. Caribbean.

CUBAN STONE CRAB
Menippe nodifrons
Stone Crabs – Menippidae
SIZE: carapace to 7.5 cm (3 in.)

ID: Carapace heavy and somewhat lumpy near front with prominent bi-lobed projection between eyes; two round nodules below each eye and two broadly rounded lobes behind on the edge of the carapace; reddish to purple with pale netlike marking formed by nodules on the palms of claw arms; black claws. Inhabit shallow near-shore waters. Occasional S. E. Florida, Caribbean.

Spray & Neck Crabs

Percnon gibbesi
Spray Crabs – Plagusiidae
SIZE: carapace to 3 cm
(1¼ in.)
ID: Flat, reddish-brown
mottled carapace with
yellow to white central
vertical line; long banded
walking legs extend to the
side; **horizontal yellow line
runs across front of carapace
below eyes.** Inhabit shallow
rocky shorelines, frequently
take shelter beneath spines
of Long-spined Urchin,
Diadema antillarum. Abundant
Florida, Bahamas, Caribbean.
Also Pacific Coast of Central
America. Invasive species in
Mediterranean.

TIDAL SPRAY CRAB
Plagusia depressa
Spray Crabs – Plagusiidae
SIZE: carapace to 2.5 cm
(1 in.)
ID: Flat carapace with long
walking legs extending to
side; color variable from light
reddish with numerous dark
red dots and gray tubercles,
to olive or bluish green with
brown to black tubercles; red
to purple highlights on legs
and claw tips. Inhabit rocky
shorelines and tidepools.
Uncommon Florida, Bahamas,
Caribbean; also Gulf of Mexico.

YELLOWLINE ARROW CRAB
Stenorhynchus seticornis
Neck Crabs – Inachidae
SIZE: to 6.5 cm (2½ in.)
ID: Small triangular body with alternating white, brown and black stripes; long pointed rostrum; long, slender, tan spiderlike legs; purple-tipped claws. Inhabit a variety of habitats including reefs from 10 to 130 ft. Abundant Florida, Bahamas, Caribbean.

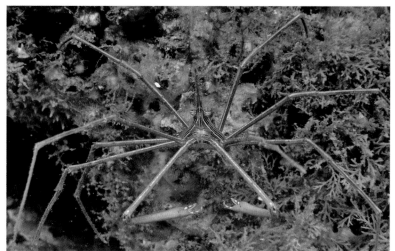

FALSE ARROW CRAB   *Metoporhaphis calcarata*
SIZE: carapace to 1 cm (³/₈ in.)   Neck Crabs – Inachidae
ID: Small dirty gray to yellowish triangular carapace covered with pointed protrusions; long, spiderlike legs; claw arms short and stocky when compared with legs. Variety of habitats to 300 ft. Uncommon Florida, Caribbean; also Gulf of Mexico.

SHORTFINGER NECK CRAB   *Podochela sidneyi*
SIZE: carapace to 2 cm (³/₄ in.)   Neck Crabs – Inachidae
ID: Small tan triangular carapace with rounded rostrum; claw arms covered with hair; body and legs typically covered with bryozoans and algae [photo]. Often on seafans and gorgonians to 450 ft. Occasional Florida, Caribbean.

NECK CRABS   *Podochela* spp.
SIZE: carapace to 2 cm (³/₄ in.)   Neck Crabs – Inachidae
ID: Because of extensive covering of living organisms difficult to identify genus members to species. Generally found living in association with organisms they employ as decorations: **BL**-Sponge, **BR**- Hydroids. Occasional Florida, Bahamas, Caribbean.

Decorator Crabs

SPONGY DECORATOR CRAB
Macrocoeloma trispinosum
Decorator Crabs –
Mithracidae
SIZE: to 5 cm (2 in.)
ID: Triangular tan to red or brown carapace with indention on each side behind eye; two indentations on rear carapace; body typically covered with decoration, primarily sponge, leaving openings for eyes to protrude, also frequently decorate with hydroids and algae. Nocturnal; inhabit reefs and man-made structures from 10 to 225 ft. Occasional Florida, Bahamas, Caribbean.

ROUGHNOSE DECORATOR CRAB
Leptopisa setirostris
Decorator Crabs –
Mithracidae
SIZE: length to 2.5 cm (1 in.)
ID: Triangular orange to red carapace with central ridge of tubercles ending with two slightly curved spines; two white-tipped elongate rostrum horns (almost touch), covered with bristles, extend from front of carapace; white appendages; walking legs become shorter toward rear; typically decorate with sponge or algae. Nocturnal; inhabit reefs from 6 to 240 ft. Uncommon to rare S. Florida, Bahamas, Caribbean.

BANDED CLINGING CRAB
Mithraculus cinctimanus
Decorator Crabs –
Mithracidae
SIZE: carapace to 1.8 cm
($^{3}/_{4}$ in.)
ID: Oval whitish to tan or brown carapace and walking legs heavily bristled (bristles become less prominent with age); walking legs and claw arms white with brown to red banding; claw pincers white with prominent dark band. **MR**- Juvenile: Densely covered with hairlike bristles. Inhabit patch reefs from 10 to 45 ft.; often in association with anemones, especially Giant Anemone, *Condylactis gigantea*, and Sun Anemone, *Stichodactyla helianthus*. Common S. Florida, Bahamas, Caribbean.

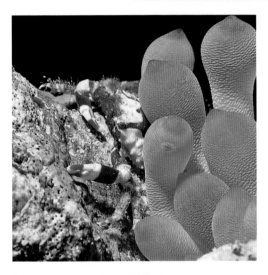

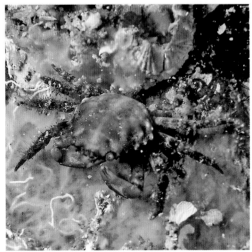

RED-RIDGED CLINGING CRAB   *Mithraculus forceps*
SIZE: carapace to 1.8 cm ($^{3}/_{4}$ in.) Decorator Crabs – Mithracidae
ID: Shiny oval carapace with three forward angling grooves; orange, brown, red to olive; bristled walking legs; stout claw arms with two forward pointing spines on inside of first section. Reef from 10 to 45 ft. Common S. Florida, Bahamas,

Spider Crabs

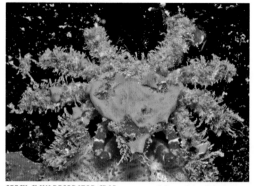

SPECK-CLAW DECORATOR CRAB *Microphrys bicornutus*
SIZE: carapace to 1.8 cm (³/₄ in.) Decorator Crabs – Mithracidae
ID: Typically heavily decorated leaving only claw arms exposed;
claw arms red with narrow white banding; two horns project
from front of head. Nocturnal; reefs from 20 to 130 ft. Common
S. Florida, Bahamas, Caribbean.

NODOSE CLINGING CRAB *Mithraculus coryphe*
SIZE: carapace to 2.5 cm (1 in.) Decorator Crabs – Mithracidae
ID: Mottled green and white, occasionally red; carapace bumpy
with median furrows; walking legs with vague white bands and
bristles; rear-pointing spines line first section of claw arms. Reefs
and rubble to 300 ft. Occasional Florida, Bahamas, Caribbean.

GREEN CLINGING CRAB *Mithraculus sculptus*
SIZE: carapace to 1.8 cm (³/₄ in.) Decorator Crabs – Mithracidae
ID: Olive-green carapace and appendages; back covered with
smooth, rounded nodules; walking legs heavily bristled; two
large spines on inside of first section of claw arms. Rubble and
reefs to 40 ft. Common S. Florida, Bahamas, Caribbean.

CORAL CLINGING CRAB *Mithrax hispidus*
SIZE: carapace to 15 cm (6 in.) Decorator Crabs – Mithracidae
ID: Tan to red; carapace and walking legs often covered with
sponge and algae; first section of stout claw arms heavily
spined; tubercles around eyes. Nocturnal; various habitats
from shallows to 215 ft. Common Florida, Bahamas, Caribbean.

CHANNEL CLINGING CRAB
Mithrax spinosissimus
Decorator Crabs –
Mithracidae
SIZE: to 18 cm (7 in.)
ID: Large; red to purplish; rough, nearly circular carapace with spines lining front and sides; all three sections of claw arms bear short spines; about ten blunt spines on front edge of wrist section before claws; claws curved with wide gape. **MR-** Occasionally covered with algae. Often in caves or under ledge overhangs during the day; forage in the open at night. Occasional Florida, Bahamas, Caribbean.

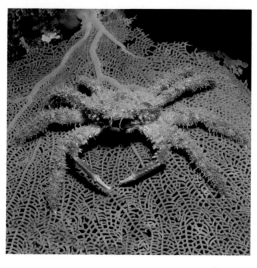

HAIRY CLINGING CRAB *Mithrax pilosus*
SIZE: carapace to 10 cm (4 in.)   Decorator Crabs – Mithracidae
ID: Reddish brown and bristled carapace and appendages; numerous spines on walking legs and claw arms; sharp spines line front edge of wrist section before claws. Inhabit caves and recesses from 15 to 45 ft. Rare Florida, Bahamas, Caribbean.

PAVED CLINGING CRAB *Mithrax verrucosus*
SIZE: carapace to 1.8 cm (¾ in.)   Decorator Crabs – Mithracidae
ID: Carapace with thick covering of granules and bristles; walking legs covered with long bristles; first two sections of claw arms bear long spines, third section smooth. Shallow habitats to 30 ft. Occasional Florida, Bahamas, Caribbean.

141

Decorator Crabs

FURCATE SPIDER CRAB
Stenocionops furcatus
Decorator Crabs –
Mithracidae
SIZE: to 14 cm (5½ in.)
ID: Tan to red body and appendages; bumpy carapace with four long, pointed spines on each side and two between the eyes (seldom seen because of decoration); long, thin claw arms smooth except for a few spines on first section; purplish brown claws; decorate with a variety of organisms including sponge, tunicates, algae and the Hitchhiking Anemone, *Calliactis tricolor.* Nocturnal; inhabit reefs and rocky areas to 350 ft. Occasional Florida, Bahamas, Caribbean; also Gulf of Mexico.

PRICKLY SPIDER CRAB   *Stenocionops spinimanus*
SIZE: carapace to 13 cm (5 in.)   Decorator Crabs – Mithracidae
ID: Pear-shaped convex carapace with numerous spines and bristles; walking legs with bristles but no spines; claw arms heavily spined except smooth claws; develop spines with age. Various habitats from 100 to 750 ft. Uncommon S. Florida, Caribbean.

STALKEYE SUMO CRAB   *Ethusa mascarone americana*
SIZE: to 1.8 cm (¾ in.)   Sumo Crabs – Dorippidae
ID: Flat fuzzy grayish carapace; long slender white eyestalks with dark centers; first pair walking legs long and stout, last two pair used to hold decoration; pink claws. Sand and rubble from shallows to 270 ft. Uncommon S. Florida, Caribbean.

CRYPTIC TEARDROP CRAB
Pelia mutica
Decorator Crabs – Pisidae
SIZE: carapace to 1.8 cm
(³/₄ in.)
ID: Red triangular carapace typically decorated with bits of red sponge; **claw arms purplish blue with black specks.** Nocturnal; inhabit reefs and manmade structures such as pier pilings from 20 to 130 ft. Common Florida, Bahamas, Caribbean.

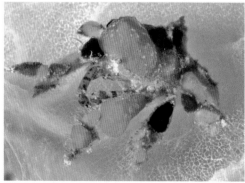

SOUTHERN TEARDROP CRAB   *Pelia rotunda*
SIZE: carapace to 1.2 cm (¹/₂ in.)   Decorator Crabs – Pisidae
ID: Much the same size and shape as Cryptic Teardrop Crab [previous]. Can be distinguished by **brown banding** rather than purplish blue on claw arms. Inhabit reefs and manmade structures from 6 to 120 ft. Uncommon S. Caribbean.

SHORTHORN DECORATOR CRAB   *Chorinus heros*
SIZE: carapace to 4.5 cm (1³/₄ in.)   Decorator Crabs – Pisidae
ID: Golden brown oblong carapace with two prominent spines in front and two smaller spines on each side; walking legs with bristles; claw arms long, smooth and unmarked. Rubble and grass from 15 to 150 ft. Uncommon S. Florida, Caribbean.

143

Sponge, Spider & Imitator Crabs

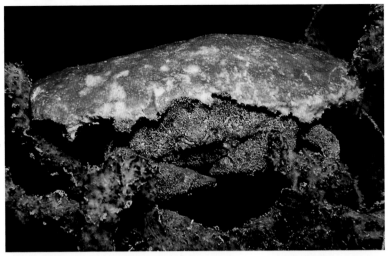

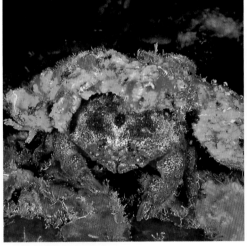

REDEYE SPONGE CRAB
Dromia erythropus
Sponge Crabs – Dromiidae
SIZE: to 8 cm (3 1/4 in.)
ID: Thick dome-shaped carapace covered with short bristles from tan to red; dark spot on middle front of carapace; stout claws tipped with red; carry living sections of sponge held in place by modified last pair of walking legs. Nocturnal; disturbed by direct beam from divers' lights. Inhabit reefs and pier pilings to 1200 ft. Occasional Florida, Bahamas, Caribbean; also Gulf of Mexico.

HAIRY SPONGE CRAB
Moreiradromia antillensis
Sponge Crabs – Dromiidae
SIZE: to 6.5 cm (2 1/2 in.)
ID: Thick dome-shaped carapace covered with coat of short reddish bristles; slender walking legs, last pair longer and modified to bend across back to hold living sponge cap in place; claw arms stout; small dark eyes on white stalks. Hide by day beneath sponge caps; nocturnal; disturbed by direct beam from divers' lights. Reef and pier pilings from shallows to 130 ft. Rare Florida, E. and S. Caribbean; also Gulf of Mexico.

ROUGH SHELLBACK CRAB *Hypoconcha parasitica*
SIZE: to 2.5 cm (1 in.) Sponge Crabs – Dromiidae
ID: One of three species in genus that carries a single clam valve on back held in place by modified last pair of walking legs; pinkish tan carapace ringed with bristles. Sand and shell beds to 300 ft. Uncommon Florida, Bahamas, Caribbean.

GREEN ALGAE CRAB *Thersandrus compressus*
SIZE: carapace to 2.5 cm (1 in.) Spider Crabs – Majidae
ID: Flat dark green oval carapace with heavy covering of green bristles on head and walking legs. Live and feed on Paddle Blade Alga, *Avrainvillea longicaulis*, to 30 ft. Occasional Bahamas, Caribbean.

RED SPIDER CRAB *Teleophrys* sp.
SIZE: carapace to 5 cm (2 in.) Spider Crabs – Majidae
ID: Rounded, slightly bumpy, carapace; first two sections of claw arms rough with blunt spines, third section smooth. Identification to species can't be made without clear view of walking legs. Rare; known from Bonaire.

RED-WHITE SPIDER CRAB
Epialtus kingsleyi
Imitator Crabs – Epialtidae
SIZE: carapace to 1.1 cm (³/₈ in.)
ID: Flattened red and white carapace with prominent pointed rostrum and pointed projections on sides; claw arms long and thick, largely smooth and cylindrical become wider toward claws; claws short, thick and strongly arched. Known from S. Florida.

Box, Liver & Porcelain Crabs

FLAME BOX CRAB *Calappa flammea*
SIZE: to 10 cm (4 in.) Box Crabs – Calappidae
ID: Oval dome-shaped cream-colored carapace with wavy reddish brown to lavender lines that form network pattern becoming more open toward rear. Sand to 250 ft; often bury. Occasional Florida, Bahamas, Caribbean; also Gulf of Mexico.

OCELLATE BOX CRAB *Calappa ocellata*
SIZE: to 10 cm (4 in.) Box Crabs – Calappidae
ID: Dark brown to reddish brown or lavender network pattern with enclosed yellowish speckling covers carapace. Sand to 250 ft.; often bury. Occasional Florida, Bahamas, Caribbean.

YELLOW BOX CRAB *Calappa sulcata*
SIZE: to 14 cm (5½ in.) Box Crabs – Calappidae
ID: Yellowish tan to white carapace shorter than wide; crest on upper palm with 6 teeth and shorter tooth near wrist; 4 large pointed triangular teeth on elbow. Sand and mud to 600 ft. Occasional Florida, Bahamas, Caribbean; also Gulf of Mexico.

TORTUGA BOX CRAB *Calappa tortugae*
SIZE: to 5 cm (2 in.) Box Crabs – Calappidae
ID: Lumpy oval tan to yellowish carapace with large lump behind each eye with deep furrow behind extending to rear edge of carapace; lumpy palm lined on top with 6 to 8 rounded teeth. Sand from 40 to 700 ft. Florida, E. Caribbean; also Gulf of Mexico.

SHAMEFACE HEART CRAB *Cryptosoma balguerii*
SIZE: to 7.5 cm (3 in.) Box Crabs – Calappidae
ID: White rough carapace with purple markings, concave toward rear; walking legs white with purple and yellow highlights edged with bristles; often encrusted. Sand from 3 to 45 ft.; frequently bury. Occasional Florida, Bahamas, Caribbean.

CALICO BOX CRAB *Hepatus epheliticus*
SIZE: to 7.5 cm (3 in.) Liver Crabs – Hepatidae
ID: Smooth tan carapace with large contrasting reddish brown spots. Inhabit tidal creek bottoms and offshore to 70 ft. Often with attached Hitchhiking Anemone, *Calliactis tricolor*. Occasional Florida, uncommon N. Caribbean; also Gulf of Mexico

REDBACK PORCELAIN CRAB
Petrolisthes politus
Porcelain Crabs –
Porcellanidae
SIZE: carapace to 1.5 cm
(⅝ in.)
ID: Smooth shiny brownish carapace with numerous small blue spots; upper walking legs have spines, bristles and reddish joints; claw arms blue with red highlights; red claw tips. Usually inhabit rubble and rocks from shallows to 660 ft. Like other family members, feed at night just inside openings of restrictive crevices capturing planktonic food by repeatedly extending fanlike mouth parts known as setae. Occasional S. Florida, Bahamas, Caribbean.

CHARMING PORCELAIN CRAB   *Petrolisthes amoenus*
SIZE: carapace to 1 cm (⅜ in.) Porcelain Crabs – Porcellanidae
ID: Carapace and claw arms blue to tan with dark spotting and orange highlights; white-banded walking legs. **MR-** Juvenile. Inhabit gorgonians, sponges, and finger corals (*Porites*) from shallows to 460 ft. Occasional Caribbean.

BLUE PORCELAIN CRAB   *Petrolisthes caribensis*
SIZE: carapace to 6 mm (¼ in.) Porcelain Crabs – Porcellanidae
ID: Pale blue ridged carapace, claw arms and upper legs with red-brown markings forming wavy transverse lines; lower legs banded; claw arms lined with tan bristles. Inhabit finger corals (*Porites*) to 20 ft. Uncommon Florida, Caribbean.

RED PORCELAIN CRAB   *Petrolisthes marginatus*
SIZE: carapace to 1.2 cm (½ in.) Porcelain Crabs – Porcellanidae
ID: Reddish brown with loose scattering of dark spots; thin, paired white bands on lower walking legs; dark claws with red outline. Live beneath stones and inside crevices of sand and rubble from shallows to 60 ft. Uncommon Caribbean.

147

Porcelain Crabs

BANDED PORCELAIN CRAB
Petrolisthes galathinus
Porcelain Crabs –
Porcellanidae
SIZE: carapace to 1.8 cm
(³/₄ in.)
ID: Orange to brown, gray
or white with dark red to
purple transverse ridges;
white bands near tips of
walking legs; claw arms
large with large pointed
teeth along inner edge and
smaller teeth along outer
edge. Hide beneath stone
slabs or inside narrow
cracks from 10 to 175 ft.
Occasional Florida, Bahamas,
Caribbean.

GREEN PORCELAIN CRAB *Petrolisthes armatus*
SIZE: carapace to 1.2 cm (¹/₂ in.) Porcelain Crabs – Porcellanidae
ID: Carapace, claw arms and upper walking legs greenish tan
with network of thin dark lines and blue highlights; dark claws;
scattered bristles on legs and claw arms. Hide under rocks and
inside narrow crevices. Occasional Florida, Bahamas, Caribbean.

RED-WHITE PORCELAIN CRAB *Petrolisthes jugosus*
SIZE: carapace to 4 mm (¹/₈ in.) Porcelain Crabs – Porcellanidae
ID: Round granulated carapace and claw arms fuchsia with
scattered white spots; banded walking legs; claw tips white.
Hide under coral rubble and rocks in shallows to 10 ft.
Uncommon S. Florida, Caribbean.

PENTAGONAL PORCELAIN CRAB *Megalobrachium soriatum*
SIZE: carapace to 6 mm (¹/₄ in.) Porcelain Crabs – Porcellanidae
ID: Somewhat pentagonal lumpy cream to orange carapace;
rough rounded claw arms and walking legs. Hide beneath
rocks, coral and inside canals of sponge from shore to 560 ft.
Uncommon to rare Florida, Caribbean.

RIISE PORCELAIN CRAB *Pachycheles riisei*
SIZE: carapace to 6 mm (¹/₄ in.) Porcelain Crabs – Porcellanidae
ID: Smooth red carapace and claw arms with white walking
legs, claws and sides of carapace; robust granulated claw arms
of equal size. Intertidal; live beneath rocks and inside crevices
of coral. Occasional S. Florida, Caribbean.

SPINY PORCELAIN CRAB *Parapetrolisthes tortugensis*
SIZE: carapace to 3 mm (¹/₈ in.)   Porcelain Crabs – Porcellanidae
ID: Carapace and slender claw arms (3 time length of carapace) with dark red speckling and orange and blue highlights; white-banded legs. Inhabit finger corals (*Porites*) and branching sponges from 30 to 130 ft. Rare Bahamas, Caribbean.

STRIPED PORCELAIN CRAB *Porcellana sigsbeiana*
SIZE: carapace to 2.5 cm (1 in.)   Porcelain Crabs – Porcellanidae
ID: Shiny white carapace with reddish longitudinal mottling forming a white "Y"; bluish gray spotting; short robust claw arms. From 50 to 1,200 ft. Uncommon Bahamas, E. Caribbean.

SPOTTED PORCELAIN CRAB
Porcellana sayana
Porcelain Crabs –
Porcellanidae
SIZE: carapace to 1.8 cm
(³/₄ in.)

ID: Light red to reddish brown carapace, claw arms and walking legs with prominent pattern of white to blue spots outlined with red. May be free-living, but commonly associate with Giant Hermit Crab, *Petrochirus diogenes* [next page], Stareye Hermit Crab, *Dardanus venosus* [next page], Queen Conch, *Lobatus gigas*, and **BL**-sea stars from 10 to 100 feet. Occasional Florida, Bahamas, Caribbean.

Hermit Crabs

GIANT HERMIT
Petrochirus diogenes
Left-handed Hermits –
Diogenidae
SIZE: to 20 cm (8 in.)
ID: Largest Caribbean hermit; reddish gray to reddish brown claws of nearly equal size (left slightly larger) texture resembles overlapping scales; red and white banded antennae. Inhabit sand and seagrass from 3 to 100 ft. Occasional Florida, Bahamas, Caribbean.

BAREYE HERMIT   *Dardanus fucosus*
SIZE: to 13 cm (5 in.)   Left-handed Hermits – Diogenidae
ID: Reddish purple with red highlights. **MR-** Distinctive eyes blue with horizontal black bar and tuft of bristles above eye. Sand, seagrass, coral and shell rubble from 2 to 440 ft. Occasional Florida, Caribbean.

STAREYE HERMIT
Dardanus venosus
Left-handed Hermits –
Diogenidae
SIZE: to 13 cm (5 in.)
ID: Lavender to pink and orange with numerous tan bristles; distinctive dark starlike design on blue eyes; legs banded and with white spots. Shells often encrusted with Hitchhiking Anemone, *Calliactis tricolor.* Nocturnal; Shells and anemone often home to Spotted Porcelain Crab, *Porcellana sayana.* Sand, seagrass, coral and shell rubble from 2 to 130 ft. Occasional Florida, Bahamas, Caribbean.

RED-BANDED HERMIT *Paguristes erythrops*
SIZE: to 10 cm (4 in.)   Left-handed Hermits – Diogenidae
ID: Cream to tan with red bands and large spots; Antennae and eyestalks gold; eyes blue; equal-size claws. A variety of habitats from 2 to 130 ft. Occasional Caribbean.

BLUE-EYE HERMIT *Paguristes sericeus*
SIZE: to 6.5 cm (2½ in.)   Left-handed Hermits – Diogenidae
ID: Reddish with bright red eyestalks and small brilliant blue eyes: flattened equal-size claws. Inhabit sand and rubble from 30 to 450 ft. Similar Red Banded Hermit [previous] has gold eyestalks. Occasional Florida, Bahamas, Caribbean.

WHITESPECKLED HERMIT *Paguristes puncticeps*
SIZE: to 13 cm (5 in.)   Left-handed Hermits – Diogenidae
ID: Carapace, legs, claws and eyestalks red-brown to brown covered with raised white speckles; bristles on carapace; equal-size claws. Inhabit a variety of habitats from 2 to 130 ft. Occasional S. Florida, Bahamas,Caribbean.

RED REEF HERMIT *Paguristes cadenati*
SIZE: to 2 cm (¾ in.)   Left-handed Hermits – Diogenidae
ID: Bright red legs; carapace and claw arms with shallow indentations; may have some white spots; greenish eyes on pale eyestalks. Inhabit coral reefs. Common S. Florida, Bahamas, Caribbean.

ORANGECLAW HERMIT *Calcinus tibicen*
SIZE: to 2 cm (¾ in.)   Left-handed Hermits – Diogenidae
ID: Legs and claw arms orange, red, tan, brown, or bluish green; lower legs white with brown bands; orange eyestalks have white tips; left claw much larger than right. Reefs and rock to 100 ft. Occasional S. Florida, Bahamas, Caribbean.

Hermit Crabs

TRICOLOR HERMIT *Clibanarius tricolor*
SIZE: to 1.2 cm (¹/₂ in.)   Left-handed Hermits – Diogenidae
ID: Blue carapace, legs and eyestalks; black equal-size claw arms with white bumps; legs with red joints, last section white. Prefer intertidal zones of rock and rubble. Occasional S. Florida, Bahamas, Caribbean.

HAIRY HERMIT Undetermined
SIZE: to 2.5 cm (1 in.)   Left-handed Hermits – Diogenidae
ID: Pale orange legs and claw arms covered with densely packed tan bristles; claws with white tips; eyestalks and antennae maroon with white banding. Rare; photograph taken at 30 feet on coral reef in Grand Cayman.

CANDY-STRIPED HERMIT *Pylopaguropsis mollymullerae*
SIZE: to 2.4 cm (¹/₄ in.)   Right-handed Hermits – Paguridae
ID: White legs and eye stalks with red stripes; giant right spoon-like claw reddish brown with red stripe bordered with equal width white stripes. Near or on reefs 25-55ft. Currently known only from Bonaire..

RIDGECLAW HERMIT *Phimochirus randalli*
SIZE: to 7.5 cm (3 in.)   Right-handed Hermits – Paguridae
ID: Orange legs, eyestalks and claw arms; thin white bandlike markings on legs and claw arms; white-tipped claws. Near coral reefs from 50 to 300 ft. Uncommon Florida, Bahamas, scattered locations in Caribbean; also Gulf of Mexico.

SMOOTHCLAW HERMIT
Phimochirus leurocarpus
Right-handed Hermits –
Paguridae
SIZE: to 2.5 cm (1 in.)
ID: Red legs and eyestalks with purple highlights; legs banded white; red and white claw arms with purple specks. Sand and rubble from 20 to 600 ft. Identification tentative. Uncommon S. Florida, Bahamas, central Caribbean to Venezuela.

RED-STRIPED HERMIT *Phimochirus holthuisi*
SIZE: to 2.5 cm (1 in.)   Right-handed Hermits – Paguridae
ID: White legs with brown longitudinal lines; eyestalks white with brown bands; upper claw arm white with circular lines; blue eyes. Coral reefs from 20 to 65 ft. Occasional S. Florida, Bahamas, Caribbean.

SHORTFINGER HERMIT *Pagurus brevidactylus*
SIZE: to 1.8 cm (³/₄ in.)   Right-handed Hermits – Paguridae
ID: Tan, reddish brown and lavender legs and claw arms with a scattering of bristles; banded antennae; long pale eyestalks narrow toward red eyes. Hard bottoms from 6 to 750 ft. Uncommon Florida, Bahamas, Caribbean.

RETICULATED HERMIT
Iridopagurus reticulatus
Right-handed Hermits –
Paguridae
SIZE: to 5 mm (¹/₄ in.)

ID: Small; translucent tan with bristles on equal-size claw arms (right slightly larger) with brown reticulated pattern; pale eyestalks with brown band near base and another just below cream-colored eyes. Sand from 3 to 125 ft.; occasionally bury. Common Florida, Bahamas, E. Caribbean to South America.

RINGEYE HERMIT *Iridopagurus* sp.1
SIZE: to 5 mm (¹/₄ in.)   Right-handed Hermits – Paguridae
ID: Small; dark band encircles base of bluish eyes; brown-banded translucent tan claw arms heavily bristled; legs light blue with thin longitudinal lines and a few bristles. Sand to 30 ft.; occasionally bury. Uncommon Caribbean.

SPOTEYE HERMIT *Iridopagurus* sp.2
SIZE: to 5 mm (¹/₄ in.)   Right-handed Hermits – Paguridae
ID: Small; numerous red spots on cream-colored eyes; translucent legs and claw arms with white scrawled areas, brown banding and translucent bristles. Sand to 30 ft; occasionally bury. Known from St. Vincent.

153

Squat Lobsters, Mole Crabs, Mysids, Isopods & Amphipods

COMMON SQUAT LOBSTER   *Munida pusilla*
SIZE: to 1.2 cm (¹/₂ in.)   Squat Lobsters – Galatheidae
ID: Like all family members, long claw arms held straight out
from body; red to brown with wide white stripe extending
length of carapace. Variety of sheltered habitats; often in
groups. Common to occasional Florida, Bahamas, Caribbean.

MOLE CRABS
SIZE: carapace to 5 cm (2 in.)   Mole Crabs – Albuneidae
ID: Stocky body from chalky white to orangish tan; robust front
legs without claws; bristled antennae longer than body. Bury
backward in shallow sand often in surf zones with feeding
antennae above surface. Common but rarely sighted.

MYSIDS
SIZE: to 2 mm (¹/₁₆ in.)   Mysids – Order Mysida
ID: Tiny shrimplike crustaceans; most commonly seen as tiny
translucent specks clustered around shelter or urchins. Often
mistaken for fish larvae. Three W. Altantic reef species.
Common Florida, Bahamas, Caribbean.

ISOPODS
SIZE: to 2.5 cm (1 in.)   Isopods – Order Isopoda
ID: Typically less than ½ in. flattened oval bodies; unstalked eyes;
head fused with first segment of thorax; no carapace; each of 7
thoracic segments bears pair of walking or clinging legs. 5 pairs
of branched respiratory organs. Occasional throughout range.

Mysida, Isopoda & Amphipoda/Crustacea/Arthropoda

CYMOTHOID ISOPODS *Anilocra* spp. or *Renocila* spp.
SIZE: to 2.5 cm (1 in.) Isopods – Cymothoidae
ID: Tan to dark brown bodies of overlapping plates; attach to specific regions on heads of several species of fishes; usually in pairs, largest female. Not parasitic or harmful to hosts. At least 12 species in two genera in W. Atlantic. Occasional throughout range.

AMPHIPODS
SIZE: to 5 mm (¼ in.) Amphipods – Order Amphipoda
ID: Typically laterally compressed with 13 segments; two pairs of antennae; head fused to thorax but head and thorax usually distinct; 7 pairs of thoracic legs of two types, first two bear pincers, 5 pairs for locomotion. Occasional throughout range.

SKELETON SHRIMPS *Caprella* spp.
SIZE: to 1.2 cm (½ in.) Skeleton Shrimps – Caprellidae
ID: Long thin jointed bodies with two sets of antennae; large grasping claws, saclike gills below. Backward facing hooks on last 3 segments. Often form large groups on hydroids, sponges, algae, mooring lines. Suborder of amphipods. Uncommon.

Mantis Shrimps

DARK MANTIS
Neogonodactylus curacaoensis
Smashing Mantis Shrimps – Gonodactylidae
SIZE: to 7 cm (2³/₄ in.)

ID: Light to dark green or brown with some white spots on back and greenish blue edges on abdominal segments; blue, red and white raptorial claw arms; yellow to tan walking legs; **base of eyestalks orange;** tail reddish orange with blue outline. Active during day; use blunt raptorial claws to smash shells of gastropods and the exoskeletons of crustaceans. Coral reefs from 10 to 150 ft. Uncommon Florida, Caribbean.

SWOLLENCLAW MANTIS   *Neogonodactylus oerstedii*
SIZE: to 5 cm (2 in.) Smashing Mantis Shrimp – Gonodactylidae
ID: White with brown to dark green mottling; 4 spines extend from tail; purple spot near base of blunt raptorial arms. Rubble and living coral reef from intertidal to 60 ft., typically shallow. Occasional S. Florida, Bahamas, Caribbean.

HAVANA MANTIS   *Odontodactylus havanensis*
SIZE: to 7 cm (2³/₄ in.) Smashing Mantis Shrimps – Gonodactylidae
ID: White with red to green mottling; blunt, red and white raptorial claws; **green and red antennal scales with dark red or black spot;** blue-green base of eyes. Rubble from 60 to 120 ft. Uncommon S. Florida, Bahamas, Caribbean.

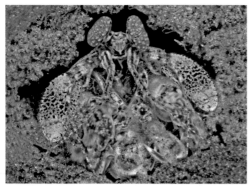

SCALY-TAILED MANTIS *Lysiosquilla scabricauda*
SIZE: to 30 cm (12 in.) Spearing Mantis Shrimps – Lysiosquillidae
ID: Large with dark banding on body; gold and **dark speckled antennal scales;** double-lobed, tan eyes with white spotting. Inhabit burrows where they spear passing fish; seldom leave burrows. Occasional Florida, Bahamas, Caribbean.

REEF MANTIS *Lysiosquillina glabriuscula*
SIZE: to 18 cm (7 in.) Spearing Mantis Shrimps – Lysiosquillidae
ID: Mottled dark brown to reddish brown to tan; dark double-lobed eyes. Inhabit burrows in sand near reefs from 15 to 75 ft. Identification tentative. Occasional S. Florida, Bahamas, Caribbean.

CILIATED FALSE SQUILLA *Pseudosquilla ciliata*
SIZE: to 9 cm (3½ in.) False Mantis Shrimps – Pseudosquillidae
ID: Color and markings vary to match habitat, mottled or solid brown, black, green or orange with speckling, spots, bands or two wide stripes. Often in open on sand, rubble or grass; juv. inhabit small holes in reef rock. Common Florida, Bahamas, Caribbean.

Barnacles, Horseshoe Crabs & Sea Spiders

SMOOTH GOOSENECK BARNACLE *Lepas anatifera*
SIZE: to 4 cm (1½ in.)   Gooseneck Barnacles – Lepadidae
ID: Five smooth translucent white to bluish shell plates encase animal. Attach by stalks that can reach an inch in length. Normally attach in clusters to floating objects such as buoys, driftwood, and ships from 0 to 130 ft. Common worldwide.

GROOVED GOOSENECK BARNACLE *Lepas anserifera*
SIZE: to 4 cm (1½ in.)   Gooseneck Barnacles – Lepadidae
ID: Five translucent radially grooved, whitish blue shell plates edged with orange; short orange attachment stalk no more than one inch in length. Frequently attach to floating driftwood, buoys, ship bottoms to 130 ft. Common Florida, Bahamas, Caribbean.

BLACK CORAL BARNACLE *Oxynaspis gracilis*
SIZE: to 1.2 cm (½ in.)   Gooseneck Barnacles – Oxynaspididae
ID: Stalk and flattened shell reddish brown to dark gray; hump on back of shells where they join. Grow in clusters on Feather Black Coral, *Antipathes pennacea*, and Bushy Black Coral, *A. caribbeana*, from 45 to 130 ft. Occasional Caribbean.

SESSILE BARNACLES
SIZE: to 4 cm (1½ in.)   Sessile Barnacles – Balanidae
ID: Permanently attach shell to substrate. Outer shell composed of one to eight plates, depending on genus most genera observed by divers have six. Six featherlike legs flick in and out of opening to feed. Common worldwide.

REDNETTED BARNACLE *Megabalanus* sp.
SIZE: to 4 cm (1½ in.)   Sessile Barnacles – Balanidae
ID: Permanently attach shell to substrate in large clumps; reddish net pattern. Need collection of specimen for species identification. A variety of shallow habitats including rocky areas from intertidal to 60 ft. Common worldwide.

HORSESHOE CRAB *Limulus polyphemus*
SIZE: to 60 cm (2 ft.)   Horseshoe Crabs – Limulidae
ID: Yellowish brown to gray horseshoe-shaped head and carapace, small abdomen, long pointed tail. Feed on clams and crustaceans in shallow water. Mate in spring. Not crabs, more closely related to spiders. Occasional Florida.

SEA SPIDERS

Sea Spiders –
Class Pycnogonida

SIZE: to 1.2 cm (¹/₂ in.)

ID: Superficially sea spiders look like terrestrial (true) spiders or water spiders, but are not directly related. Usually four, but often five to six pairs of long, spindly legs. Most pycnogonids measure less than half an inch, and display drab colors, however a few species can be quite striking. Often inhabit marine fouling organisms, such as hydroids and bryozoans (favored foods), attached to nautical trash and dock pilings. **ML&MR -** Egg masses are carried by the males on a special pair of appendages. Uncommon Florida, Bahamas, Caribbean.

Phylum Bryozoa

(Eck-toe-PROCK-tuh / Gr. outside anus)

Bryozoans

Bryozoans are tiny, colonial animals called zooids. **Zooids** have polyplike **tentacles** encircling the mouth; but, unlike polyps, they have a complete digestive system, including an anus that lies outside the ring of tentacles. These animals form a colonial skeleton with chambers that partition and separate one zooid from the next. These skeletal **chambers** may be **oval, tubular, vase** or **rectangular-shaped** and are usually less than 1/16 inch across. The colonies of different species vary greatly in appearance. Some look like a clump of **seaweed** or moss, while others grow as **lacy fans;** some species simply form **encrustations**. Colonies are generally white, although shades of brown, yellow, red and purple occur. Because the composition of building materials varies among species, colonies can be flexible or rigid. Rigid colonies, though calcareous, are often extremely fragile.

Because of the many variables, members of the phylum are not easily recognized as a group. Observing zooids joined together to form a colonial structure is often the best clue in recognizing a formation as bryozoan. Some species can be identified by the colony's pattern of growth, while others can be distinguished only by the shape of the individual zooids, which often requires microscopic examination.

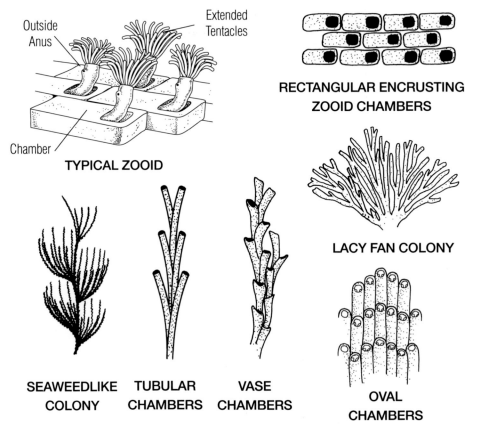

Outside Anus

Extended Tentacles

Chamber

TYPICAL ZOOID

RECTANGULAR ENCRUSTING ZOOID CHAMBERS

LACY FAN COLONY

SEAWEEDLIKE COLONY

TUBULAR CHAMBERS

VASE CHAMBERS

OVAL CHAMBERS

WHITEFAN BRYOZOAN
Reteporellina evelinae
Bryozoans – Phidoloporidae
SIZE: colonies to 5 cm (2 in.)
ID: White fan-shaped rigid and quite fragile colonies. Protected areas of coral reefs including bases of coral heads, inside recesses, and beneath ledge overhangs from 25 to 100 ft. Common Caribbean.

TANFAN BRYOZOAN
Scrupocellaria sp.
SIZE: colonies to 3 cm (1¼ in.)
Bryozoans – Candidae
ID: Fan-shaped tan colonies often grow in patches; somewhat flexible. Only genus to form tan fanlike structures along the Gulf Coast of Florida where common from 15 to 100 ft.; identification to species requires laboratory examination.

BROWNFAN BRYOZOAN
Bugula simplex
SIZE: colonies to 3 cm (1¼ in.)
Bryozoans – Bugulidae
ID: Flexible brown fan-shaped colonies with red tips and occasional bars. Protected areas of coral reefs: around bases of coral heads, inside recesses, and beneath ledges from 25 to 100 ft. Common Florida Keys, Bahamas, Caribbean.

PURPLE REEF FAN
Bugula minima
Bryozoans – Bugulidae
SIZE: colonies to 5 cm (2 in.)
ID: Purple fan-shaped colonies with flexible widely spaced branches. Protected areas of reefs from 25 to 100 ft. Occasional Caribbean; uncommon Florida.
SIMILAR SPECIES: Purple Fan Bryozoan, *B. neritina*, impossible to distinguish from the Purple Reef Fan, but grows in bays and harbors rather than reefs. Occasional Florida; rare Caribbean.

Bryozoans

PURPLE-TUFTED BRYOZOAN *Bugula neritina*
SIZE: colonies to 5 cm (2 in.) Bryozoans – Bugulidae
ID: Dark purple to reddish or brownish purple tufts form flexible branching bushlike colonies; small pearly-white beads along branches. Typically a fouling organism in harbors and bays; occasionally on reefs. Uncommon Florida, Bahamas, Caribbean.

SPIRAL-TUFTED BRYOZOAN *Bugula turrita*
SIZE: colonies to 30 cm (12 in.) Bryozoans – Bugulidae
ID: Light orangish brown to tan flexible bushy seaweedlike colonies; secondary branches form spiral around stems. Dock pilings, seagrass, shipwrecks and rock reefs from shallows to 90 ft. Common N. Florida; occasional S. Florida.

SEAWEED BRYOZOAN
Caulibugula dendrograpta
Bryozoans – Bugulidae
SIZE: colonies to 45 cm (18 in.)
ID: White to light gray or tan flexible bushy seaweedlike colonies with circular fanlike secondary branches. Dock pilings, seagrass beds, shipwrecks and rocky reefs from 10 to 30 ft. Common Florida; occasional Bahamas, Caribbean; also circumtropical.

WHITE TANGLED BRYOZOAN *Bracebridgia subsulcata*
SIZE: colonies to 13 cm (5 in.) Bryozoans – Adeonidae
ID: Calcareous rigid fragile mass of thin white cylindrical branches. Deep walls, beneath ledge overhangs, mooring lines and black coral trees from 50 to 100 ft. Occasional Florida, Bahamas, Caribbean.

TANGLED RIBBON BRYOZOAN *Membranipora* sp.
SIZE: colonies to 13 cm (5 in.) Bryozoans – Membraniporidae
ID: Rigid yet flexible white branching ribbon-shaped colonies; tiny rectangular zooid chambers are distinctive of genus. Deep walls, beneath ledge overhangs, mooring lines and black coral trees from 50 to 130 ft. Uncommon Caribbean.

PEARLY ORANGE ENCRUSTING BRYOZOAN
Hippopodina feegeensis
PURPLE ENCRUSTING BRYOZOAN
Schizoporella sp.
Bryozoans – Hippopodinidae & Schizoporellidae

SIZE: colonies to 7.5 cm (3 in.)

ID: Pearly Orange Encrusting Bryozoan: Encrusting colonies of distinctive pearly orange calcified zooids.

Purple Encrusting Bryozoan: Encrusting colonies of distinctive purple calcified zooids. Both species fouling organisms encrusting boat bottoms, pilings and mangrove roots, but also on reefs. Common Florida, Bahamas, Caribbean; also circumtropical.

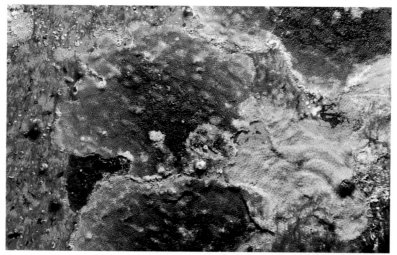

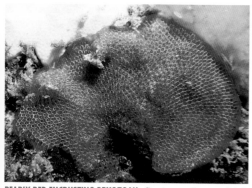

PEARLY RED ENCRUSTING BRYOZOAN *Steginoporella magnilabris*
SIZE: colonies to 7.5 cm (3 in.) Bryozoans – Steginoporellidae
ID: Thin pearly red encrustation composed of large calcified rectangular zooids with rounded ends that form shinglelike patterns. Dead areas of reefs and beneath ledges from 15 to 130 ft. Occasional Florida, Bahamas, Caribbean; also circumtropical.

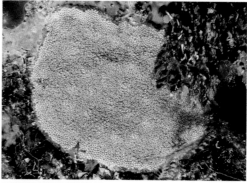

BLEEDING TEETH BRYOZOAN *Trematooecia aviculifera*
SIZE: colonies to 7.5 cm (3 in.) Bryozoans – Colatooeciidae
ID: Thin red to pink occasionally gold encrustation. (In natural light appears as a fluorescent pale green.) Calcified, rather large, tooth-shaped zooids create beaded texture. Protected areas of reefs and walls from 25 to 100 ft. Common Caribbean, Gulf of Mexico.

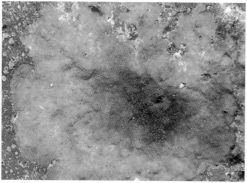

PEACH ENCRUSTING BRYOZOAN *Schizobrachiella verrilli*
SIZE: colonies to 25 cm (10 in.) Bryozoans – Schizobrachiella
ID: Peachy-orange encrustation of calcified rectangular zooids laying in long rows. Hard rocky surfaces, often mixed with encrusting coralline algae and other encrusting bryozoans from 6 to 80 ft. Occasional Florida, Bahamas, Caribbean.

TUBULARHORN BRYOZOAN *Schizoporella pungens*
SIZE: to 10 cm (4 in.) Bryozoans – Schizoporellidae
ID: Purplish brown calcified tubular branching hornlike structures. Harbors, bays, mangroves and reefs in Caribbean; inhabit rocky reefs in N. Florida from shallows to 100 ft. Occasional Florida, Bahamas, Caribbean.

163

Phylum Mollusca

(Moe-LUS-kuh / L. soft body)

Gastropods, Sea Slugs, Chitons, Bivalves, Octopuses, Squids

The Latin name Mollusca means soft body, which appropriately describes these animals because they lack a true skeleton. A majority of phylum members have an external shell for protection. Shells are made of calcium carbonate secreted from a specialized layer of the animals' outer tissues, called the **mantle.**

Snails

CLASS: Gastropoda (Gas-tro-POE-duh / Gr. stomach foot)

Snails are by far the largest class of mollusks, containing more than 35,000 species. Typically these animals secrete a tubular whorl that forms an ever-enlarging cone-shaped shell as the snail grows. Species are identified by their shells' sculpturing, color pattern, or a combination of these features. Even when on the move the majority of a snail's soft body remains hidden within its shell leaving exposed only a skirtlike **foot** for locomotion, two **tentacles** with an **eye** at each base, and a tubelike mouth, known as a proboscis. When threatened they completely withdraw inside their mobile homes. Many species have a hard disc, called an **operculum,** that covers the opening completely sealing the animals inside. The top side of the foot is called the **mantle skirt,** which is often distinctly marked and can be quite colorful. A few species, such as cowries, regularly extend their mantles over their entire porcelainlike shells.

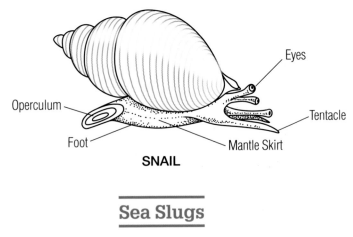

SNAIL

Sea Slugs

CLASS: Gastropoda
SUBCLASS: Opisthobranchia (Oh-PISS-toe-BRAHNK-key-uh / Gr. back or rear gills)

Most members of this subclass lack an external shell, although several orders have reduced-external, or poorly-developed internal, shells. The body is typically a thick, elongated oval only a few inches in length. The mantle, which often has colorful, ornate designs, covers the animal's back. Extending from the head is a pair of sensory tentacles, called **rhinophores;** some species also have one or two pair of **oral tentacles.**

Seahares, Order Anaspidea, have **rolled rhinophores, a pair of rolled oral tentacles** and a pair of large skin flaps on their backs, called **parapoda.** Their small internal shell is often noticeable between the skin flaps. Most have a distinct pair of black eyespots. Generally they are green to brown to blend into the algae they feed on.

Headshield Slugs, Order Cephalaspidea, have a **shield-shaped head,** but lack true rhinophores, although most have some sort of paired extensions toward the side of the head. Almost all have retained some degree of an internal or external shell, although very thin and reduced in size. Many have a pair of black eyespots.

Sidegill Slugs, Order Notaspidea, have featherlike gills hidden under the right side of their mantle skirt, and **rolled rhinophores**. Some carry an umbrellalike external shell, while others have an internal shell.

Sapsucking Slugs, Order Sacoglossa, are a diverse group distinguished by a sac in the alimentary canal that collects discarded teeth. Visually they vary greatly, although most display shades of green and all bear **rolled rhinophores**. A few species have a bubble-shaped shell, but most are shell-less. The mantles of shell-less species often form large **ruffled skin flaps.** A few have large flattened or cylindrical cerata on their backs. All feed by sucking the fluid from algae and other plants.

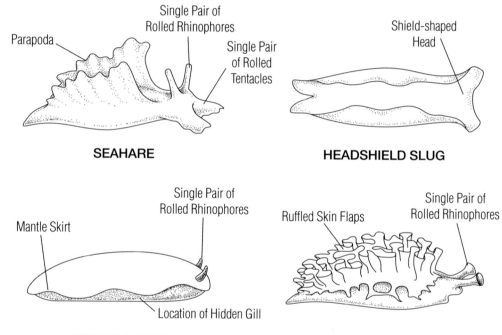

SEAHARE   HEADSHIELD SLUG

SIDEGILL SLUG   SAPSUCKING SLUG

Nudibranchs, Order Nudibranchia, can often be recognized by their "naked" external gills. All have a pair of sensory rhinophores, which most species can retract. This is by far the largest order of sea slugs, with well over 2,000 species, which is divided into four easily recognizable suborders.

Dorid Nudibranchs, Suborder Doridina, includes more species of nudibranchs than the other three suborders combined. Most can be easily recognized by branched gill structures, known as the **anal gill,** which surround the anus located on the back toward the rear of the mantle.

Dendronotid Nudibranchs, Suborder Dendronotina, can be recognized by their typically **branching paired sets of gill structures** located in rows along both sides of the mantle, as well as long sheathed rhinophores, and a **frontal veil.**

Arminid Nudibranchs, Suborder Arminina, have distinctive **bulbous-tipped rhinophores** and an **oral veil** at the front of the head. Most species display stripelike striations running the length of the mantle and have **gills beneath their mantle skirts.** A few species have numerous pointed, often bulbous, cerata that function as gills.

Aeolid Nudibranchs, Suborder Aeolidina, bear numerous elongate respiratory organs, known as **cerata,** on their backs. Near their rhinophores, a **pair of long pointed tentacles** extend from the side of their heads. The cerata of many species contain a store of stinging nematocysts (often visible through translucent tissue) harvested from cnidarian prey that serves as protection from predators.

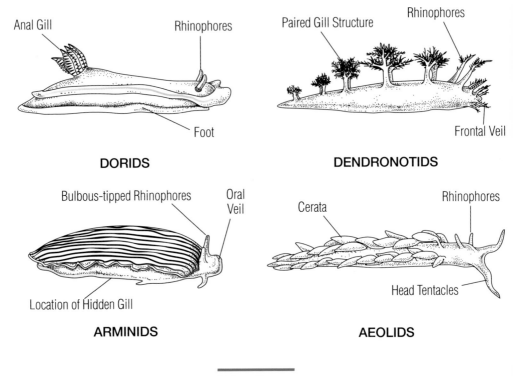

DORIDS

DENDRONOTIDS

ARMINIDS

AEOLIDS

Bivalves

CLASS: Bivalvia (Buy-VALVE-ee-uh / L. two doors)

The soft-bodied animals of this class are protected by two laterally compressed shells, called **valves,** that are hinged together by an elastic band and held tightly closed by strong adductor muscles. Species are generally identified by their valves' shape, color, marking patterns and sculpturing. When the valves are open a number of species exhibit brightly colored **curtainlike mantles.** The mantles of a few species have **tentacles** and multiple eyes or **eyespots** for sensing changes in light intensity.

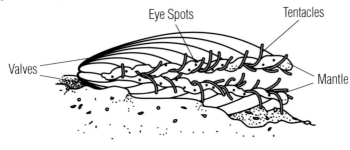

BIVALVE

Squids, Octopuses

CLASS: Cephalopoda (Sef-uh-low-POE-duh / Gr. head and foot)

Cephalopods have long arms with powerful suction cups that are used to capture prey. All are carnivores that have a pair of powerful, beaklike jaws used to crush or tear food. Of all the invertebrates, cephalopods have the most highly evolved nervous system, including vision similar to vertebrates. None have external shells except for a small group known as chambered nautiluses that do not inhabit the Tropical Western Atlantic. Cephalopods can propel their bodies by rapidly expelling jets of water from the mantle cavity through a ventral tubular **funnel**. Cephalopods are known for the ability to swiftly and dramatically change the color patterns as well as the skin texture of their bodies. Changes in color patterns, used primarily for camouflage and intra-species communications, are generated by the expansion or contraction of specialized pigment cells known as chromatophores.

Squids, Order Teuthida, have elongate streamlined bodies and **eight arms** and **two feeding tentacles** that are longer than the arms, and typically retracted. Running along the sides are stabilizing **swim fins** that are often enlarged toward the rear body.

Octopuses, Order Octopoda, have bulbous bodies with **eight arms.** They are primarily bottom-dwellers that use their arms and **suction cups** to move about, although they have the ability to jet backwards when threatened. They are known to be the most intelligent of invertebrate animals.

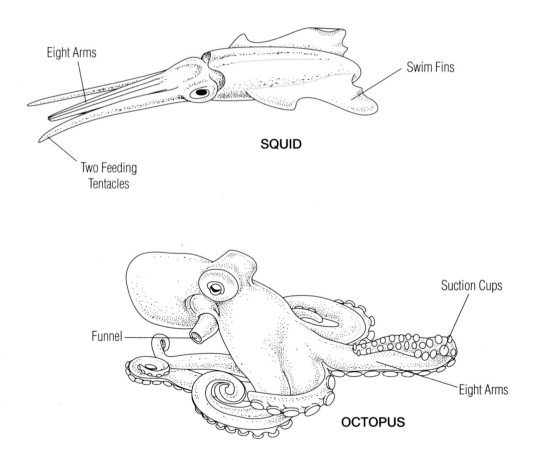

Eight Arms

Swim Fins

SQUID

Two Feeding
Tentacles

Suction Cups

Funnel

Eight Arms

OCTOPUS

QUEEN CONCH *Lobatus gigas*
SIZE: to 30 cm (12 in.)   Conchs – Strombidae
ID: Large shell with short conical spire and blunt spikes; orangish exterior, rosy pink aperture. Pair of long spotted eyestalks with tentacle below often visible. Seagrass and sand from 40 to 100 ft. Common S. Florida, Bahamas, Caribbean.

HAWKWING CONCH *Lobatus raninus*
SIZE: to 12 cm (4½ in.)   Conchs – Strombidae
ID: Mottled brown shell with short conical spire and two spikes on last whorl; reddish aperture's upper lip expanded and extends upward. Seagrass and sand, often near reefs from 3 to 80 ft. Occasional S. Florida, Bahamas, Caribbean.

ROOSTERTAIL CONCH *Lobatus gallus*
SIZE: to 13 cm (5 in.)   Conchs – Strombidae
ID: Orangish shell with white blotching and reddish cream aperture; **long narrow extension of aperture's upper lip.** Seagrass and sand, often around shallow patch reefs from 3 to 20 ft. Rare S. Florida, Bahamas, Caribbean.

MILK CONCH *Lobatus costatus*
SIZE: to 15 cm (6 in.)   Conchs – Strombidae
ID: Thick whitish shell with short conical spire and large rounded spikes; cream lip and aperture. Seagrass and sand from 3 to 40 ft. Common to occasional S. Florida, Bahamas, Caribbean.

FLORIDA FIGHTING CONCH *Strombus alatus*
SIZE: to 13 cm (5 in.)   Conchs – Strombidae
ID: Orangish brown shell with knoblike spikes on next-to-last whorl and pointed spikes on final whorl. Aperture's upper lip slants down. Seagrass and sand from 3 to 20 ft. Common Florida.

WEST INDIAN FIGHTING CONCH *Strombus pugilis*
SIZE: to 10 cm (4 in.)   Conchs – Strombidae
ID: Tan to orange shell with small pointed concave spire; large last whorl; row of spines on each whorl; two notches near front of lip; long foot enables it to jump. Seagrass and sand from 3 to 180 ft. Common Caribbean; occasional S. Florida, Bahamas.

KING HELMET *Cassis tuberosa*
SIZE: to 30 cm (12 in.) Helmets – Cassidae
ID: Shell light tan, often with reddish wavy, net pattern and 7 to 8 bands on outer lip; flattened lip around aperture forms triangle. Shallow sand flats from 10 to 35 ft. Occasional Florida, Bahamas, Caribbean; rare where over-collected.

EMPEROR HELMET *Cassis madagascariensis*
SIZE: to 35 cm (14 in.) Helmets – Cassidae
ID: Cream to brown shell with short spire (about 10 whorls); 3 rows of knobs on body whorl; pear-shaped inner lip with rounded outer edge; about 11 blunt projections on inside of outer lip. Seagrass and sand from 10 to 35 ft. Uncommon Florida, Bahamas, Caribbean.

FLAME HELMET *Cassis flammea*
SIZE: to 15 cm (6 in.) Helmets – Cassidae
ID: Cream with brown zigzags and mottling; short spire with about 7 whorls; row of blunt knobs on shoulder with smaller row below. Seagrass and sand from 10 to 35 ft. Uncommon S. Florida, Bahamas, Caribbean.

RETICULATE COWRIE HELMET *Cypraecassis testiculus*
SIZE: to 7.5 cm (3 in.) Helmets – Cassidae
ID: Gray to orange or brown shell with 5 whorls and short spire; long narrow aperture; strongly toothed rolled-in outer lip; narrow longitudinal ridges crossed by transverse indentations. Sand to 30 ft. Occasional Florida, Bahamas, Caribbean.

SCOTCH BONNET *Semicassis granulata*
SIZE: to 10 cm (4 in.) Helmets – Cassidae
ID: Pale yellow to cream shell with **brown squarish spots forming encircling whorls** and transverse encircling ribs; black markings on eye tentacles. Sand from 20 to 80 ft. Occasional Florida, Bahamas, Caribbean.

Moon Snails, Tritons, Ceriths, Wentletraps

COLORFUL MOON SNAIL   *Naticarius canrena*
SIZE: to 6.5 cm (2½ in.)   Moon Snails – Naticidae
ID: Smooth white shell with 3 whorls forming flat spire; **several brown bands often intersected by zigzags.** Body whitish with reddish brown lines toward front and blotches toward rear. Sand to 20 ft. Occasional Florida, Bahamas, Caribbean.

MILK MOON SNAIL   *Polinices lacteus*
SIZE: to 4 cm (1½ in.)   Moon Snails – Naticidae
ID: Milky white to pink oval shell with rounded spire; slightly convex whorls and large rounded body whorl; **body milky white and unmarked.** Primarily inhabit shallow sand, but to 210 ft. Occasional Florida, Bahamas, Caribbean.

LESSER-GIRDLED TRITON   *Cymatium succinctum*
SIZE: to 5 cm (2 in.)   Tritons – Ranellidae
ID: Wide yellowish brown shell tapering at both ends with projecting canal, convex whorls and raised outer lip; transverse dark and light ribs; often with covering of hairlike projections. Sand and rubble 10 to 60 ft. Occasional circumtropical.

LIP TRITON   *Cymatium labiosum*
SIZE: to 2.5 cm (1 in.)   Tritons – Ranellidae
ID: Reddish to yellowish brown shell with long spire; 3 ridges per whorl give a triangular look; small aperture with short canal; mantle white with dark spots. Rock and sand from 20 to 80 ft. Occasional Florida, Bahamas, Caribbean.

ATLANTIC HAIRY TRITON   *Cymatium martinianum*
SIZE: to 10 cm (4 in.)   Tritons – Ranellidae
ID: Exterior of tan to reddish **shell covered with short hairlike projections;** transverse ribs; dark brown between white teeth on aperture lip. Coral reefs from 20 to 80 ft. Occasional Florida, Bahamas, Caribbean.

DWARF HAIRY TRITON   *Cymatium vespaceum*
SIZE: to 5 cm (2 in.)   Tritons – Ranellidae
ID: Orange to yellowish white shell with a pointed apex and 5 to 6 whorls; small aperture with thick-toothed lips and long canal. Sand and rubble from 15 to 100 ft. Uncommon Florida, Bahamas, Caribbean.

ATLANTIC TRITON'S TRUMPET   *Charonia variegata*
SIZE: to 38 cm (15 in.)   Tritons – Ranellidae
ID: Large pointed cream to brown spiral shell; body mottled reddish brown; banded yellow and black tentacles. **ML&MR-** Juvenile: Yellowish orange with dark posterior. Occasional to rare S.E. Florida, Caribbean.

STOCKY CERITH   *Cerithium litteratum*
SIZE: to 4.5 cm (1³/₄ in.)   Ceriths – Cerithiidae
ID: Whitish to yellow, orange or rusty brown shell with numerous small dark squarish markings; prominent short spikes on spire. Numerous similar-appearing species; most are more elongate. Intertidal to 100 ft. Abundant S. Florida, Bahamas, Caribbean.

ANGULATE WENTLETRAP   *Epitonium angulatum*
SIZE: to 7.5 cm (3 in.)   Wentletraps – Epitoniidae
ID: White, elongate spiral shell with approximately 6 non-overlapping whorls; 9 or 10 bladelike, longitudinal ribs; translucent mantle. Sand near shallow reefs to 10 ft. Common Florida; also Gulf of Mexico.

ATLANTIC PARTRIDGE TUN *Tonna pennata*
SIZE: to 15 cm (6 in.) Tuns – Tonnidae
ID: White to tan shell can be unpatterned [right],or with pale to dark brown bandlike markings; short spire and large inflated body whorl with encircling ribs. Sand near coral reefs from 60 to 200 ft. Occasional S. Florida, Bahamas, Caribbean.

GIANT TUN
Tonna galea
Tuns – Tonnidae
SIZE: to 18 cm (7 in.)
ID: Large globular shell with low spire of about 5 whorls and a very large body whorl; large oval aperture; white to yellowish or reddish brown often with brown mottling; often ridges between grooves give appearance of banding; foot white with dark mottling. Sand near reef and rubble to 110 ft. Uncommon Florida, Caribbean. .

COFFEE BEAN TRIVIA *Trivia pediculus*
SIZE: to 3 cm (1¼ in.) Bean Cowries – Triviidae
ID: Transverse ribs run across central groove on back of white shell often with dark blotches; mantle dark gray to brown often with bulbous projections; foot dark with thin white streaks. Reefs from 2 to 80 ft. Occasional Florida, Bahamas, Caribbean.

ATLANTIC DEER COWRIE
Macrocypraea cervus
Cowries – Cypraeidae
SIZE: to 13 cm (5 in.)
ID: Lustrous reddish brown shell (more bulbous than shell of similar-appearing Measled Cowrie [next]) covered with white spots and occasionally light or dark bands; mantle black, gray or brown with numerous fleshy, spikelike projections, often white blotches. Shells of young banded without spots. Reefs, recesses, often on underside of ledges to 40 ft. Occasional Florida, Caribbean.

MEASLED COWRIE   Macrocypraea zebra
SIZE: to 10 cm (4 in.)   Cowries – Cypraeidae
ID: Lustrous yellowish red to brown shell covered with whitish spots and occasionally banded; tan to grayish mottled mantle with numerous fleshy projections (some multi-branched). Reef recesses from 6 to 35 ft. Occasional S.E. Florida, Caribbean.

ATLANTIC YELLOW COWRIE   Erosaria acicularis
SIZE: to 4 cm (1 1/2 in.)   Cowries – Cypraeidae
ID: Lustrous yellow-brown shell with lighter blotches; mantle reddish brown with numerous long fleshy forked projections (often lighter color than mantle). Rubble; often under rocks from 10 to 50 ft. Occasional Florida, Bahamas, Caribbean.

ATLANTIC GRAY COWRIE   Talparia cinerea
SIZE: to 4 cm (1 1/2 in.)   Cowries – Cypraeidae
ID: Lustrous, tan to brown or mauve shell with dark flecks and two wide vague bands; mantle solid or mottled from black to mauve with short fleshy projections and white specks. Reefs from 20 to 50 ft. Occasional S. Florida, Bahamas, Caribbean.

FLAMINGO TONGUE
Cyphoma gibbosum
Allied Cowries – Ovulidae
SIZE: to 2.5 cm (1 in.)

ID: Cream-white mantle, often covered with orangish or gray rectangular areas with black outlines, or orangish fingerprint like design with black margins, or black oval areas with orangish vertical stripes, **all have a white mantle foot "skirt" with dark lines coming from under the shell toward the edge of the skirt** that often has a orangish to gold outer edge. The shell is a polished white, but is usually covered by a closed mantle. Juveniles are more elongate with fewer mantle markings. Feed on gorgonians from 6 to 45 ft. Common Florida, Bahamas, Caribbean.

Note: Formerly each of the different pattern mantels was considered a difference species, but in 2017 it was determined all were the same species with the similar foot skirt. They included Fingerprint Cyphoma, *C. signatum*, Blackband Cyphoma, *C. christahemmenae* and Spotted Cyphoma, *C.mcgintyi*.

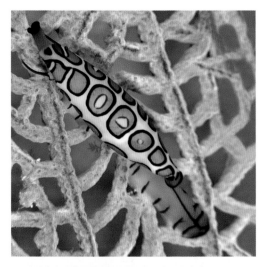

BLACKBAND CYPHOMA *Cyphoma christahemmenae*
SIZE: to 1.5 cm (⁵/₈ in.) Allied Cowries – Ovulidae
ID: Mantle yellowish and white with transverse black lines; shell beige with pink canal. Attach to a variety of hosts from shallows to 100 ft. Rare central Caribbean to Venezuela.

SPOTTED CYPHOMA *Cyphoma mcgintyi*
SIZE: to 2.5 cm (1 in.) Allied Cowries – Ovulidae
ID: Mantle white with gray to black, usually rounded spots, with darker outlines; shell white. Feed on gorgonians from 20 to 80 ft. Occasional to rare Florida, Bahamas.

WHITE-SPOTTED CYPHOMA *Cyphoma* sp.1
SIZE: to 2 cm (³/₄ in.) Allied Cowries – Ovulidae
ID: Mantle black with a **scattering of white dots;** foot white with transverse black streaks; shell tapers toward front. Photograph taken in Grand Cayman.

BULLROARER CYPHOMA
Cyphoma rhomba
Allied Cowries – Ovulidae
SIZE: to 2.5 cm (1 in.)
ID: Mantle white with **pink to lavender spots with dark outlines of variable shapes and sizes;** shell dorsal surface reddish violet; the aperture white; long curved aperture with narrow smooth outer lip. Feed on sea whips from 15 to 80 ft. Rare S. Florida.

Allied Cowries

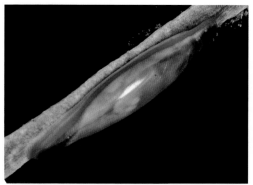

BAHAMA SIMNIA *Cymbovula bahamaensis*
SIZE: to 1.5 cm (⁵/₈ in.)   Allied Cowries – Ovulidae
ID: Small elongate shell with a narrow aperture running length; glossy, usually purplish white or pale purple, with an **orange to reddish orange border.** Feed on sea plumes and sea rods from 3 to 30 ft. Rare S. Florida, Bahamas, Caribbean.

WEST INDIAN SIMNIA
Cymbovula acicularis
Allied Cowries – Ovulidae
SIZE: to 1.2 cm (¹/₂ in.)
ID: Mantle shades of purple, yellow or green with fine scattering of white specks and occasionally branched white papillae; **fine reticulated pattern;** shells white, yellow, green or lavender with thin white border encircling narrow aperture that runs length. Feed on sea fans and other gorgonians from 5 to 50 ft.; mantle can change color to match host. Occasional Florida, Bahamas, Caribbean.

ONETOOTH SIMNIA
Simnialena uniplicata
Allied Cowries – Ovulidae
SIZE: to 2 cm (³/₄ in.)
ID: Unmarked mantle either purple, yellow, black or green; thin glossy white to yellowish, pink or purple shell with narrow aperture that runs length. Feed on sea fans and other gorgonians to 30 ft.; can change color to match host. Occasional Florida, Bahamas, Caribbean.

YELLOW SIMNIA
Cymbovula sp.1
SIZE: to 2 cm (³/₄ in.)
Allied Cowries – Ovulidae
ID: Yellow mantle with orange specks. Either an undescribed species or color variant of West Indian Simnia, *C. acicularis* [facing page]. Feed on sea fans to 30 ft. Rare; known from Cayman Islands and St. Vincent.

ORANGE-SPOTTED SIMNIA
Cymbovula sp.2
SIZE: to 2 cm (³/₄ in.)
Allied Cowries – Ovulidae
ID: Mantle white with round somewhat **oblong orange markings of irregular size and shape**. Feed on sea fans to 30 ft. Rare; known from Cayman Islands and St. Vincent.

PINK-CIRCLED SIMNIA
Cymbovula sp.3 .
Allied Cowries – Ovulidae
SIZE: to 2 cm (³/₄ in.)
ID: Mantle white with irregular-shaped **pink circle markings outlined in red;** shell elongate and tapered toward ends. Feed on gorgonians. Photographed at 30 ft. in Dominica.

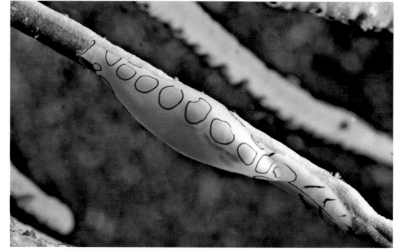

HORSE CONCH
Pleuroploca gigantea
Tulip Snails – Fasciolariidae
SIZE: to 60 cm (24 in.)
ID: Spindle-shaped shell white to tan or salmon with long conical spire bearing small knobs; shell can have flaky texture; body cream to reddish orange with vague white blotching. Although they can grow to 30 in., more typically from 10 to 14 in. Seagrass and sand from 3 to 100 ft.; larger individuals tend to inhabit deep water. Common Florida; also Gulf of Mexico.

TRUE TULIP
Fasciolaria tulipa
SIZE: to 25 cm (10 in.)
Tulip Snails – Fasciolariidae
ID: Spindle-shaped shell gray, green or brown with thin dark spiral stripes and longitudinal lines; often with black or tan blotches; body red, brown or black with white speckles. Seagrass and sand to 35 ft. Occasional Florida, Bahamas, Caribbean.

MUSIC VOLUTE
Voluta musica
Volutes – Volutidae
SIZE: to 7.5 cm (3 in.)
ID: Thick, cream to reddish brown or black shell with short conical spire and blunt spikes; **distinct series of lines resembling musical score encircle mid-shell;** Whitish mantle with gold and black markings. Rubble, mud and sand to 50 ft. Nocturnal. Occasional central and E. Caribbean to Colombia and Venezuela.

BEADED PHOS *Antillophos candeanus*
SIZE: to 2.5 cm (1 in.) True Whelks – Buccinidae
ID: Elongate white to brown shell with 13 to 20 radial ribs forming "beads" at intersections; oval aperture with slightly flaring outer lip with wavy edge. Sand from 6 to 250 ft. Uncommon Florida, Bahamas, Caribbean.

LIGHTNING WHELK *Busycon sinistrum*
SIZE: to 40 cm (16 in.) True Whelks – Buccinidae
ID: Unlike most snails the pear-shaped **shell spirals left rather than right;** low conical spire with nodules on the shoulder of each whorl; long oval aperture with slightly twisted canal. Sand from shore to 10 ft. Uncommon Florida and Yucatan.

GAUDY CANTHARUS *Gemophos auritulus*
SIZE: to 3.5 cm (1½ in.) True Whelks – Buccinidae
ID: Shell cream with orange-brown to black mottling; even conical spire with about 9 axial ribs per whorl; intersections of ribs and chords produce a series of "knobs" near posterior of body whorl. Intertidal. Common S. Florida, Caribbean.

SPINY CARIBBEAN VASE *Vasum capitellum*
SIZE: to 7.5 cm (3 in.) Vase Snails – Turbinellidae
ID: White and brown to reddish brown shell with 9 coarse spiral cords on body whorl; teeth on last whorl of spire and body are long and often curved. Sand and reef flats from intertidal to 30 ft. Uncommon Caribbean.

ARROW DWARF TRITON *Tritonoharpa lanceolata*
SIZE: to 5 cm (2 in.) Nutmeg Snails – Cancellariidae
ID: Elongate tan to yellowish white shell with orange-brown blotches; 5 to 6 whorls with many thin spiral and axial ribs and 1 to 2 axial ridges on body whorl. Rocky areas to 50 ft. Uncommon Florida, Bahamas, Caribbean.

CROWN CONCH *Melongena corona*
SIZE: to 13 cm (5 in.) Crown Conchs – Melongenidae
ID: Brown to gray shell with bluish black to yellow bands; 5 to 6 whorls, the last few have sharp spines; bluish white mantle with dark markings. Rock and sand from shore to 35 ft. Occasional Florida; also Gulf of Mexico.

Murex Snails, Dove Snails

APPLE MUREX   *Chicoreus pomum*
SIZE: to 12 cm (4¾ in.)   Murex Snails – Muricidae
ID: Heavy shell with elevated conical spire; 5 to 7 convex whorls with axial ribs; large aperture with thick slightly flared outer lip with scalloped edge. Sand and rock of intertidal zone; feeds on oysters. Common Florida, Bahamas, Caribbean.

WEST INDIAN MUREX   *Chicoreus brevifrons*
SIZE: to 15 cm (6 in.)   Murex Snails – Muricidae
ID: Ornate shell with spines along outer lip; large body whorl and pointed conical spire with 5 whorls; frequently encrusted. Protected areas of rubble and rocks from 10 to 80 ft. Common to occasional Florida Keys, Caribbean; also Gulf of Mexico.

LACE MUREX
Chicoreus dilectus
Murex Snails – Muricidae
SIZE: to 7.5 cm (3 in.)
ID: Shell with 3 prominent rows of leaflike projections, one along edge of outer lip, one on opposite side with a short third row between; small round aperture. Sand and mud bottoms of protected areas; often under rocks to 500 ft. Common Florida; occasional Bahamas, W. Caribbean.

GIANT EASTERN MUREX   *Hexaplex fulvescens*
SIZE: to 18 cm (7 in.)   Murex Snails – Muricidae
ID: White to yellowish brown shell with thin brown transverse lines; 7 or 8 whorls and long constricted canal; 7 to 9 ridges, each with erect hollow spines. Sand and rock from 6 to 35 ft. Common Florida; also Gulf of Mexico.

REAPER MUREX   *Vokesimurex messorius*
SIZE: to 5 cm (2 in.)   Murex Snails – Muricidae
ID: Shell with 3 prominent ridges per whorl that slope to a long upturned canal; each longitudinal ridge has long curved spine at shoulder; canal with 3 to 4 short spines. Hard and soft bottoms from 3 to 120 ft. Uncommon S. Florida, Caribbean.

SHORT CORALSNAIL
Coralliophila abbreviata
Murex Snails – Muricidae
SIZE: to 5 cm (2 in.)
ID: White to gray ribbed shell with low spire; toothed outer lip; yellow/orange operculum. To feed extend long proboscis into the mouths of fourteen different species of stony corals. Identification tentative; several similar-appearing species. Common S. Florida, Bahamas, Caribbean

ORANGESTRIPE MUREX   *Muricopsis deformis*
SIZE: to 6 mm (¼ in.)   Murex Snails – Muricidae
ID: Small; orange to yellow transverse ridges separated by **dark brown to black bands;** oval with short spire and several longitudinal ribs. Rock or coral reefs to 180 ft. Uncommon Bahamas, W. Caribbean.

SHARPRIB DRILL   *Eupleura sulcidentata*
SIZE: to 2.5 cm (1 in.)   Murex Snails – Muricidae
ID: Gray, brown or tan occasionally with narrow spiral brown bands; curved spines on spire whorls and on shoulder; long, almost closed, siphon canal. Seagrass and mud to 20 ft. Occasional S. Florida, Bahamas, Caribbean.

WEST INDIAN DOVESNAIL   *Columbella mercatoria*
SIZE: to 2.5 cm (1 in.)   Dove Snails – Columbellidae
ID: Compact triangular shell quite variable in color; long, narrow, curved aperture; thick outer lip with 12 rounded white teeth on inner edge. Seagrass, rocks and coral reefs to 30 ft. S. Florida, Bahamas, Caribbean.

PURPLE PYRENE   *Minipyrene dortimor*
SIZE: to 3 mm (⅛ in.)   Dove Snails – Columbellidae
ID: Tiny purple to pink biconical shell with short 6-whorl spire; long, narrow straight aperture; narrow siphon canal. Sand and coral; depth range unrecorded. Rare S. Caribbean.

Cone Snails

FLORIDA CONE
Conus floridanus
Cone Snails – Conidae
SIZE: to 4 cm (1½ in.)
ID: Yellowish brown shell with white and brown blotches; occasionally encircled with several lines composed of dashes [pictured]; a wide pale band often encircles central body; pale brown mantle and orange snout. Cone shells secrete neurotoxic venom that is delivered by a single radular tooth that resembles a small harpoon. Although the venom of some Indo-Pacific cone shells can be fatal, the wounds of Western Atlantic species are painful, but not life threatening. Handle with care! Sand to 50 ft. Common Florida.

AGATE CONE   *Conus ermineus*
SIZE: to 13 cm (5 in.)   Cone Snails – Conidae
ID: Shell grayish white to bluish to orange with irregular mottling of brown, bluish black, or dark gray, thin spiral and axial threads on the body whorl. Sand to 175 ft.; one of few fish-eating cones in Caribbean. S. Florida, Bahamas, Caribbean.

TORTUGAS CONE   *Conus anabathrum burryae*
SIZE: to 1.6 cm (⅝ in.)   Cone Snails – Conidae
ID: Shell pink, white, yellowish orange or violet with broken band of axial streaks or blotches at midbody; moderately high spire with straight to slightly concave outline. Sand and rubble to 35 ft. Rare; known from Dry Tortugas, Florida.

CROWN CONE
Conus regius
Cone Snails – Conidae
SIZE: to 6 cm (2¼ in.)
ID: Shell mottled and **blotched with yellow, red, purple or brown and white;** spire with 7 or 8 knobbed whorls; maroon mantle with dark speckles. Coral reefs from 10 to 80 ft. Occasional S. Florida, Caribbean.

BERMUDA CONE *Conus mindanus*
SIZE: to 5 cm (2 in.) Cone Snails – Conidae
ID: Shell white with pale yellow or orange blotches and thin dashed spiral line; prominent spiral groves near base. Sand to 500 ft. Uncommon Florida, Bahamas, Caribbean.

JASPER CONE *Conus jaspideus*
SIZE: to 2.5 cm (1 in.) Cone Snails – Conidae
ID: Shell white with reddish brown or yellowish mottling; brown spots on shoulder; a high, stepped pointed spire one-third shell length. Seagrass and sand from 3 to 60 ft. Occasional S. Florida, Bahamas, Caribbean.

MATCHLESS CONE
Conus cedonulli
Cone Snails – Conidae
SIZE: to 7.5 cm (3 in.)
ID: Shell with short pointed spire of approximately 7 whorls; large cone-shaped body whorl; brick red with **numerous encircling lines of spots and several pale blotches.** Red, lightly speckled mantle. Sand to 500 ft. Rare E. Caribbean.

CARROT CONE *Conus daucus*
SIZE: to 3.5 cm (1½ in.) Cone Snails – Conidae
ID: Shell **yellow to orange**; low spire; occasionally with white to brown mottling; a pale band often encircles central shell; low spire. Sand to 70 ft. Uncommon Florida, Bahamas, Caribbean.

CARDINAL CONE *Conus cardinalis*
SIZE: to 3.5 cm (1½ in.) Cone Snails – Conidae
ID: Shell color highly variable: body whorl orange to reddish occasionally with bands or blotches; can be khaki-green with pale shoulder knobs and irregular white patches around midbody. Sand to 70 ft. Rare S. Florida and Caribbean.

Margin Snails

PRINCESS MARGINELLA *Persicula catenata*
SIZE: to 7 mm (¹/₄ in.) Margin Snails – Cystiscidae
ID: Small glossy oval shell with flattened spire; translucent grayish white encircled with about 7 spiral rows of "teardrops" above with **inverted brown "V's" pointing toward outer lip.** Sand to 180 ft. Uncommon Florida, Bahamas, Caribbean.

WAVY MARGINELLA *Persicula fluctuata*
SIZE: to 7 mm (¹/₄ in.) Margin Snails – Cystiscidae
ID: Small glossy oval shell with flattened spire; light tan to cream with 16 to 18 wavy longitudinal **brown lines.** Sand from 6 to 50 ft. Uncommon to rare Florida, Bahamas, Caribbean.

DECORATED MARGINELLA *Persicula pulcherrima*
SIZE: to 9 mm (³/₈ in.) Margin Snails – Cystiscidae
ID: Small glossy oval shell with flattened spire; gray to cream with 5 wide bands of wavy brown lines separated by narrow white bands marked with brown dashes; occasionally pink blotches. Sand from intertidal to 300 ft. Rare E. Florida, Caribbean.

RIDGED MARGINELLA *Eratoidea sulcata*
SIZE: to 5 mm (¹/₄ in.) Margin Snails – Marginellidae
ID: Small white shell with pronounced axial ribs; 4 whorls including large body whorl often marked with 2 to 3 orange-brown bands; teeth on outer lip. Seagrass and sand from 30 to 220 ft. Rare Caribbean.

WHITE-BANDED MARGINELLA *Volvarina albolineata*
SIZE: to 8 mm (³/₈ in.) Margin Snails – Marginellidae
ID: Small glossy white cylindrical shell with short spire and rounded apex; **3 wide reddish brown to yellow spiral bands.** Mantle white with reddish brown spots. Sand and beneath rocks from 3 to 170 ft. Occasional Florida, Bahamas, Caribbean.

GLOWING MARGINELLA *Prunum pruinosum*
SIZE: to 1.2 cm (¹/₂ in.) Margin Snails – Marginellidae
ID: Small lustrous white shell with white spots and blotches and 3 faint diffuse yellowish bands; translucent mantle blotched with white. Seagrass and sand from 5 to 20 ft. Occasional Caribbean.

ORANGE MARGINELLA
Prunum carneum
Margin Snails –
Marginellidae
SIZE: to 2.5 cm (1 in.)
ID: Orange shell with **two narrow whitish bands at midbody;** teardrop-shaped body whorl; translucent mantle with white spots and orange and white speckles. Sand, rocks, mud and algae to 40 ft. Often beneath rocks. Uncommon S.E. Florida, Caribbean.

WHITE-SPOTTED MARGINELLA   *Prunum guttatum*
SIZE: to 2.5 cm (1 in.)   Margin Snails – Marginellidae
ID: Glossy cream to mauve shell with numerous white spots; thick outer lip with two brown bands; mantle translucent with white spotting. Sand near reefs from 3 to 30 ft. Occasional S.E. Florida, Caribbean.

OBLONG MARGINELLA   *Prunum oblongum*
SIZE: to 2.5 cm (1 in.)   Margin Snails – Marginellidae
ID: Pink to orangish shell with teardrop-shaped body whorl; grayish translucent mantle with speckles; orangish and white spots on proboscis. Sand and reefs to 40 ft. Uncommon Caribbean.

MILKY MARGINELLA   *Volvarina lactea*
SIZE: to 9 mm (³/₈ in.)   Margin Snails – Marginellidae
ID: Small cylindrical white shell with short spire and rounded white apex; outer lip smooth and thin with 3 folds; mantle translucent gray with white to dark patches. Rocks and coral to 20 ft. S. Florida, Bahamas, Caribbean.

PALLID MARGINELLA   *Volvarina pallida*
SIZE: to 6 mm (¹/₄ in.)   Margin Snails – Marginellidae
ID: Small thin glossy white shell with low spire and rounded apex; smooth outer lip; cream mantle with black, white and gray blotches and pale orange shading. Sand and reefs to 35 ft. Uncommon S.E. Florida, Bahamas, Caribbean.

Olive Snails, Augers, Top Snails

SNOWY DWARF OLIVE
Olivella nivea
Olive Snails – Olividae
SIZE: to 2 cm (³/₄ in.)
ID: Small glossy conical shell with well developed spire and deep channels between whorls; white to yellowish tan with irregular dark spiral markings; often 1 or 2 dark bands. Sand from shallows to 150 ft. Uncommon Florida, Bahamas, Caribbean.

LETTERED OLIVE   *Oliva sayana*
SIZE: to 6.5 cm (2¹/₂ in.)   Olive Snails – Olividae
ID: Glossy cylindrical shell with pointed conical spire of 4 or 5 whorls; cream with numerous brown zigzag markings and yellowish triangles; dark markings often form two spiral bands. Sand and rubble; often bury. Common Florida.

NETTED OLIVE   *Oliva reticularis*
SIZE: to 5 cm (2 in.)   Olive Snails – Olividae
ID: Glossy cylindrical shell with short pointed apex of 4 whorls; light brown netted pattern over cream to white; often 2 or 3 dark bands; rarely all white. Sand near patch and back reefs; often bury. Common Florida, Bahamas, Caribbean.

FLAME AUGER
Terebra taurina
Augers – Terebridae
SIZE: to 15 cm (6 in.)
ID: Long, slender conical shell with 28 ribbed convex whorls progress from small and ribbed at the point to large, smooth and slanted; yellowish white with broad, often interrupted reddish brown spiral rows. Occasional to uncommon S. Florida, Bahamas, Caribbean.

CARIBBEAN TEGULA
Tegula hotessieriana
Top Snails – Trochidae
SIZE: to 1.3 cm (¹/₂ in.)
ID: Broadly conical with relatively high spire; rounded whorls crossed by approximately 35 equal-sized threads with **alternating red/white or brown/white dashes;** purplish brown, tan or reddish with blotches. Beneath rocks or in sand to 35 ft. Uncommon S. Florida, Bahamas, Caribbean.

GEM TEGULA   *Tegula gruneri*
SIZE: to 2 cm (³/₄ in.)   Top Snails – Trochidae
ID: Broadly conical with low spire; spiral riblets of alternating red and white blotches on white to gold; occasionally brown, yellow or pink with white markings; Rock and sand to 35 ft. Uncommon Bahamas, Caribbean.

SILKY TEGULA   *Tegula fasciata*
SIZE: to 2 cm (³/₄ in.)   Top Snails – Trochidae
ID: Broadly conical with 4 or 5 smooth rounded whorls; reddish, tan to black mottling with some white blotches; spiral lines of alternating reddish and white dashes. Beneath rocks from shallows to 20 ft. S. Florida, Bahamas, Caribbean.

CHOCOLATE-LINED TOPSNAIL   *Calliostoma javanicum*
SIZE: to 3 cm (1¹/₄ in.)   Top Snails – Calliostomatidae
ID: Numerous thin tan, slightly raised and occasionally beaded ribs separated by well-defined chocolate-brown lines; occasional red to reddish orange highlights; sharp spire. Sand and shallow reefs to 35 ft. Rare Florida Keys, Caribbean.

MOTTLED TOPSNAIL   *Calliostoma jujubinum*
SIZE: to 3 cm (1¼ in.)   Top Snails – Calliostomatidae
ID: Conical shell with sharply pointed apex; 8 to 10 whorls with finely beaded spiral ribs; tan to reddish purple, usually darker toward spire; flat base with spiral threads. Reefs and beneath rocks to 25 ft. Occasional Florida, Bahamas, Caribbean.

GULF STREAM TOPSNAIL   *Calliostoma scalenum*
SIZE: to 4 cm (1½ in.)   Top Snails – Calliostomatidae
ID: Conical shell with sharply pointed apex; about 10 whorls, each with finely beaded spiral ribs; reddish brown with a few irregular dark and white streaks. Calcareous substrates from 80 to 260 ft. Uncommon to rare Florida, Caribbean.

CHESTNUT TURBAN   *Turbo castanea*
SIZE: to 5 cm (2 in.)   Turban Snails – Turbinidae
ID: Turban-shaped with short pointed spire; 5 or 6 whorls with beads, knobs, or scales; variable orangish, greenish or light brown with dark brown or white blotches; often encrusted. Sand or rubble to 20 ft. Common Florida, Bahamas, Caribbean.

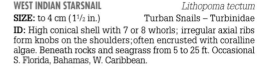

WEST INDIAN STARSNAIL   *Lithopoma tectum*
SIZE: to 4 cm (1½ in.)   Turban Snails – Turbinidae
ID: High conical shell with 7 or 8 whorls; irregular axial ribs form knobs on the shoulders;often encrusted with coralline algae. Beneath rocks and seagrass from 5 to 25 ft. Occasional S. Florida, Bahamas, W. Caribbean.

FILOSE TURBAN   *Turbo cailletii*
SIZE: to 4 cm (1½ in.)   Turban Snails – Turbinidae
ID: Conical with short spire; reddish with yellowish brown to white blotches; many smooth to slightly beaded spiral ribs (about 12 on body whorl); wide circular aperture. Near coral reefs from 12 to 240 ft. Rare Florida, Bahamas, W. Caribbean.

TUSK SNAILS   *Dentalium* sp.
SIZE: to 9 cm (3½ in.)   Tusk Snails – Dentaliidae
ID: Nearly 20 species/subspecies of tusk shells in the Tropical West Atlantic. All are shaped somewhat like an elephant's tusk; open at both ends. Identification to species requires close exam. Sandy shallows to 100 ft. Common Florida, Bahamas, Caribbean.

LONGSPINE STARSNAIL *Astralium phoebium*
SIZE: to 6.5 cm (2½ in.) Turban Snails – Turbinidae
ID: Flat star-shaped shell with 6 or 7 whorls; large flat triangular spines around periphery; silvery white to whitish yellow with tan, orange, or pinkish blotches. Seagrass; usually shallow, but to 100 ft. Uncommon Florida, Bahamas, Caribbean.

STRONG-RIBBED FALSE CUP-AND-SAUCER *Cheilea striata*
SIZE: to 2.5 cm (1 in.) Hoof Snails – Hipponicidae
ID: Caplike grayish white shell with irregularly concentric ridges crossed by fine radial lines; wavy margin; glossy white interior. Beneath rocks from shallows to 170 ft. Uncommon Florida, Bahamas, Caribbean.

COMMON SUNDIAL
Architectonica nobilis
Sundials –
Architectonicidae
SIZE: to 5 cm (2 in.)
ID: Circular, somewhat flattened shell with 6 or 7 whorls and 4 or 5 spiral ribs (usually beaded); white to tan with some purplish areas and uniformly spaced reddish brown markings on spirals. Sand from shallows to 130 ft. Occasional Florida, Caribbean.

SHARP EULIMA *Melanella hypsela*
SIZE: to 1.3 cm (½ in.) Parasitic Snails – Eulimidae
ID: Glossy white elongate tapered shell with about 12 whorls. **Parasitize sea cucumbers;** generally attach near the mouth; often in clusters. Seagrass and sand from 20 to 120 ft. Occasional S. Florida, Bahamas, Caribbean.

FLORIDA WORMSNAIL *Vermicularia knorrii*
SIZE: opening to 6 mm (¼ in.) Worm Snails – Turritellidae
ID: Long curving tube shell; bury in sponge or coral rock with only tip exposed; only head and tentacles can be seen. Extend mucus thread to feed. Often grow in clusters in shallow, more solitary at depths to 60 ft. Common Florida, Bahamas, Caribbean.

Keyhole Limpets, True Limpets, Lamellaries

SPECKLED FLESHY LIMPET
Lucapina sowerbii
Keyhole Limpets –
Fissurellidae
SIZE: to 3 cm (1¼ in.)
ID: Slightly elevated oblong shell with straight sides and rounded ends; about 60 radiating ribs; large rounded opening "keyhole" at apex; fleshy orangish speckled mantle covers the entire shell. Intertidal; often found in pairs beneath rocks. Although keyhole limpets superficially resemble limpets the two groups are not directly related. The intertidal animals do not have an operculum, instead use a muscular foot to attach to rocks. The top opening is for respiration and to eliminate waste. Occasional S. Florida, Bahamas, Caribbean.

SHIELD FLESHY LIMPET　　　　　*Lucapina aegis*
SIZE: to 4 cm (1½ in.)　　　Keyhole Limpets – Fissurellidae
ID: Thin depressed cap-shaped oblong shell with about 40 major radial ribs; narrow oblong keyhole bears tiny teeth on margin; pinkish foot and fleshy mantle. Attached to hard bottom and beneath rocks. Uncommon Florida, Bahamas, Caribbean.

CANCELLATE FLESHY LIMPET　　　　　*Lucapina suffusa*
SIZE: to 4 cm (1½ in.)　　　Keyhole Limpets – Fissurellidae
ID: Slightly depressed oblong shell with many alternating large and small radiating ribs and a finely-toothed margin; dark edged keyhole slightly off center; fleshy cream to orange mantle. Low-tide line to 70 ft. Common Florida, Bahamas, Caribbean.

CAYENNE KEYHOLE LIMPET　　　　　*Diodora cayenensis*
SIZE: to 4.5 cm (1¾ in.)　　　Keyhole Limpets – Fissurellidae
ID: Elevated oval shell with prominent radial ribs; dumbbell-shaped keyhole slightly forward of central apex; translucent gray mantle. Low-tide line to 90 ft. Common Florida, Bahamas, Caribbean.

META KEYHOLE LIMPET　　　　　*Diodora meta*
SIZE: to 1.5 cm (⅝ in.)　　　Keyhole Limpets – Fissurellidae
ID: Moderately raised oval shell with 37 to 39 beaded radial ribs; nearly round keyhole slightly forward of apex; long humped posterior; short straight anterior slope. Mantle translucent gray. Uncommon S. Florida, Caribbean; also Gulf of Mexico.

KNOBBY KEYHOLE LIMPET *Fissurella nodosa*
SIZE: to 4.5 cm (1³/₄ in.) Keyhole Limpets – Fissurellidae
ID: Moderately elevated oval shell with concentric rows of nodules on 20 to 22 radial ribs; deeply scalloped margin; dumbbell-shaped opening at apex. Attach to intertidal rocks. Common S. Florida, Bahamas, Caribbean.

EIGHTRIB LIMPET *Hemitoma octoradiata*
SIZE: to 3 cm (1¹/₄ in.) Keyhole Limpets – Fissurellidae
ID: Highly elevated grayish white oval shell with 8 main radial ribs and 1 to 5 smaller ribs between; central apex without keyhole; green mantle, turquoise foot, orange tentacles. Attach to intertidal rocks. Common S.E. Florida, Bahamas, Caribbean.

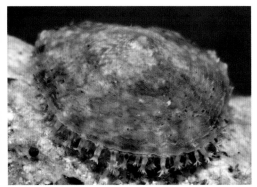

SPOTTED LIMPET *Patelloida pustulata*
SIZE: to 2.5 cm (1 in.) True Limpets – Lottiidae
ID: Thick moderately elevated oval shell with slightly pointed (closed) apex; a few coarse low radial ribs and weak concentric ridges; White exterior with reddish spots or bars. Attach to intertidal rocks. Common Florida, Bahamas, Caribbean.

TRANSPARENT LAMELLARIA *Lamellaria perspicua*
SIZE: to 4 cm (1¹/₂ in.) Lamellarias – Velutinidae
ID: Thin smooth translucent to white shell with about 8 whorls; orange to reddish brown body envelops shell. Tide pools to 180 ft.; feed on colonial tunicates. Occasional Florida, Bahamas, Caribbean.

LAMELLARIAS *Lamellaria* spp.
SIZE: to 4 cm (1¹/₂ in.) Lamellarias – Velutinidae
ID: Small thin slightly flattened shells with earlike apertures; fleshy non-retractile mantles completely cover shells. Living specimens difficult to identify from photographs. Tide pools to 400 ft. Occasional Florida, Bahamas.

Bubble Snails

SIZE: to 6 cm (2¼ in.)

ID: Thin pale bubblelike shell with black or brown spirals; broad reddish brown to reddish ruffled mantle skirt with white or blue margin. Glands secrete unpalatable acid; feed on polychaete worms. Nocturnal; sand to 20 ft. Uncommon Florida, Caribbean.

MINIATURE MELO   *Micromelo undatus*
SIZE: to 3 cm (1¼ in.)   Bubble Snails – Aplustridae
ID: White to yellow oval shell with network of dark red lines; translucent mantle with white blotches often outlined with green and yellow. Nocturnal; shallow sand; feed on polychaete worms. Uncommon Florida, Bahamas, Caribbean.

FLAPPING DINGBAT   *Gastropteron chacmol*
SIZE: to 4 mm (⅛ in.)   Bubble Snails – Gastropteridae
ID: Tiny oval body with short bilobed head shield and central cleft; folds red to black with thin margin, occasionally blotched; parapodia fold meeting on back; siphon curves forward over head. Sand to 30 ft.; bury. Uncommon Florida, Bahamas, Caribbean.

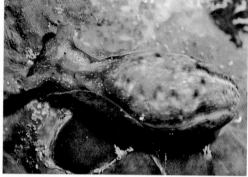

STRIATE BUBBLE   *Bulla striata*
SIZE: to 4 cm (1½ in.)   Bubble Snails – Bullidae
ID: Body and shell mottled brown to gray with white flecks; shell sculptured with widely spaced parallel grooves. Nocturnal; sand and mud; frequently bury; feed on algae. Occasional Florida, Bahamas, Caribbean.

WESTERN STRIATE BUBBLE   *Bulla occidentalis*
SIZE: to 5 cm (2 in.)   Bubble Snails – Bullidae
ID: Elongate translucent brown to gray with white spots on head and parapodia; often retract into whitish shell with brown reticulated markings. Nocturnal; shallow sand and seagrass. Uncommon Florida, Caribbean.

ELEGANT GLASSY BUBBLE   *Haminoea elegans*
SIZE: to 4 cm (1½ in.)   Bubble Snails – Haminoeidae
ID: Elongate translucent yellowish tan to gray with dark and light spotting; deeply notched cephalic shield; large parapodia cover front of shell; delicate mottled brownish shell with closely spaced spirals. Occasional Florida, Bahamas, Caribbean.

AMBER GLASSY BUBBLE   *Haminoea succinea*
SIZE: to 2 cm (¾ in.)   Bubble Slugs – Haminoeidae
ID: Gray to brown body and translucent shell with black speckling; parapodia barely extend up sides of shell. Often bury in sand and mud of intertidal areas. Uncommon Florida, Caribbean.

Headshield Slugs

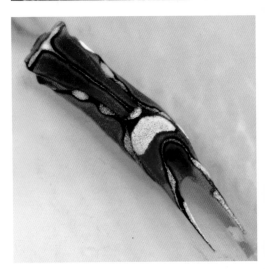

LEECH AGLAJA   *Chelidonura hirundinina*
SIZE: to 2.5 cm (1 in.)   Headshield Slugs – Aglajidae
ID: Elongate golden or orange to reddish brown or black with two equal length tails; two blue to turquoise stripes on back outlined in black, **central stripe forms "T" before head;** wide white band on back. Sand and seagrass to 60 ft. Occasional Florida, Caribbean.

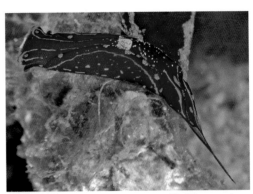

CUBAN AGLAJA   *Chelidonura cubana*
SIZE: to 1 cm (³/₈ in.)   Headshield Slugs – Aglajidae
ID: Small elongate red to black with orange stripes and spots; **lines of widely spaced blue spots on margin of parapodia;** unequal length tails; wide white band on back. Shallow sand; often bury. Known from Cuba and Cayman Islands.

BEROLINA AGLAJA
Chelidonura berolina
Headshield Slugs –
Aglajidae
SIZE: to 1.2 cm (½ in.)
ID: Black body with highly variable markings; often covered with white, orange and/or blue spotting and blotches; some individuals almost solid black with edges of parapodia outlined with yellow or orange; unequal length tails, one long and tapered to a point, the other short and rounded. Shallow sand. Uncommon Bahamas, Caribbean.

NORMAN'S AGLAJA   *Chelidonura normani*
SIZE: to 8 mm (³/₈ in.)   Headshield Slugs – Aglajidae
ID: Small, brown to black with orange outline on parapodia and across head; some with white or yellow spotting and blotching; occasional blue markings on parapodia; tails of unequal length. Sand to 7 ft. Rare Bahamas.

Headshield Slugs

PAINTED AGLAJA   *Philinopsis depicta*
SIZE: to 6.5 cm (2½ in.)   Headshield Slugs – Aglajidae
ID: Broad body with two lateral lobes below head and **raised lobes at middle and rear of body;** dark brown with orange and blue-edged parapodia and random white markings. Shallow sand. Uncommon Florida, Bahamas, Caribbean.

ROCK AGLAJA
Philinopsis petra
Headshield Slugs –
Aglajidae
SIZE: to 2.5 cm (1 in.)
ID: Narrow elongate body highly variable from yellow to dark brown and occasionally green with some yellow and white spotting and blotching; wide parapodia; lateral lobe on each side of head; two short pointed tail lobes. Shallow sand. Uncommon Florida, Bahamas, Caribbean.

ANNE'S AGLAJA   *Spinoaglaja anneae*
SIZE: to 2.5 cm (1 in.)   Headshield Slugs – Aglajidae
ID: Brownish orange to yellow with white speckling and blotching. Similar to Rock Aglaja [previous] swollen at midbody and wider parapodia; **line of 3 blotches on head.** Shallow sand. Uncommon Bahamas.

PUSA AGLAJA *Philinopsis pusa*
SIZE: to 5 cm (2 in.) Headshield Slugs – Aglajidae
ID: Stocky gray, tan to brown with white speckling; wide parapodia often edged with black and blue; upturned lobe at midbody; two short equal-length lobes on rear. Shallow sand. Uncommon Florida, Caribbean.

STRIATED AGLAJA *Navanax aenigmaticus*
SIZE: to 5 cm (2 in.) Headshield Slugs – Aglajidae
ID: Yellow to red, olive or dark gray with fine white lines or mottling; lateral lobe on each side of head; equal length pointed tails; **single row of tiny blue spots on edge of parapodia.** Rocks and sand to 30 ft. Occasional Florida, Bahamas, Caribbean.

BLACK AGLAJA *Aglaja felis*
SIZE: to 2.5 cm (1 in.) Headshield Slugs – Aglajidae
ID: Long narrow jet black body occasionally with white lines or blotches on back; rounded tails of unequal length; somewhat rounded head. Shallow sand. Common to occasional Bahamas, Caribbean.

Seahares

ID: Dark brown with white to gold spots; occasionally black-centered blue spots; covered with cream to black branching papillae, which can be quite thin and hairlike. **ML-** Juvenile: Papillae covering not as thick as that of adults. **MR-** Breeding aggregation. Note variations in color. Sand, rubble and algae to 50 ft. Occasional Florida, Caribbean; tend to be more common in S.E. Caribbean.

WARTY SEACAT   *Dolabrifera dolabrifera*
SIZE: to 6.5 cm (2½ in.)   Seahares – Notarchidae
ID: Pale green to dark brown compact muscular body wider toward rear; covered with thin netlike lines; a few papillae; short rolled rhinophores and oral tentacles. Sand and rubble with algae from 15 to 30 ft. Uncommon Florida, Bahamas, Caribbean.

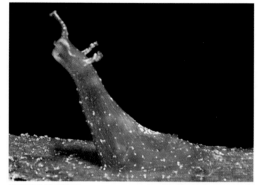

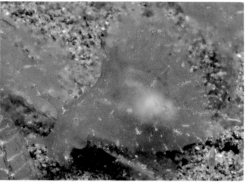

EMERALD LEAFSLUG *Phyllaplysia smaragda*
SIZE: to 2.5 cm (1 in.) Seahares – Notarchidae
ID: Dark green with scattering of tiny white tubercles; white blotch on back; rhinophores and tips of tentacles whitish. Shallow seagrass. Occasional Florida, Bahamas.

PINBALL SEAHARE *Notarchus punctatus*
SIZE: to 3.5 cm (1½ in.) Seahares – Notarchidae
ID: Translucent yellowish tan pear-shaped body with scattering of unbranched papillae (internal organs visible). Shallow sand and seagrass; good swimmer. Uncommon Florida, Caribbean.

STRIATED SEAHARE
Stylocheilus striatus
Seahares – Notarchidae
SIZE: to 4.5 cm (1¾ in.)
ID: Translucent with thin striping varying from yellow to tan, reddish brown or black; typically a scattering of **blue spots circled with red rings**; inflated central body with long tapering tail; often numerous papillae. **BR-** Breeding aggregation. Sand and rubble from shallows to 100 ft. Occasional Florida, Bahamas, Caribbean.

Seahares

ID: Brown to gray with white speckling and blotches; inflated central body with long tail; **parapodia and tips of rolled rhinophores and tentacles edged with black and/or blue.** Nocturnal; sand and rubble with algae from 10 to 40 ft. Uncommon Florida, Bahamas, Caribbean.

WHITE-SPOTTED SEAHARE *Aplysia* cf. *parvula*
SIZE: to 3.5 cm (1½ in.) Seahares – Aplysiidae
ID: The interior edges of irregular parapodia on back lined with black and/or blue; light brown with numerous white blotches and spots; tips of rhinophores and oral tentacles dark. Sand and rubble with algae to 20 ft. Rare Caribbean.

ATLANTIC BLACK SEAHARE
Aplysia cross
Seahares – Aplysiidae
SIZE: to 36 cm (14 in.)
ID: Dark maroon to black, occasionally with some spotting, speckles and streaks; large muscular mantle with skin flaps on back. Algal habitats from 10 to 80 ft. **ML-** Occasionally spread parapodia like wings and swim vigorously; can discharge cloud of harmless purple ink. Uncommon Florida, Bahamas, Caribbean.

SPOTTED SEAHARE
Aplysia dactylomela
Seahares – Aplysiidae
SIZE: to 20 cm (8 in.)
ID: Yellowish tan to green with **numerous black ring spots;** ruffled parapodia generally remain closed over back; can discharge a harmless cloud of purple ink. Sand and seagrass with algae to 120 ft. Occasional Florida, Bahamas, Caribbean.

Seahares

MOTTLED SEAHARE
Aplysia brasiliana
Seahares – Aplysiidae
SIZE: to 25 cm (10 in.)
ID: Translucent yellowish tan to reddish, gray, green or black with white mottling. Occasional black spotting on sides of parapodia. Sand and seagrass in sheltered bays; vigorous swimmer; can discharge cloud of either purple or white ink secreted from different sets of glands. Uncommon Florida, Caribbean.

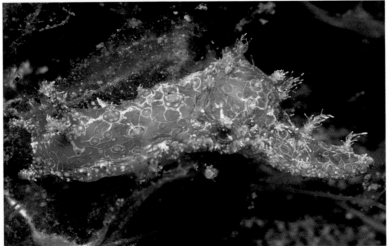

BABA'S SEAHARE
Petalifera ramosa
Seahares – Aplysiidae
SIZE: to 7 cm (2³/₄ in.)
ID: Translucent green to tan with scattering of low conical tubercles some with multi-branching papillae; tubercles often encircled with interconnecting network of thin pale lines. Seagrass, sand and silt to 35 ft. Occasional Florida, Bahamas, Caribbean.

WALKING SEAHARE *Aplysia juliana*
SIZE: to 15 cm (6 in.) Seahares – Aplysiidae
ID: Tan to reddish brown with white mottling. Can "walk" by configuring rear of parapodia into suction disc allowing it to elevate and extend its body to move forward; can discharge harmless white cloud. Uncommon Florida, E. and S. Caribbean.

TURTLE GRASS SEAHARE *Phyllaplysia engeli*
SIZE: to 1.8 cm (³/₄ in.) Seahares – Aplysiidae
ID: Translucent green rounded flattened body may be smooth or warty; numerous thin white lines; papillae may be present or absent; occasionally green with pinkish blotches. Shallow seagrass and algae. Occasional Bahamas, Caribbean.

GEOGRAPHIC SEAHARE
Siphonota geographica
Seahares – Aplysiidae
SIZE: to 17 cm (6 ³/₄ in.)

ID: Green to tan with white or dark line markings that range from tight intricate reticulated patterns to widely spaced wavy lines, Shallow sand with algae. Uncommon Florida, Caribbean.

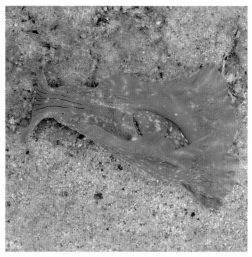

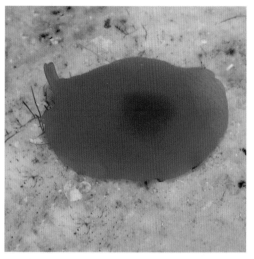

APRICOT SIDEGILL SLUG *Berthellina engeli*
SIZE: to 8 cm (3¼ in.) Sidegill Slugs – Pleurobranchidae
ID: Smooth oval, somewhat translucent pale yellow to deep orange or bright red body. Rolled rhinophores and wide flattened curving oral tentacles. Sand, rubble and reefs to 100 ft.; often beneath rocks. Occasional S. Florida, Caribbean.

AGASSIZ'S BERTHELLA *Berthella agassizii*
SIZE: to 2.5 cm (1 in.) Sidegill Slugs – Pleurobranchidae
ID: Low-profile dusky white to brown translucent oval body; rolled rhinophores and oral tentacles; gill on lower right side of body. Reef and rubble; feed on sponges. Occasional Caribbean.

STARRY BERTHELLA *Berthella stellata*
SIZE: to 1.8 cm (¾ in.) Sidegill Slugs – Pleurobranchidae
ID: Translucent white with scatterings of slightly raised whitish papillae; usually a poorly defined elongated white marking across back. Shallow sand and rubble; often beneath rocks. Uncommon Bahamas, Caribbean.

WARTY PLEUROBRANCH *Pleurobranchus areolatus*
SIZE: to 15 cm (6 in.) Sidegill Slugs – Pleurobranchidae
ID: Numerous rounded tubercles occasionally forming either dark reddish brown to translucent yellow and golden brown clusters. Rocky shallows and rubble; often beneath rocks. Uncommon S. Florida, Bahamas, Caribbean.

ATLANTIC PLEUROBRANCH *Pleurobranchus atlanticus*
SIZE: to 12 cm (4¾ in.) Sidegill Slugs – Pleurobranchidae
ID: Large reddish brown to white and yellow oval with numerous tubercles of two sizes; row of scattered larger tubercles, encircled with dark rings, run along each side of back; short stocky rhinophores not fused. Common Bahamas, Caribbean.

INCONSPICUOUS PLEUROBRANCH
Pleurobranchaea inconspicua
Sidegill Slugs – Pleurobranchaeidae
SIZE: to 6 cm (2 ¼ in.)
ID: White to tan or brown with a scattering of numerous white spots; wide oral veil tapering to a straight leading edge; elongate, widely spaced rhinophores. Sand to 300 ft. Occasional Florida, Caribbean.

AMERICAN TYLODINA   *Tylodina americana*
SIZE: to 1.2 cm (½ in.)   Umbrella Shells – Tylodinidae
ID: Reddish brown to dark brown conical shell with radiating protrusions; yellowish body and smooth rhinophores. Rare Florida, Caribbean.

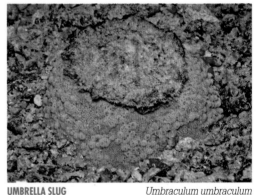

UMBRELLA SLUG   *Umbraculum umbraculum*
SIZE: to 28 cm (11 in.)   Umbrella Shells – Umbraculidae
ID: Large soft body variable from tan to black, orange or yellow covered with rounded tubercles; round shell considerably smaller than animal typically encrusted. Tapered rhinophores just beneath shell. Uncommon Florida, Bahamas, Caribbean.

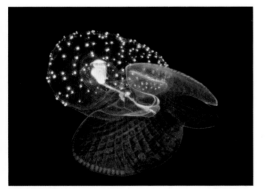

SEA BUTTERFLY   *Corolla* sp.
SIZE: to 4 cm (1½ in.)   Sea Butterflies – Cymbuliidae
ID: A translucent gelatinous planktonic opisthobranch with a tiny transparent internal shell; parapodia have developed into large winglike structures. Near surface waters at night, often in large numbers; feed with mucus webs. Inhabit all oceans.

SEA ANGELS   *Cliopsidae* spp.
SIZE: to 4 cm (1½ in.)   Sea Angels – Cliopsidae
ID: A translucent gelatinous planktonic opisthobranch without a shell; parapodia have developed into small winglike structures. Near surface waters at day and night; carnivores, feed on sea butterflies. Inhabit all oceans.

Sapsucking Slugs

LETTUCE SLUG
Elysia crispata
Sapsucking Slugs –
Plakobranchidae
SIZE: to 10 cm (4 in.)
ID: Skin ruffles on back resemble leaf lettuce; ruffles extremely variable in color, often green, blue or pastel; large pale blotches along sides of mantle; large rolled rhinophores. **MR-** Juvenile: Parapodia less ruffled when young. Reefs and rock to 40 ft; feed on algae. Common Florida, Bahamas, Caribbean.

ORNATE ELYSIA
Elysia ornata
Sapsucking Slugs –
Plakobranchidae
SIZE: to 5 cm (2 in.)
ID: Usually shades of green to pale orange to nearly white with numerous black and white speckles; margins of ruffled parapodia orange and black; pale yellow and orange rolled rhinophores tipped with black. Reef and rock from shallows to 100 ft.; feed on algae. Occasional Florida, Bahamas, Caribbean.

CAULERPA ELYSIA   *Elysia subornata*
SIZE: to 4 cm (1½ in.)   Sapsucking Slugs – Plakobranchidae
ID: Elongate green to tan, orange or yellow with scattering of short white papillae; thin brown edge on ruffled parapodia; Reef and rock to 100 ft.; feed on *Caulerpa* algae. Occasional Florida, Bahamas, Caribbean.

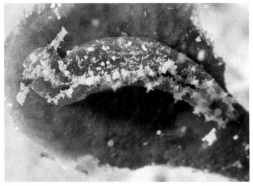

TUCA ELYSIA   *Elysia tuca*
SIZE: to 4 cm (1½ in.)   Sapsucking Slugs – Plakobranchidae
ID: Elongate green to brownish with tiny white papillae lining parapodia edges, which, for the most part, remain closed over the back; **white patch on head extends onto rhinophores.** Feed on *Halimeda* algae. Uncommon Florida, Caribbean.

ZULEICA'S ELYSIA   *Elysia zuleicae*
SIZE: to 1.8 cm (¾ in.)   Sapsucking Slugs – Plakobranchidae
ID: Elongate green to tan with **dark dots** and numerous white papillae surrounded by white patches; closed ruffled parapodia lined with white and orange, occasionally with thin dark edge. Feed on *Udotea* algae from 15 to 65 ft. Occasional Caribbean.

Sapsucking Slugs

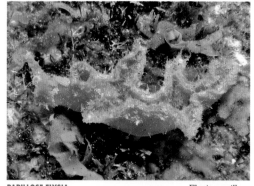

PAPILLOSE ELYSIA *Elysia papillosa*
SIZE: to 4 cm (1½ in.) Sapsucking Slugs – Plakobranchidae
ID: Elongate green to reddish brown with open parapodia edged with ragged white band of papillae; conical papillae scattered over body and head. Feed on *Halimeda, Penicillus* and *Udotea* algae. Occasional Florida, Caribbean.

SHY ELYSIA *Elysia timida*
SIZE: to 1.8 cm (¾ in.) Sapsucking Slugs – Plakobranchidae
ID: White to greenish white **with reddish specks**; body and long rhinophores covered with tubercles. Feed on *Padina* and *Acetabularia* algae. Uncommon Florida, Bahamas, Caribbean.

UNDESCRIBED *Elysia* sp.
SIZE: to 1.8 cm (¾ in.) Sapsucking Slugs – Plakobranchidae
ID: Greenish brown with numerous small white tubercles and scattering of green dots; ruffled parapodia lined with fine papillae form pinkish margin and turquoise submargin. Known from Grand Cayman.

CLARK'S ELYSIA
Elysia clarki
Sapsucking Slugs –
Plakobranchidae
SIZE: to 5 cm (2 in.)
ID: Dark green with **pale round and oval spots giving it a somewhat reticulated appearance;** open ruffled parapodia with wide solid or broken margin can be either translucent, orange or green. Feed on *Halimeda* and *Penicillus* algae. Uncommon S. Florida, Caribbean.

LINED ELYSIA *Elysia pratensis*
SIZE: to 1.8 cm (³/₄ in.)   Sapsucking Slugs – Plakobranchidae
ID: Elongate dark green to greenish yellow with **numerous thin dark or light lines** on body, head and rhinophores; thin dark line on margin of ruffled parapodia; rhinophores with yellowish tips. Seagrass to 25 ft. Occasional Florida, Bahamas, Caribbean.

PAINTED ELYSIA
Thuridilla picta
Sapsucking Slugs –
Plakobranchidae
SIZE: to 3 cm (1¹/₄ in.)
ID: Elongate with brilliant stripes and bands of red, blue, green and yellow; **white "Y" on head extends onto rhinophores ending with blue, black and red banding;** ruffled parapodia. Rubble and sand near patch reefs to 35 ft. Occasional Florida, Bahamas, Caribbean.

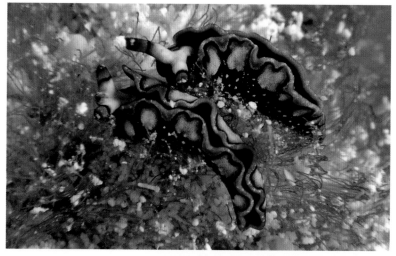

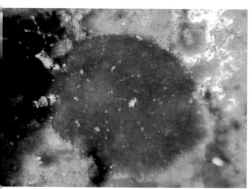

MIMIC BOSELLIA *Bosellia mimetica*
SIZE: to 7 mm (¹/₄ in.)   Sapsucking Slugs – Boselliidae
ID: Shades of green with parapodia typically flattened; scattering of tiny white papillae; short stout white rhinophores. Inhabit alga *Halimeda tuna*. Uncommon Florida, Bahamas, Caribbean.

LINEDSHELL LOBIGER *Lobiger souverbii*
SIZE: to 3 cm (1¹/₄ in.)   Sapsucking Slugs – Oxynoidae
ID: Shades of green; central bulbous shell with thin dark lines and blue dots; **shell bordered by four extended lobes of parapodia** covered with white papillae. Feed on *Caulerpa* algae to 35 ft. Occasional Florida, Caribbean.

Sapsucking Slugs

ANTILLES OXYNOE *Oxynoe antillarum*
SIZE: to 3.5 cm (1½ in.) Sapsucking Slugs – Oxynoidae
ID: Yellowish green with hidden central bulbous shell and elongate tail; often dark speckling and conical papillae; generally blue spots on rhinophores and lining mantle; thin pale line above eye. Feed on *Caulerpa* algae to 35 ft. Occasional Florida, Caribbean.

PATRICK'S COSTASIELLA *Costasiella patricki*
SIZE: to 1 cm (³⁄₄ in.) Sapsucking Slugs – Oxynoidae
ID: Numerous pale green cerata with pale blue, black ringed spots cover body, near tip is a small orange ring (similar Eyespot Costasiella [next] have larger orange rings); tiny close-set black eyes between rhinophores. Feed on green algae. Rare S. Florida and Bahamas.

EYESPOT COSTASIELLA *Costasiella ocellifera*
SIZE: to 1 cm (³⁄₈ in.) Sapsucking Slugs – Limapontiidae
ID: Covered with long tapering green, or black to white cerata with translucent tips and white spots; long tapering rhinophores with dark spotting; tiny black close-set eyes on head. Feed on green algae. Uncommon Florida, Bahamas, Caribbean.

BURNT PLACIDA *Placida cremoniana*
SIZE: to 1.2 cm (½ in.) Sapsucking Slugs – Limapontiidae
ID: Pale orange with numerous pointed orange and bluish black cerata; scroll-like black rhinophores with whitish or blue posterior; **dark patch on side of head.** Filamentous algae along shallow exposed coastlines. Rare Florida.

BLUE STILIGER *Ercolania* cf. *coerulea*
SIZE: to 6 mm (¼ in.) Sapsucking Slugs – Limapontiidae
ID: Numerous blunt translucent heavily speckled cerata extend from yellowish to green body; long thin tapering translucent rhinophores. Possible variant of *E. coerulea.* Rare Florida Caribbean.

CROSSBEARER HERMAEA *Hermaea cruciata*

SIZE: to 5 mm (¹/₄ in.)   Sapsucking Slugs – Stiligeridae

ID: Translucent with white spots and orange to brown markings; long transparent cerata with brown digestive glands visible. Filamentous red algae in very shallow water. Rare to uncommon Florida, Caribbean.

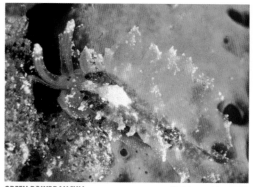

GREEN POLYBRANCHIA *Polybranchia viridis*

SIZE: to 7 cm (2³/₄ in.)   Sapsucking Slugs – Caliphyllidae

ID: Wide front of green body tapers to pointed rear; broad transparent leaflike cerata with small papillae and white patches; long translucent rhinophores tipped with white papillae. Nocturnal. Uncommon Florida, Caribbean.

HARLEQUIN GLASS SLUG *Cyerce cristallina*

SIZE: to 7.5 cm (3 in.)   Sapsucking Slugs – Caliphyllidae

ID: Numerous large translucent leaflike cerata with spotting become tan to burgundy toward tapering tips; cerata bordered with brown or white. Algal bottoms from 3 to 45 ft. Rare Florida, Bahamas, Caribbean.

ANTILLES GLASS SLUG
Cyerce antillensis
Sapsucking Slugs –
Caliphyllidae
SIZE: to 6 cm (2¹/₄ in.)

ID: Green to yellowish tan inflated leaflike cerata tipped with tubercles and tiny papillae; **dark streaks on side of broad head run down elongate antennae.** Feed on *Halimeda* algae. Uncommon Florida, Bahamas, Caribbean.

Dorid Nudibranchs

CARIBBEAN SPANISH DANCER
Hexabranchus morsomus
Dorid Nudibranchs –
Hexabranchidae
SIZE: to 12 cm (4³/₄ in.)
ID: Large; white to orange,
red or purple with occasional
mottling; when disturbed flare
bright red mantle border.
Closely related to Spanish
Dancer, *H. sanguineus*, from
the Indo-Pacific. Nocturnal;
reefs and sand from 20 to 100
ft. Uncommon Caribbean.

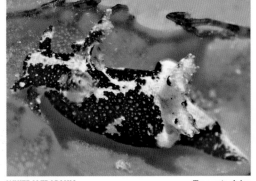

SMALLWOOD'S OKENIA   *Okenia zoobotryon*
SIZE: to 8 mm (³/₈ in.) Dorid Nudibranchs – Goniodorididae
ID: Translucent white with brown to green spots; series of
round translucent papillae; long tapered rhinophores with
whitish tips and ridges on upper anterior surface. Reefs to 20 ft;
feed on bryozoans. Uncommon Florida, Caribbean.

WHITE-V TRAPANIA   *Trapania dalva*
SIZE: to 1.2 cm (¹/₂ in.) Dorid Nudibranchs – Goniodorididae
ID: Dark brown and white; numerous orange spots with tiny
yellow papillae encircled with dark ring; white blotching around
gill and head; **white "V" branching from gill to each rhinophore.**
Nocturnal; reefs to 40 ft. Uncommon Florida, Bahamas, Caribbean.

ELLEN'S TRAPANIA
Trapania bonellenae
Dorid Nudibranchs –
Goniodorididae
SIZE: to 2.5 cm (1 in.)
ID: Dark gray to brown with
network of thin white
interlaced stripes; white patch
in front of large bushlike gill
structure; a **rear-curved
appendage on each side of
rhinophore.** Sponges to 40 ft.
Rare; known from Bonaire.

ORANGEGILL TAMBJA   *Tambja* cf. *stegosauriformis*
SIZE: to 5 cm (2 in.)   Dorid Nudibranchs – Polyceridae
ID: Elongate dark brown with large oblong green spots with dark green edges; black-edged green flap at front of head; gill structure orange with black tips. Reef from 3 to 40 ft. Rare; known from Venezuela.

RICE'S ROBOASTRA   *Roboastra ricei*
SIZE: to 5 cm (2 in.)   Dorid Nudibranchs – Polyceridae
ID: Bright yellow with dark slightly raised tubercles; mantle skirt edged with green and blue; five non-retractable yellow, blue and red gill branches arranged in semicircle at mid-back. Sponges from 50 to 85 ft. Uncommon Florida.

FEATHERED THECACERA   *Thecacera pennigera*
SIZE: to 2.5 cm (1 in.)   Dorid Nudibranchs – Polyceridae
ID: Translucent white with orange spots and black dots; pair of elongate appendages extend behind gill structure and a shorter pair extend from each side of rhinophores. Rare Florida, Caribbean.

PACIFIC THECACERA   *Thecacera pacifica*
SIZE: to 3 cm (1¼ in.)   Dorid Nudibranchs – Polyceridae
ID: Translucent dusky gold with pair of elongate appendages behind gill cluster; large black and white tubercle at rear; black-lined gill structure. Rare; known from Texas Flower Garden Banks in Gulf of Mexico.

HARLEQUIN POLYCERA   *Polycera chilluna*
SIZE: to 2.5 cm (1 in.)   Dorid Nudibranchs – Polyceridae
ID: Bluish gray to black with series of continuous and broken yellow stripes; long tapering tail; six tapered yellow appendages extend from lower head; black-tipped rhinophores and gill branches. Rare Florida, Venezuela.

HUMM'S POLYCERA   *Polycera hummi*
SIZE: to 1.8 cm (¾ in.)   Dorid Nudibranchs – Polyceridae
ID: Translucent tan with thin black streaks forming undefined stripes from head to tail; four elongate appendages with blue and orange bands located on each side of gill and two additional pairs branching from each side of head. Uncommon Florida.

213

Dorid Nudibranchs

ODHNER'S POLYCERA *Polycera odhneri*
SIZE: to 2.5 cm (1 in.)   Dorid Nudibranchs – Polyceridae
ID: Light green to dark brown with numerous red or yellow oval spots; scattering of papillae; rhinophores have cup-like ridges. Algae and floats of *Sargassum*. Rare Florida, Bahamas, Caribbean.

PAPILLOSE POLYCERA *Polycera rycia*
SIZE: to 1.2 cm (½ in.)   Dorid Nudibranchs – Polyceridae
ID: Whitish with numerous brown spots and scattering of papillae; four short appendages, usually with blue and orange bands, extend from head and another located on each side of gill structure. Reefs. Uncommon Florida, Bahamas.

STRIPED POLYCERA *Polycera sp.*
SIZE: to 1.2 cm (½ in.)   Dorid Nudibranchs – Polyceridae
ID: Pale orange with red lines and numerous large yellow conical tubercles; several large papillae behind gill structure; bulbous rhinophores with thin projection on tips. Known from Dry Tortugas in Gulf of Mexico.

LUCAYAN PLOCAMOPHERUS *Plocamopherus lucayensis*
SIZE: to 4 cm (1½ in.)   Dorid Nudibranchs – Polyceridae
ID: Red to orange or brown with scattering of white-tipped papillae; 8 to 10 tiny appendages with branching white tips on front of head; rhinophores extend from short sheaths; gill branches tipped with white papillae. Rare E. Florida, Bahamas.

GOLDCROWNED SEA GODDESS *Felimare acriba*
SIZE: to 4.5 cm (1¾ in.)   Dorid Nudibranchs – Chromodorididae
ID: Yellowish gold with complex pattern of blue circles, ovals and spots on back; notably ruffled white to pink mantle skirt with yellow outer edge. Shallow rocks and reefs from 10 to 35 ft. Uncommon Caribbean; rare S. Florida.

BLACK-BARRED SEA GODDESS   *Felimare cf. acriba*
SIZE: to 6 cm (2¼ in.) Dorid Nudibranchs – Chromodorididae
ID: Differs from *Hypselodoris acriba* [previous] by having thin black transverse bars crossing mantle margin. May be color variant of *H. acriba*. Specimen analysis is required. Shallow rocks and reefs from 10 to 35 ft. Uncommon Caribbean; rare S. Florida.

ZEBRA SEA GODDESS   *Felimare zebra*
SIZE: to 18 cm (7 in.) Dorid Nudibranchs – Chromodorididae
ID: Orange with numerous broken lines; smooth blue rhinophores; gill branches blue with orange trim; mantle skirt edged with irregular blue line. Feed on sponge *Dysidea etheria* from shallows to 65 ft. Common Bermuda.

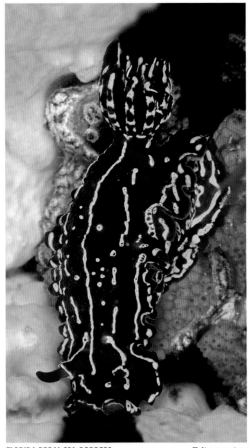

FLORIDA REGAL SEA GODDESS   *Felimare picta*
SIZE: to 13 cm (5 in.) Dorid Nudibranchs – Chromodorididae
ID: Navy blue to deep purple with brilliant yellow to gold irregular stripes; large blue and gold featherlike gill branches extend from a raised base. Reefs; feed on sponges to 130 ft. Common to occasional Florida.

Dorid Nudibranchs

PURPLE-SPOTTED SEA GODDESS   *Felimare marci*
SIZE: to 2.5 cm (1 in.)   Dorid Nudibranchs – Chromodorididae
ID: Yellow gold to reddish brown with concentrated pattern of blue to purple circles, ovals and spots on back; white unruffled mantle skirt with series of random dark blotches or dark spots. Reefs with algae from 12 to 45 ft. Uncommon Caribbean.

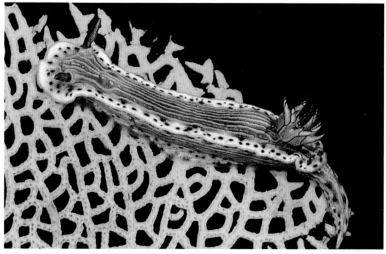

BLACK-SPOTTED SEA GODDESS
Felimare bayeri
Dorid Nudibranchs –
Chromodorididae
SIZE: to 6 cm (2¼ in.)
ID: Blue back with parallel golden stripes; white skirt edged with gold with black spots. Live in association with sponges in genus *Dysidea*. Uncommon Florida, Caribbean.

GOLD-LINED SEA GODDESS   *Felimare ruthae*
SIZE: to 2.5 cm (1 in.)   Dorid Nudibranchs – Chromodorididae
ID: Black to blue back with golden lines; **black on back spills over onto gold-lined white mantle skirt;** irregular blue spotting on back; white or black gill branches with contrasting edging. Reefs in moderate current to 65 ft. Occasional Caribbean.

216

PURPLE-CROWNED SEA GODDESS
Felimare kempfi
Dorid Nudibranchs – Chromodorididae
SIZE: to 2.5 cm (1 in.)
ID: Back grayish to blue with broad bright-white central stripe extending from before rhinophores to gill structure; large and small dark spots on each side of white area; rhinophores purple; gill structure purple with white trim; blue rear foot with black spots. Reefs from 25 to 75 ft.; feed on sponges. Uncommon S. Florida, Bahamas, Caribbean.

OLGA'S SEA GODDESS — *Felimare olgae*
SIZE: to 3.5 cm (1½ in.) Dorid Nudibranchs – Chromodorididae
ID: Yellowish to cream back with orange to brown patches and numerous **bright blue spots surrounded by smaller black spots;** white mantle skirt with blue and black spots; blue spots bordering pointed rear foot. Reefs. Uncommon Florida.

SUNSET SEA GODDESS — *Felimare sp.*
SIZE: to 3.5 cm (1½ in.) Dorid Nudibranchs – Chromodorididae
ID: Three gold to reddish lines on white back; often blue to black patches; white mantle skirt with orange margin and some black spotting; rhinophores white and blue. Sand and rubble near reefs. Uncommon Florida, Caribbean.

ROYAL SEA GODDESS
Felimida regalis
Dorid Nudibranchs – Chromodorididae
SIZE: to 3.5 cm (1½ in.)
ID: Reddish brown with dense covering of dark specks and a few white dots toward white mantle skirt edged in yellow; rhinophores and gill same color as body. Rocks and reefs to 33 ft; feed on sponges. Uncommon Caribbean.

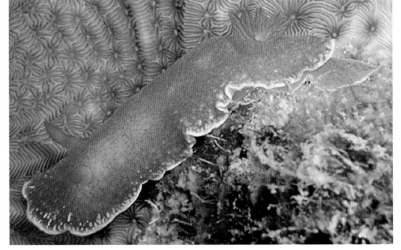

Dorid Nudibranchs

HARLEQUIN SEA GODDESS
Felimida clenchi
Dorid Nudibranchs –
Chromodorididae
SIZE: to 3.5 cm (1½ in.)
ID: White to yellowish with **large patch of red on back that extends at numerous points onto mantle skirt;** blue spots of various sizes circled in red; white gill branches with reddish trim. Rock and sand to 40 ft. Occasional Florida, Bahamas, Caribbean.

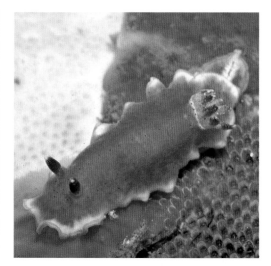

BINZA SEA GODDESS   *Felimida binza*
SIZE: to 3 cm (1¼ in.) Dorid Nudibranchs – Chromodorididae
ID: Pale to dark blue back covered with network of red to yellow lines; white mantle skirt edged in red; pointed blue rear foot with central yellow streak; purple and white rhinophores and gill structure. Sand to 35 ft. Uncommon Florida, Caribbean.

NEONA SEA GODDESS   *Felimida neona*
SIZE: to 3 cm (1¼ in.) Dorid Nudibranchs – Chromodorididae
ID: Pale blue back covered with network of golden lines trimmed in red, some **lines extended to edge of white mantle skirt;** white rhinophores and gill structure white with purple tips. Patch reefs and hard bottom to 35 ft. Uncommon Florida, Caribbean.

GRAHAM'S SEA GODDESS   *Felimida grahami*
SIZE: to 2 cm (¾ in.)   Dorid Nudibranchs – Chromodorididae
ID: White to pink or orange with dense covering of dark specks; white mantle skirt with yellow margin; **rounded rear foot with thin dark central line;** gill branches whitish with dark tips. Shallow coral rubble to 15 ft. Rare Florida, Caribbean.

218

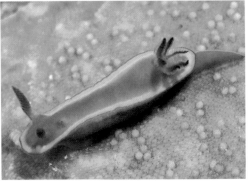

STRAWBERRY SEA GODDESS   *Felimida fentoni*
SIZE: to 2.5 cm (1 in.)   Dorid Nudibranchs – Chromodorididae
ID: Whitish with heavy covering of reddish pigment and orange centered yellow spots; thin yellow to orange line on mantle margin. Feed on sponges to at least 30 ft. Known from eastern Gulf of Mexico.

REDLINE BLUE SEA GODDESS   *Risbecia nyalya*
SIZE: to 3.5 cm (1½ in.) Dorid Nudibranchs – Chromodorididae
ID: Dark blue with red and yellow edged mantle skirt; rhinophores and gill structure purplish blue. Reefs from 6 to 30 ft. Occasional Florida, Bahamas, Caribbean.

TUBERCULATE SEA GODDESS   *Mexichromis multituberculata*
SIZE: to 2 cm (¾ in.)   Dorid Nudibranchs – Chromodorididae
ID: White to yellowish with **numerous purple-tipped tubercles of various sizes;** white skirt edged with purple markings; rhinophores and gill structure white with purple tips. A common Pacific species, rare in Caribbean; known from Puerto Rico.

EVELINE'S SEA GODDESS   *Tyrinna evelinae*
SIZE: to 3 cm (1¼ in.)   Dorid Nudibranchs – Chromodorididae
ID: Translucent white with scattering of orange spots that become larger toward skirt; rhinophores and gill structures white. Under rocks to 15 ft. Uncommon Caribbean.

RED-TIPPED SEA GODDESS
Doriprismatica sedna
Dorid Nudibranchs –
Chromodorididae
SIZE: to 5 cm (2 in.)
ID: White; ruffled mantle skirt with red and yellow edging; rhinophores and gill structure white with red trim. Rocks and reefs from 10 to 50 ft. Pacific species, probably introduced to the Tropical Western Atlantic. Uncommon S. Florida, Bahamas, Caribbean.

Dorid Nudibranchs

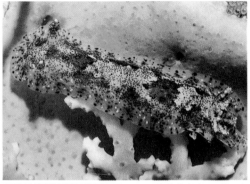

PALE CADLINA *Cadlina rumia*
SIZE: to 1.2 cm (¹/₂ in.)   Dorid Nudibranchs – Cadlinidae
ID: Translucent white oval with wide mantle skirt; numerous tiny yellow-tipped tubercles and a few larger yellow mantle glands; fanlike gill structure edged in pale yellow. Intertidal species. Uncommon Florida, Caribbean.

BROWN-SPECKLED APHELODORIS *Aphelodoris antillensis*
SIZE: to 3 cm (1¹/₄ in.)   Dorid Nudibranchs – Dorididae
ID: Yellow to brown back with dark or light speckling and large brown patches; mantle skirt yellow with brown blotches; white-tipped rhinophores with yellow and brown markings. Reefs from 6 to 12 feet. Uncommon Florida, Bahamas, Caribbean.

LEATHER-BACKED PLATYDORIS *Platydoris angustipes*
SIZE: to 15 cm (6 in.)   Dorid Nudibranchs – Discodorididae
ID: Flat oval with raised central area; reddish tan to orange or purple with some white speckling and occasional white blotches; gill structure tan. Reefs to 25 ft.; feed on red sponges. Occasional Florida, Bahamas, Caribbean.

BROWN DISCODORIS *Discodoris evelinae*
SIZE: to 10 cm (4 in.)   Dorid Nudibranchs – Discodorididae
ID: Flat oval with raised central area; cream or beige to almost black with white or dark brown blotching; rhinophores and gill structures white tipped. Under rocks from 12 to 30 ft. Occasional Florida, Bahamas, Caribbean.

NETWORK GEITODORIS *Geitodoris immunda*
SIZE: to 4.5 cm (1³/₄ in.) Dorid Nudibranchs – Discodorididae
ID: Flat oval with raised central area; orangish brown with textured surface of ridges and rounded tubercles; white-tipped rhinophores. Under rocks. Uncommon Florida, Caribbean.

HANS AND ROSA'S CARMINODORIS *Carminodoris hansrosaorum*
SIZE: to 5.5 cm (2¹/₄ in.)   Dorid Nudibranchs – Dorididae
ID: Flat oval with raised central area; covered with rounded tubercles with pale tips, those toward outside encircled with white at base; **four gill branches at the front, two at the rear whitish outside and orange inside.** Rare; known from Florida, Bonaire.

BLOTCHED DIAULULA *Diaulula greeleyi*
SIZE: to 5 cm (2 in.)   Dorid Nudibranchs – Discodorididae
ID: Flat oval with raised central area; yellow to yellowish brown with numerous patches of dark brown to black; surface has a fuzzy appearance due to ciliated tubercles; rhinophore and gill encircled by raised sheaths. Uncommon Florida, Bahamas, Caribbean.

HUMMELINCK'S DIAULULA *Diaulula hummelincki*
SIZE: to 5 cm (2 in.)   Dorid Nudibranchs – Discodorididae
ID: Flat oval with raised central area; translucent white to pinkish with numerous gray or pinkish blotches; numerous rounded tubercles and ciliated tubercles some with white tips; mantle skirt edged with white papillae. Uncommon S. Caribbean.

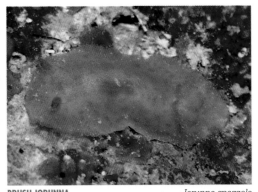

BRUSH JORUNNA *Jorunna spazzola*
SIZE: to 1.5 cm (⅝ in.)   Dorid Nudibranchs – Discodorididae
ID: Flat oval with raised central area; translucent gray with diffuse patches and ciliated tubercles; white papillae near edge of mantle skirt; rhinophores and gill structure gray with brown spots and white tips. Reefs. Uncommon Florida, Bahamas, Caribbean.

ORANGE THORDISA *Thordisa diuda*
SIZE: to 3.5 cm (1½ in.)   Dorid Nudibranchs – Discodorididae
ID: Flat oval with raised central area; dusky orange with rough texture due to covering of tubercles. Rocks and rubble. Uncommon Florida, Bahamas, Caribbean.

ORANGEBALL TARINGA *Taringa telopia*
SIZE: to 4 cm (1½ in.)   Dorid Nudibranchs – Discodorididae
ID: Yellow to orange or dark brown with scattering of darker blotches and ciliated tubercles; gill structure translucent; rhinophores brown with white specks and tips. Shallow sand. Rare Caribbean.

FUZZY ROSTANGA *Rostanga byga*
SIZE: to 1.8 cm (¾ in.)   Dorid Nudibranchs – Discodorididae
ID: Orange to reddish orange with rough texture created by ciliated tubercles; lamellate rhinophores same color as body occasionally with white tips. Rocks and rubble. Occasional Florida, Bahamas, Caribbean.

Dorid Nudibranchs

MAGAGNA DENDRODORIS
Dendrodoris magagnai
Dorid Nudibranchs –
Dendrodorididae
SIZE: to 2.5 cm (1 in.)
ID: Raised oval encircled with ruffled mantle skirt; light bluish gray with light yellow rounded tubercles and black patches on back; mantle skirt edged in yellow with black spots and blotches. Reefs to 60 ft. Rare; known from Costa Rica.

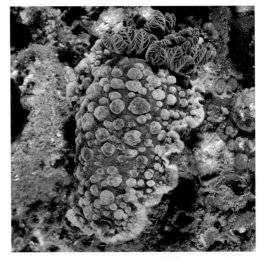

WARTY DENDRODORIS *Dendrodoris warta*
SIZE: to 11 cm (4¼ in.) Dorid Nudibranchs – Dendrodorididae
ID: Large oval with a concentrated covering of large rounded tubercles; highly ruffled mantle skirt; large gill structure same color as body. Occasional west coast of Florida.

LEMON DROP *Doriopsilla pharpa*
SIZE: to 1.8 cm (¾ in.) Dorid Nudibranchs – Dendrodorididae
ID: Small yellow to orange oval with numerous rounded tubercles; brown spotting on rhinophores. Feed on sponges in genus *Cliona*; reefs to 50 ft. Uncommon Florida, Caribbean.

BLACK-SPOTTED CERATOPHYLLIDIA *Ceratophyllidia papilligera*
SIZE: to 3 cm (1¼ in.) Dorid Nudibranchs – Phyllidiidae
ID: White to light blue back covered with dark blue spots of various sizes; largest spots surround large tubercles; rhinophores with dark tips and pale base. Rocks and reefs to 100 ft. Uncommon Florida, Bahamas, Caribbean.

SMILING ARMINA
Armina sp.
Arminid Nudibranchs –
Arminidae
SIZE: to 5 cm (2 in.)
ID: An undescribed species in the family Arminidae, which is characterized by narrow black and white ridges on back. Sand; feed on sea pens. Uncommon Caribbean.

Dendronotid Nudibranchs

GRAPECLUSTER DOTO   *Doto uva*
SIZE: to 1.2 cm (¹/₂ in.) Dendronotid Nudibranchs – Dotidae
ID: Dark body with white spotting; row of cerata along each side formed by clusters of tubercles; dark smooth rhinophores with white specks extend from white edged sheaths. On Feather Bush Hydroid from 15 to 60 ft. Occasional Florida, Bahamas, Caribbean.

VARADERO DOTO
Doto varaderoensis
Dendronotid Nudibranchs – Dotidae
SIZE: to 1.2 cm (¹/₂ in.)
ID: Creamy pink with white spots on back; two rows of densely packed cerata composed of translucent-white oval tubercles; smooth rhinophores with white spotting. Feed on hydroids to 20 ft. Occasional S. Florida, Caribbean.

WILDE'S DOTO   *Doto wildei*
SIZE: to 8 mm (³/₈ in.) Dendronotid Nudibranchs – Dotidae
ID: Small translucent gray to dark brown with white spotting on back; cerata formed by clusters of rounded tan tubercles with white tops; long dark rhinophores with white spotting extend from short white-spotted sheaths. Hydroids to 20 ft. Rare S. Caribbean.

BLACKSTALK DOTO   *Doto curere*
SIZE: to 8 mm (³/₈ in.) Dendronotid Nudibranchs – Dotidae
ID: Small translucent gray with dark patches on back; cerata formed by clusters of rounded translucent tubercles with blue and orange highlights; smooth slender black rhinophores with white tips. Hydroids to 20 ft. Rare Florida, Caribbean.

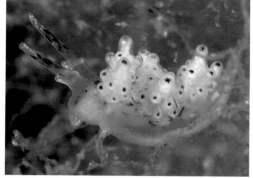

WAVE BREAKING DOTO *Doto fluctifraga*
SIZE: to 8 mm (³/₈ in.) Dendronotid Nudibranchs – Dotidae
ID: Translucent white; cerata formed by bulbous tubercles with black spot at tips; black streaks on back and rhinophores. Hydroids to 20 ft. Rare Florida.

PITA DOTO *Doto pita*
SIZE: to 7 mm (¹/₄ in.) Dendronotid Nudibranchs – Dotidae
ID: Small elongate translucent gray with some dark patches on back; elongate cerata formed by irregularly sized tubercles. Hydroids to 20 ft. Rare Florida, Caribbean.

UNDESCRIBED *Doto* sp.1
SIZE: to 8 mm (³/₈ in.) Dendronotid Nudibranch – Dotidae
ID: Small translucent brown with small dark blotches and white specks; cerata formed by clusters of tan tubercles with blue highlights and black specks; smooth tan rhinophores white toward tips. Hydroids to 20 ft. Known from Florida.

UNDESCRIBED *Doto* sp.2
SIZE: to 1.2 cm (¹/₂ in.) Dendronotid Nudibranch – Dotidae
ID: Elongate black body with tan edges and white specks; cerata formed by cluster of orangish tubercles with pale tops; smooth thin blackish rhinophores. Hydroids to 20 ft. Known from Florida.

UNDESCRIBED *Doto* sp.3
SIZE: to 1.2 cm (¹/₂ in.) Dendronotid Nudibranchs – Dotidae
ID: Elongate tan and dark brown body; row of whitish cerata formed by clusters of rounded tubercles with bluish highlights; smooth rhinophores purplish with white dots. Hydroids to 20 ft. Known from Florida.

UNDESCRIBED *Doto* sp.4
SIZE: to 7 mm (¹/₄ in.) Dendronotid Nudibranchs – Dotidae
ID: Small orangish body with white specks; cerata formed by clusters of whitish tubercles with orange highlights; long translucent rhinophores with white speckling. Hydroids to 30 ft. Known from St. Vincent.

225

Dendronotid Nudibranchs

TATTY SLUG *Janolus comis*

SIZE: to 1 cm (³/₈ in.) Dendronotid Nudibranchs – Proctonotidae

ID: Flattened tan body covered with white speckles; pointed translucent cerata covered with papillae; rough stocky rhinophores extend from ridge. Uncommon Florida, Bahamas, Caribbean.

CRISSCROSS TRITONIA *Tritonia bayeri*

SIZE: to 1 cm (³/₈ in.) Dendronotid Nudibranchs – Tritoniidae

ID: Translucent with network of thin reticulated lines on back; branched cerata along sides; four appendages flare from front of head. Inhabit areas with gorgonians to 50 ft. Uncommon Florida, Bahamas, Caribbean.

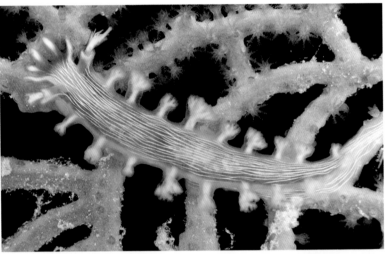

HAMNER'S TRITONIA
Tritonia hamnerorum
Dendronotid Nudibranchs –
Tritoniidae

SIZE: to 1.5 cm (⁵/₈ in.)

ID: Elongate with pale back covered with numerous thin interweaving lines; cerata tufts extend from narrow translucent mantle skirt running along sides of body; three appendages between tentacles flare from front of head; rhinophores extend from long sheaths. Inhabit sea fans to 50 ft. Occasional Florida, Bahamas, Caribbean.

WELLS' TRITONIA *Tritonia wellsi*

SIZE: to 1 cm (³/₈ in.) Dendronotid Nudibranchs – Tritoniidae

ID: Wide flat gray to reddish brown body tapering to point covered with white speckling; short tufts of cerata along sides; somewhat rounded veil with short projections extending from front of head. Inhabit gorgonians. Uncommon Florida, Caribbean.

UNDESCRIBED *Tritonia sp.*

SIZE: to 1 cm (³/₈ in.) Dendronotid Nudibranchs – Tritoniidae

ID: Reddish orange body tapering to point covered with network of scrawled white lines; short stocky cerata topped with a ring of papillae extend from sides; extremely long translucent orange rhinophore sheaths. Known from Roatan.

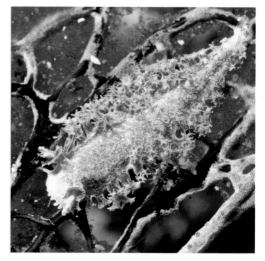

TUFTED TRITONIOPSIS *Tritoniopsis frydis*
SIZE: to 2 cm (³/₄ in.) Dendronotid Nudibranchs – Tritoniidae
ID: Flat body white to orange with highly branched flattened cerata lining sides; rounded veil with short projections extend from head. Feed on gorgonians from 30 to 120 ft. Uncommon Florida, Bahamas, Caribbean.

TASSELED BORNELLA
Bornella calcarata
Dendronotid Nudibranchs –
Bornellidae
SIZE: to 6.5 cm (2¹/₂ in.)
ID: Elongate body red to orange with network of thin lines; scattering of white rounded tubercles; paired sets of cerata with elongate red and white tubercles; multibranched veil extends from front of head; stocky multibranched rhinophores. Reef; feed on hydroids. Uncommon Florida, Bahamas.

HYDROID LOMONOTUS
Lomanotus vermiformis
Dendronotid Nudibranchss
– Lomanotidae
SIZE: to 3.5 cm (1¹/₂ in.)
ID: Elongate body brown with numerous thin interlaced white lines; dense covering of tall pointed and inflated translucent cerata; long pointed dark rhinophores extend from tall translucent sheaths. Hydroids to 30 ft. Uncommon Florida, Bahamas.

Dendronotid & Aeolid Nudibranchs

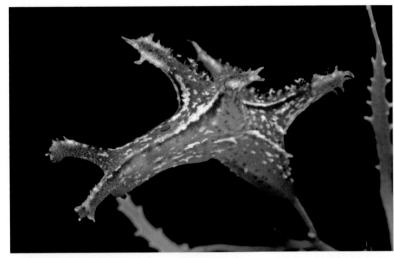

SARGASSUM NUDIBRANCH
Scyllaea pelagica
Dendronotid Nudibranchs –
Scyllaeidae
SIZE: to 10 cm (4 in.)
ID: Translucent brown, green or golden with two flattened elongate lobes extending from each side of the body; occasional bright blue spots; single flattened lobe centered near rear used for swimming; some light red spotting and a few tiny tubercles; two long tubular rhinophore sheaths with fluted tips extend from head. Inhabit floats of *Sargassum* weed, and occasionally algae on mooring lines; feed on hydroids. Seasonally common Florida, Bahamas, Caribbean.

WARD'S NOTOBRYON   *Notobryon* cf. *wardi*
SIZE: to 6.5 cm (2½ in.) Dendronotid Nudibranchs – Scyllaeidae
ID: Translucent yellowish brown with two unequal-sized pairs of large flattened mantle lobes, front pair larger; a single flattened lobe centered near rear used for swimming; large rhinophore sheaths. Indo-Pacific species; rare Florida, Caribbean.

WHITE-SPOTTED HANCOCKIA   *Hancockia ryrca*
SIZE: to 1.5 cm (⅝ in.) Dendronotid Nudibranchs – Hancockiidae
ID: Elongate translucent gray with some dark blotching and white specks; rhinophore sheaths with wide rims lined with projections; widely separated cerata formed by translucent papillae. Hydroids. Uncommon Bahamas, Caribbean.

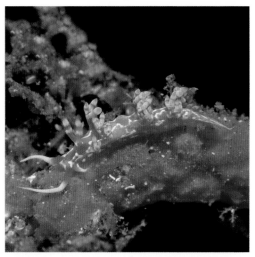

ENGEL'S FLABELLINA *Flabellina engeli*
SIZE: to 2.5 cm (1 in.)   Aeolid Nudibranchs – Flabellinidae
ID: Long thin tapering body with elaborate white pattern on purple to orange background; paired sets of orange-banded cerata; **white patch between long white tentacles** and banded rhinophores. Feed on hydroids. Occasional Florida, Caribbean.

DUSHIA FLABELLINA
Flabellina dushia

Aeolid Nudibranchs –
Flabellinidae

SIZE: to 2 cm (³/₄ in.)

ID: Long thin tapering white body with paired clusters of elongate cerata; color of cerata varies between individuals; smooth white to blue elongate rhinophores and tentacles. Feed on hydroids. Occasional Florida, Bahamas, Caribbean.

Aeolid Nudibranchs

PURPLERING FLABELLINA *Flabellina marcusorum*
SIZE: to 3 cm (1¼ in.)   Aeolid Nudibranchs – Flabellinidae
ID: Red to orange with numerous long thin white-tipped cerata with purple bands; rhinophores grooved on anterior surface; long tapered antennae. Uncommon Florida, Caribbean.

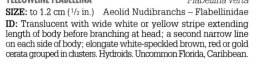

YELLOWLINE FLABELLINA *Flabellina verta*
SIZE: to 1.2 cm (½ in.)   Aeolid Nudibranchs – Flabellinidae
ID: Translucent with wide white or yellow stripe extending length of body before branching at head; a second narrow line on each side of body; elongate white-speckled brown, red or gold cerata grouped in clusters. Hydroids. Uncommon Florida, Caribbean.

HAMANN'S FLABELLINA
Flabellina hamanni
Aeolid Nudibranchs – Flabellinidae
SIZE: to 3 cm (1¼ in.)
ID: Translucent reddish orange; cerata translucent toward base with purple band beneath yellow top, similarily marked rhinophores and tentacles: rhinophores grooved on anterior surface. Feed on hydroids. Uncommon Bahamas, Caribbean.

UNDESCRIBED
Flabellina sp.1
Aeolid Nudibranchs –
Flabellinidae
SIZE: to 1.8 cm (³/₄ in.)
ID: Elongate tapering reddish orange body with dense clusters of cerata along each side of body; cerata dark orange with white tips; thin purple line runs length of midbody; long rhinophores and tentacles orange at base turning purple with white tips. Feed on hydroids. Known from S. Florida.

UNDESCRIBED   *Flabellina* sp.2
SIZE: to 1.8 cm (³/₄ in.)   Aeolid Nudibranchs – Flabellinidae
ID: Translucent white with white stripe running length of back that divides at head with each branch extending onto tentacles; discrete clusters of thin white-tipped maroon cerata along each side. Feed on hydroids. Known from S. Florida.

UNDESCRIBED   *Flabellina* sp.3
SIZE: to 1.8 cm (³/₄ in.)   Aeolid Nudibranchs – Flabellinidae
ID: Translucent with white stripe running length of back that divides at head with each branch extending onto tentacles; dense clusters of long cerata with red band and white tips; light blue tentacles and tapering tail. Known from S. Florida.

CONE EUBRANCHUS   *Eubranchus coniclus*
SIZE: to 5 mm (¹/₄ in.)   Aeolid Nudibranchs – Eubranchidae
ID: Translucent gray with brown speckling; bulbous cerata with numerous tubercles and pointed tip; short tentacles; smooth rhinophores with one or two dark bands. Feed on hydroids. Rare Florida, Caribbean.

Aeolid Nudibranchs

FRINGEBACK DONDICE
Dondice occidentalis
Aeolid Nudibranchs –
Facelinidae
SIZE: to 5 cm (2 in.)
ID: Variable in color and markings; most frequently pinkish to yellow with **white or blue line extending down center of back and a shorter second and third line running parallel on each side;** several clusters of elongate cerata often banded with white or blue tips; white or orange line on head often forms into a white patch. Reef, rubble and mangroves to 100 ft.; feed on cnidarians. Occasional Florida, Bahamas, Caribbean.

CASSIOPEA DONDICE   *Dondice parguerensis*
SIZE: to 5 cm (2 in.)   Aeolid Nudibranchs – Facelinidae
ID: Inhabit the tentacles of Upside-down Jellyfish, *Cassiopea* spp.; very similar to Fringe-back Dondice [previous]; translucent gray with white stripe extending down center of back; white ring near tips of cerata. Uncommon Florida, Caribbean.

GAUDY BABAKINA   *Babakina anadoni*
SIZE: to 1 cm (3/8 in.)   Aeolid Nudibranchs – Facelinidae
ID: Pinkish translucent gray; white area on head between rhinophores and tentacles; bulbous blue-and-red banded cerata with white tips; rhinophores bulbous, lamellate and fused at base. Feed on hydroids to 20 ft. Rare Bahamas, Caribbean.

CHRISTMAS TREE HYDROID LEARCHIS   *Learchis poica*

SIZE: to 3 cm (1¼ in.)   Aeolid Nudibranchs – Facelinidae

ID: Transparent white to orange with wide white stripe extending down center of back and past rhinophores to tentacles; numerous clusters of black cerata. Feed on Christmas Tree Hydroids from 1 to 60 ft. Occasional Florida, Bahamas, Caribbean.

EVELINE'S LEARCHIS
Learchis evelinae

Aeolid Nudibranchs – Facelinidae

SIZE: to 1.5 cm (⅝ in.)

ID: Translucent gray; broad white area on head extends over sides with orange patch below; translucent reddish or brown white-tipped cerata; upper portion of smooth rhinophores and tentacles white. Feed on hydroids. Uncommon Florida, Caribbean.

NIPPLED PALISA   *Palisa papillata*

SIZE: to 1.5 cm (⅝ in.)   Aeolid Nudibranchs – Facelinidae

ID: Gray to orange with numerous white spots; bulbous pale blue cerata with thin orange band topped with white nipple; thick white and orange tentacles; stout rhinophores with nipplelike tips. Feed on hydroids to 40 ft. Rare Florida, Caribbean.

Aeolid Nudibranchs

LYNX PHIDIANA
Phidiana lynceus
Aeolid Nudibranchs –
Facelinidae
SIZE: to 4.5 cm (1³/₄ in.)

ID: Translucent gray to orange with central stripe on back (occasionally absent); central stripe divides between rhinophores and curves toward base of long smooth orange and gray tentacles; cerata dark with white tips. Shallow rocky habitats. Occasional Florida, Bahamas, Caribbean.

LONG-EARED FAVORINUS   *Favorinus auritulus*
SIZE: to 1.2 cm (¹/₂ in.)   Aeolid Nudibranchs – Facelinidae
ID: Translucent white to orange with white markings on body; bulbous cerata; blue and white area on head; smooth tentacles; rhinophores with inflated ring beneath white tips. Feed on sea slug eggs to 45 ft. Uncommon Florida, Bahamas, Caribbean.

WHITE-SPECKLED PAULEO   *Pauleo jubatus*
SIZE: to 5 cm (2 in.)   Aeolid Nudibranchs – Facelinidae
ID: Yellowish with white central stripe along center of back; numerous slightly curved bulbous cerata with white speckles and tiny translucent tips. Feed on sea rods, *Plexaurella* sp., to 100 ft. Occasional Caribbean.

ORANGE-SPOTTED NANUCA
Nanuca sebastiani
Aeolid Nudibranchs –
Facelinidae
SIZE: to 1.2 cm (¹/₂ in.)

ID: Narrow translucent green with elongate white patches generally with reddish brown lines and spots fringed with yellow on back; line of reddish brown spots and dashes along sides with white spots on skirt below; widely separated clusters of brownish cerata with thin white stripes capped with greenish band and pointed translucent tips; rhinophores ringed with raised ridges; long smooth tentacles with white markings. Shallow algae beds to 10 ft. Rare Florida, Bahamas, Caribbean.

LONGHORN AUSTRAEOLIS
Austraeolis catina
Aeolid Nudibranchs –
Facelinidae
SIZE: to 2.5 cm (1 in.)
ID: Brown to orange with fine speckling; two prominent white spots on front of head; bulbous cerata orange with brown bases and white tips; rhinophores orange at base with white tips and ringed with compact raised ridges; long smooth white tentacles with dark central band. Reefs; feed on hydroids from 30 to 100 ft. Occasional Florida, Bahamas, Caribbean.

FROSTY NOUMEAELLA   *Noumeaella kristenseni*
SIZE: to 1.8 cm (³/₄ in.)   Aeolid Nudibranchs – Facelinidae
ID: Translucent white with network of white lines on back; long thin whitish cerata with some white markings; rhinophores covered with white tubercles. Feed on hydroids to 40 ft. Uncommon Florida, Caribbean.

REDLINE GODIVA   *Godiva rubrolineata*
SIZE: to 1.8 cm (³/₄ in.)   Aeolid Nudibranchs – Facelinidae
ID: Translucent with three orange to red lines on body; dark elongate cerata in clusters; smooth rhinophores and tentacles orange to blue at base changing to white toward tips. Feed on hydroids to 20 ft. Rare Florida, Caribbean.

ORANGESPOT CRATENA   *Cratena cf. peregrina*
SIZE: to 2.5 cm (1 in.)   Aeolid Nudibranchs – Facelinidae
ID: Translucent with discreet clusters of long thin red to blue cerata with white tips; **two prominent orange patches on head;** rhinophores and tentacles become white toward tips. Feed on hydroids. Uncommon Florida.

Aeolid Nudibranchs

BLUE CUTHONA   *Cuthona caerulea*
SIZE: to 2.5 cm (1 in.)   Aeolid Nudibranchs – Tergipedidae
ID: Translucent with numerous yellowish white cerata with wide blue bands; **blue patch on head;** rhinophores with translucent base, white center and orangish brown tips. Green algae *Dictyosphaeria* sp. and *Valonia* sp. Uncommon Florida, Caribbean.

PINKLINE CUTHONA   *Cuthona* sp.1
SIZE: to 2.5 cm (1 in.)   Aeolid Nudibranchs – Tergipedidae
ID: Cream to orange back with bright orange sides and three long pink or purple lines; 7 or 8 white-tipped brown cerata extend from each side; rhinophores and tentacles translucent at base, purple center and white tips. Known from S. Florida.

ORANGE AND WHITE CUTHONA   *Cuthona* sp.2
SIZE: to 2.5 cm (1 in.)   Aeolid Nudibranchs – Tergipedidae
ID: Opaque white with pronounced hump behind head; rhinophores entirely white; short tentacles with brownish bases and white ends. Known from S. Florida.

CAYMAN CUTHONA   *Cuthona* sp.3
SIZE: to 2.5 cm (1 in.)   Aeolid Nudibranchs – Tergipedidae
ID: Opaque white body with translucent foot; cerata clusters along back orange-brown with scattered white spots and white tips. Algae and hydroids to 30 ft. Known from Grand Cayman.

CHOCOLATE CUTHONA   *Cuthona* sp.4
SIZE: to 2.5 cm (1 in.)   Aeolid Nudibranchs – Tergipedidae
ID: Brown with random white spots; base of smooth rhinophores and tentacles brown, white toward tips; inflated cerata brown at base followed by blue and yellow bands and white tips. Algae and hydroids. Known from Grand Cayman.

INDIAN AEOLIDIELLA
Aeolidiella indica
Aeolid Nudibranchs –
Aeolidiidae
SIZE: to 4 cm (1½ in.)
ID: Translucent gray to orange with several white connected oval patches on back; numerous cerata light orange with a white band just before orange tips; rhinophores and tentacles smooth. Feed on anemones. Uncommon Caribbean.

WHITE AEOLIDIELLA   *Aeolidiella alba*
SIZE: to 1.2 cm (½ in.)   Aeolid Nudibranchs – Aeolidiidae
ID: White with numerous short inflated white cerata with occasional brown areas in two rows of clusters; rhinophores translucent brown with inflated rings and small blunt tips. Feed on anemones. Known from Florida.

WARTY BAEOLIDIA   *Baeolidia nodosa*
SIZE: to 1.5 cm (⅝ in.)   Aeolid Nudibranchs – Aeolidiidae
ID: White to light green; **thin orange circles on head and open areas on back;** stocky cerata with numerous fingerlike tubercles; translucent rhinophores and tentacles with white speckling. Feed on filamentous algae. Uncommon Florida, Caribbean.

CREUTZBERG'S SPURILLA
Spurilla creutzbergi
Aeolid Nudibranchs –
Aeolidiidae
SIZE: to 3 cm (1¼ in.)
ID: Brown with fine network of white lines covering head and body; inflated brown and white cerata with vague banding and pointed tips; thick rhinophores covered with numerous tubercles. Uncommon Florida, Caribbean.

Aeolid Nudibranchs

NEAPOLITAN SPURILLA
Spurilla neapolitana
Aeolid Nudibranchs –
Aeolidiidae
SIZE: to 3.5 cm (1¹/₂ in.)
ID: Light yellow to reddish brown with heavy white spotting covering head and body; often thin brown lines on head; stocky curved cerata with some white spotting; rhinophores ridged. Occasional Florida, Caribbean.

SARGASSUM SPURILLA   *Spurilla sargassicola*
SIZE: to 3.5 cm (1¹/₂ in.)   Aeolid Nudibranchs – Aeolidiidae
ID: Light brown head, body and inflated cerata covered with white spots; head and body with thin brown lines; rhinophores translucent with series of ridges toward tips. Inhabit floats of *Sargassum.* Uncommon Florida, Bahamas, Caribbean.

TANNA CERBERILLA
Cerberilla tanna
Aeolid Nudibranchs –
Aeolidiidae
SIZE: to 2.5 cm (1 in.)
ID: Flattened gray body with blue mantle skirt; short pointed cerata with yellow to orange and brown markings; often orange or brown patch between brown rhinophores; smooth blue tentacles. Sand. Rare Florida.

GOLD-FRINGED CERBERILLA   *Cerberilla potiguara*
SIZE: to 2.5 cm (1 in.)   Aeolid Nudibranchs – Aeolidiidae
ID: Flatten bluish gray body; white skirt with blue fringe; smooth rhinophores and elongate tentacles dark blue; two gold lines between rhinophores curve toward tentacles; blue cerata with golden tips. Sand. Rare Florida and Cayman Is. to E. Caribbean,

BLUE GLAUCUS
Glaucus atlanticus
Aeolid Nudibranchs –
Glaucidae
SIZE: to 4 cm (1½ in.)
ID: Slender blue body tapering to pointed tail; small tentacles and rhinophores; groups of cerata project laterally in a single plane like fingers of an open hand. Similar-appearing Margined Glaucus, *Glaucilla marginata*, cerata arranged in multiple arching rows. Pelagic; associates with and feed on Portuguese Man-of-War; both host and prey can inflict painful sting if touched. Circumglobal in temperate and tropical waters.

Spiny Oysters, File Clams

ATLANTIC THORNY OYSTER
Spondylus americanus
Spiny Oysters –
Spondylidae

SIZE: to 14 cm (5¹/₂ in.)

ID: Numerous scattered spines (can grow to two inches, but often broken) cover surface; shells variable colors including white, yellow, orange, red and purple, but generally overgrown by a variety of organisms; mantle brown, and white. Valves typically snap shut when approached. Inhabit natural and artificial reefs, often attach under overhangs from 5 to 100 ft. Common Florida, Bahamas, Caribbean.

SPINY FILECLAM　　　　　　　　　　　*Lima lima*
SIZE: to 9 cm (3¹/₂ in.)　　　　　File Clams – Limidae
ID: White to lavender mantle and tentacles; white to tan valves deeply sculptured with numerous radiating, sharply spined ribs. Swim by snapping valves shut. Beneath rocks from 3 to 25 ft. Common Florida, Bahamas, Caribbean.

ROUGH FILECLAM
Ctenoides scabra
File Clams – Limidae
SIZE: to 9 cm (3½ in.)
ID: Brilliant red to orange-red mantle; tentacles often reddish orange, especially in shallow water and white deeper; whitish to brownish valves sculpted with numerous thin radiating ribs; valves usually hidden with only mantle and tentacles exposed. Inhabit narrow cracks and recesses from 3 to 130 ft. Common Florida, Bahamas, Caribbean.

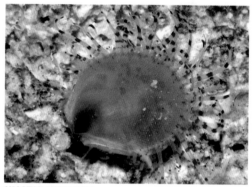

SMOOTH FLAME SCALLOP   *Ctenoides mitis*
SIZE: to 7.5 cm (3 in.)   File Clams – Limidae
ID: Oval thin-walled shell with about 90 thin scaly radial ribs; white with brown blotches; white tentacles; reddish mantle; juveniles [pictured] with banded tentacles. Beneath rocks from 5 to 25 ft. Occasional Florida, Bahamas, Caribbean.

ANTILLEAN FILECLAM   *Limaria pellucida*
SIZE: to 2.5 cm (1 in.)   File Clams – Limidae
ID: Mantle red, orange or white with white to pinkish tentacles; white valves of unequal size sculpted with small uneven radiating ribs. Beneath rocks from 5 to 25 ft. Snap valves shut to swim. Occasional Florida, Bahamas, Caribbean.

ROUGH SCALLOP   *Lindapecten muscosus*
SIZE: to 5 cm (2 in.)   Scallops – Pectinidae
ID: Fanlike valves with unequal-size wings; about 20 rounded ribs of erect scoop-shaped scales; colors variable; translucent mantle with white streaks; blue spots are simple eyes. Seagrass and sand from 10 to 150 ft. Common Florida, Bahamas, Caribbean.

THISTLE SCALLOP   *Lindapecten exasperatus*
SIZE: to 2.5 cm (1 in.)   Scallops – Pectinidae
ID: Fanlike valves with unequal-size wings; about 20 rounded ribs of flat rounded scales; variable colors. Seagrass and sand from 10 to 150 ft. Common Florida, Bahamas, Caribbean.

ATLANTIC CALICO SCALLOP   *Argopecten gibbus*
SIZE: to 3.5 cm (1½ in.)   Scallops – Pectinidae
ID: Moderately inflated almost circular shell with wings of nearly equal size; about 20 rounded radiating ribs and numerous concentric growth lines; brown and tan mantle. Sand from 5 to 300 ft. Common Florida, Bahamas, Caribbean.

LION'S PAW SCALLOP   *Nodipecten nodosus*
SIZE: to 15 cm (6 in.)   Scallops – Pectinidae
ID: Robust reddish brown to orange shell with slightly convex valves; 7 to 9 folds with blunt knoblike projections in concentric rows. Gold and brown mantle fringed with short tentacles. Sand from shallows to 500 ft. Occasional Florida, Bahamas, Caribbean.

ZIGZAG SCALLOP
Euvola ziczac

Scallops – Pectinidae

SIZE: to 10 cm (4 in.)

ID: Lower valve flat with numerous crowded ribs; white and brown blotches and some dark zigzag lines; upper valve deep cup-shaped with 18 to 20 broad low radiating ribs; both valves with wavy outer edges; tan and white mantle lined with short tentacles that regulate water flow. Inhabit sand from 3 to 25 ft. where they bury with only tentacles protruding to filter phytoplankton food. Common Florida, Caribbean.

KNOBBY SCALLOP
Caribachlamys pellucens

SIZE: to 4.5 cm (1³/₄ in.)

Scallops – Pectinidae

ID: White fan-shaped valves with 8 to 10 heavy ribs often **lined with short knobs;** white-speckled translucent to reddish tentacles; often encrusted. Beneath rocks or inside recesses from 10 to 25 ft. Uncommon Florida, Bahamas, Caribbean.

ORNATE SCALLOP
Caribachlamys ornata

SIZE: to 1.5 cm (⁵/₈ in.)

Scallops – Pectinidae

ID: Elongate rounded valves with unequal wings (one almost indiscernible); upper valve with 18 to 20 tall ribs of scales with short sharp spines; white or yellowish with red or purple spots. Beneath rocks from 3 to 65 ft. Florida, Bahamas, Caribbean.

FROND OYSTER
Dendostrea frons

Oysters – Ostreidae

SIZE: to 6.5 cm (2¹/₂ in.)

ID: **Valves interlock in zig-zag pattern.** Attach to gorgonians, dead corals and hard substrates; frequently overgrown with a variety of organisms, including sponges, hydroids, and algae from 20 to 130 ft. Common Florida, Bahamas, Caribbean.

Pen Shells, Pearl Oysters, Ark Clams, Tree Oysters

AMBER PENSHELL
Pinna camea
Pen Shells – Pinnidae
SIZE: to 25 cm (10 in.)
ID: Thin amber to gray slightly translucent fan-shaped valves with projections along upper edge; rows of short projections radiate from sides. Partially bury in mud or sand, or inhabit narrow openings in reefs, with valves only slightly exposed, from 6 to 50 ft. Anchored with chitinous threads. Occasional Florida, Bahamas; common Caribbean.

ATLANTIC WING-OYSTER   *Pteria colymbus*
SIZE: to 7.5 cm (3 in.)   Pearl Oysters – Pteriidae
ID: Long dark brown to black winglike valves extend from hinge. Typically encrusted; attach to stalks of black coral and gorgonians, most commonly sea plumes from 10 to 100 ft. Common Florida, Bahamas, Caribbean.

STIFF PENSHELL   *Atrina rigida*
SIZE: to 28 cm (11 in.)   Pen Shells – Pinnidae
ID: Fan-shaped and moderately thick valves with 25 slightly elevated radial ribs with erect tube-like spines; dark to light brown to purplish black. Partially bury in bottom with narrow tip down. Common Florida, Bahamas, Caribbean.

ATLANTIC PEARL-OYSTER   *Pinctada imbricata*
SIZE: to 6.5 cm (2½ in.)   Pearl Oysters – Pteriidae
ID: Flattened valves with concentric growth plates radiating from hinge in mottled shades of brown; irregular rows of short scaly spines along outer border; often encrusted. Rock, wrecks, sea fans from 6 to 65 ft. Common S. Florida, Bahamas, Caribbean.

EARED ARK *Anadara notabilis*
SIZE: to 9 cm (3¹/₂ in.) Ark Clams – Arcidae
ID: Thick oblong valves with about 25 radial ribs and thin evenly spaced concentric ridges; white with a brown spiny surface covering that diminishes with age. Seagrass and sand from shallows to 20 ft. Uncommon Florida, Bahamas, Caribbean.

RED-BROWN ARK *Barbatia cancellaria*
SIZE: to 6.5 cm (2¹/₂ in.) Ark Clams – Arcidae
ID: Irregularly shaped purplish brown valves with rounded ends and many slightly beaded close-set ribs forming a finely cross-hatched pattern; surface hairy, especially along radial ribs. Rock to 12 ft. Common Florida, Bahamas, Caribbean.

FLAT TREE-OYSTER *Isognomon alatus*
SIZE: to 7.5 cm (3 in.) Tree Oysters – Isognomonidae
ID: Flat and thin valves with smooth, rounded opening; **interior brown, purple or black.** Grow in clusters on mangrove roots, dock pilings, artificial reefs, gorgonians and rock to 40 ft. Common to occasional Florida, Bahamas, Caribbean.

LISTER PURSE-OYSTER *Isognomon radiatus*
SIZE: to 7 cm (2³/₄ in.) Tree Oysters – Isognomonidae
ID: Valve openings long irregular and often twisted; yellowish with a few thin radial rays. Rocks in tidal areas, but occasionally on reefs. Common to occasional Florida, Bahamas, Caribbean.

ASIAN GREEN MUSSEL *Perna viridis*
SIZE: to 10 cm (4 in.) Sea Mussels – Mytilidae
ID: Elongate smooth shell with bright green shell covering layer (periostracum); **adults brown with green margins.** Hard substrates in turbid and polluted coastal waters to 30 ft. Can be abundant; Florida, Jamaica, and Venezuela.

STUBBY SOLECURTUS *Solecurtus sanctaemarthae*
SIZE: to 3 cm (1¹/₄ in.) Razor Clams – Solecurtidae
ID: Oblong squarish white shell with a gape at each end; white body with red to orange spotting. Common Florida, Bahamas, Caribbean.

Chitons

WEST INDIAN FUZZY CHITON *Acanthopleura granulata*
SIZE: to 9 cm (3¹/₂ in.) Chitons – Chitonidae
ID: Eight overlapping plates brown when not eroded or encrusted; girdle gray, brown to green with broad dark bands; skirt covered with short coarse hairlike spines. Attach to rocks and hard substrate along shorelines. Abundant Caribbean.

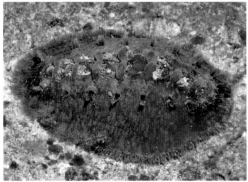

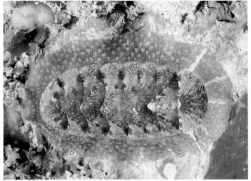

RED GLASS-HAIR CHITON *Acanthochitona hemphilli*
SIZE: to 2.5 cm (1 in.) Chitons – Chitonidae
ID: Orange-brown girdle with hairy outer margin almost covers plates; plates heart shaped and red with some spotting; tuft of bristles extends from indentation on each side of plates. Rocks from 3 to 20 ft. Occasional S. Florida, Bahamas, Caribbean.

ORNATE CHITON *Tonicia schrammi*
SIZE: to 2.5 cm (1 in.) Chitons – Chitonidae
ID: Plates ornately sculpted and patterned in gray, green, brown and crimson; wide textured **crimson girdle** with light spots and occasional bands. Rocks and hard substrate from 10 to 45 ft. Uncommon Florida, Bahamas, Caribbean.

SPENGLER'S GREEN CHITON *Chiton viridis*
SIZE: to 5 cm (2 in.) Chitons – Chitonidae
ID: Oval, cream to brownish-green with brown-streaked valves; lateral triangles with 4-5 beaded ribs. Brown-banded cream girdle has round scales. Nocturnal; rocks of intertidal zones. Common Florida, Bahamas, Caribbean.

SQUAMOSE CHITON *Chiton squamosus*
SIZE: to 7.5 cm (3 in.) Chitons – Chitonidae
ID: Plates dull gray to tan with irregular wide faint brown bands; often green to blue highlights; girdle covered with scales bearing pale grayish green bands. Rock from shore to 10 ft. Common to occasional Florida, Bahamas, Caribbean.

246

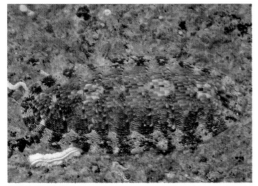

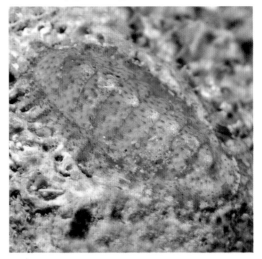

STRIOLATE CHITON　　　　　　*Ischnochiton striolatus*
SIZE: to 2.5 cm (1 in.)　　　　Chitons – Ischnochitonidae
ID: Oblong with zigzag grooves along sides; rows of threadlike bumps along sides of central plates and concentric rows of bumps on the ends; cream, gray, white, orange, brown, pink, green, purple, black. Rocks of intertidal zones. Common Caribbean.

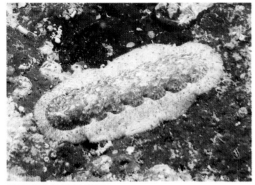

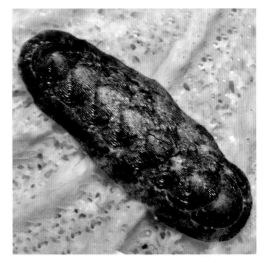

CARIBBEAN SLENDER CHITON　　*Stenoplax purpurascens*
SIZE: to 5 cm (2 in.)　　　　Chitons – Ischnochitonidae
ID: Plates gray, grayish green, light brown or cream often with green, purple, pink or white mottling; scaled girdle marbled bluish gray to brown. Occasional Caribbean, absent Central American coast.

ATLANTIC ROSE CHITON　　　*Stenoplax boogii*
SIZE: to 1.2 cm (¹/₂ in.)　　Chitons – Ischnochitonidae
ID: Oblong plates rose-pink with a scattering of cream spots, a few dots and blotches; thin longitudinal indentations at edges above girdle; narrow tan scaled girdle with irregular markings. Beneath rocks to 40 ft. Rare S.E. Florida, Bahamas, Caribbean.

ZEBRA GLASS-HAIR CHITON　　*Acanthochitona zebra*
SIZE: to 13 cm (5 in.)　　Chitons – Acanthochitonidae
ID: Oblong with **band of chevron-shaped stripes** angling backwards; girdle white with brown transverse bands; tufts of bristles border plates. On or beneath rocks to 10 ft. Occasional Florida Keys, Bahamas, Caribbean.

CARIBBEAN REEF SQUID *Sepioteuthis sepioidea*
SIZE: to 30 cm (12 in.) Inshore Squids – Loliginidae
ID: Most common squid. Oblong mantle bordered by translucent fin forming a point at the rear. Frequently change colors and patterns; brown to white, often with blue and green highlights. **ML-** Young juvenile. Common Florida, Bahamas, Caribbean.

GIANTEYE SQUID *Abralia veranyi*
SIZE: to 4.5 cm (1³/₄ in.) Midwater Squids – Enoploteuthidae
ID: Small with large eyes; tentacles nearly as long as body; translucent fins end in point; color varies from pale shades of bluish gray to brown with dark spots and speckles. Uncommon to rare Florida, Bahamas, Caribbean.

ATLANTIC BRIEF SQUID *Lolliguncula brevis*
SIZE: to 13 cm (5 in.) Inshore Squids – Loliginidae
ID: Compact with a rounded fin on each side of rear quarter of body ending in rounded tip. Color from bluish gray to brown; often display mottled spots. Inshore waters including estuaries and bays from surface to 70 ft. Uncommon Florida, Bahamas, Caribbean.

LONGFIN INSHORE SQUID *Doryteuthis pealeii*
SIZE: to 35 cm (14 in.) Inshore Squids – Loliginidae
ID: Large elongate body with rounded, somewhat triangular, fins that extend nearly half the body's length; variable markings in shades from brown to bluish gray; often display orange spots. Common Florida, Caribbean, but rarely observed by divers.

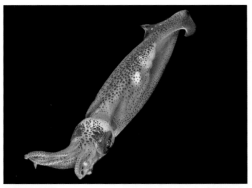

ARROW SQUID   *Loligo plei*
SIZE: to 45 cm (18 in.)   Inshore Squids – Loliginidae
ID: Triangular fins at rear of body. Juveniles: [pictured] translucent with heavy red, gold, and black spots; short arms. Nocturnal open-water species to 130 ft.; juveniles often feed near shore; adults offshore. Occasional Florida, Bahamas, Caribbean

GRASS SQUID   *Pickfordiateuthis pulchella*
SIZE: to 2.5 cm (1 in.)   Inshore Squids – Loliginidae
ID: Small with pair of rounded fins that do not join at rear of body; two rows of suckers on arms; rapidly change colors and patterns. Seagrass and patch reefs from 3 to 45 ft. Uncommon Florida, Bahamas, Caribbean.

DIAMOND BACK SQUID EGG CASE
Thysanoteuthis rhombus
Squids – Teuthoidae
SIZE: to 1.2 m (4 ft.)

ID: Long cylindrical bluish translucent mass of egg strings laid in a double helix. The eggs of nearly all oceanic squid are laid in free-floating masses, which are either without form or structured as tubes. Most inshore squids and octopuses lay eggs attached to the substrate. Uncommon Florida, Bahamas, Caribbean; also worldwide in tropical and subtropical waters.

Octopuses

Octopus vulgaris

Octopuses – Octopodidae

SIZE: to 1 m (3 ft.)

ID: **Largest and most common octopus on reef;** arms 3 to 4 times length of body; reddish brown reticulated pattern is often displayed; can alter colors and patterns quickly and dramatically; when in the open skin texture relatively smooth, but when camouflaging or in their den texture is quite rough and bumpy.. Dark ring around each sucker. Daytime foragers; dens can be located by nearby piles of discarded bivalve shells. Reefs, seagrass and rocks from 15 to 75 ft. Occasional Florida, Bahamas, Caribbean.

CARIBBEAN REEF OCTOPUS
Octopus briareus
Octopuses – Octopodidae
SIZE: to 50 cm (20 in.)

ID: Largest octopus seen on reefs at night; frequently display pale to intense iridescent blue-green cast with reddish brown blotches or mottling; no dark edge around suckers; skin texture relatively smooth; large bulging eyes; often spread skirt membrane. Nocturnal; hunt by spreading skirt over bottom structures teasing out crustaceans with tips of arms. Occasional Florida, Bahamas, Caribbean.

Octopuses

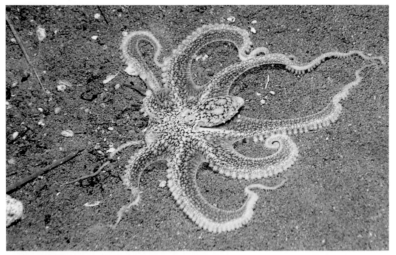

ATLANTIC LONGARM OCTOPUS
Macrotritopus defilippi
Octopuses – Octopodidae
SIZE: to 36 cm (14 in.)
ID: Long thin arms; typically brownish to blue gray with brown scrawled markings on mantle; often display row of widely spaced white spots on arms. Sand, rubble and mud where they live underground occasionally extending heads from openings; often swim across seafloor with arms trailing behind, reminiscent of a flounder. **BR-** Juvenile: Translucent with rows of reddish spots along arms; Seagrass, sand, rubble from 4 to 600 ft.; tend to be shallow. Occasional Florida, Bahamas, Caribbean.

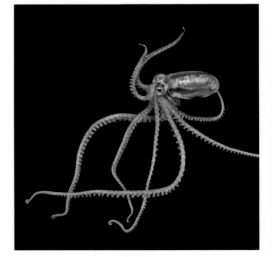

BROWNSTRIPE OCTOPUS
Amphioctopus burryi
Octopuses – Octopodidae
SIZE: to 30 cm (12 in.)

ID: Wide dark stripe extending along each arm often visible; whitish suckers line arms; reddish brown net pattern can be lightened or darkened; dark horizontal streak extends from front and back of eye; occasionally display wartlike skin papillae on mantle. Bury in sand, often surrounding body with pieces of debris such as bivalve shells. Seagrass, sand, mud from 15 to 75 ft. Uncommon Florida, Bahamas, Caribbean, but can be locally common.

Octopuses

CARIBBEAN TWOSPOT OCTOPUS   *Octopus hummelincki*
SIZE: to 25 cm (10 in.)   Octopuses – Octopodidae
ID: Blue ring around brown center situated just below eye (not always readily visible); can darken and lighten rapidly; often extend skin papillae. Coral reefs and rubble from 15 to 35 ft. Occasional Florida, Bahamas, Caribbean.

ATLANTIC PYGMY OCTOPUS   *Octopus joubini*
SIZE: to 15 cm (6 in.)   Octopuses – Octopodidae
ID: Small; red to orangish brown with pale banding across arms; skin texture smooth. **MR-** Juvenile: Identification tentative. Extremely nocturnal, seldom in open. Sand and mud, generally below 30 ft. Rare Florida, Bahamas, Caribbean.

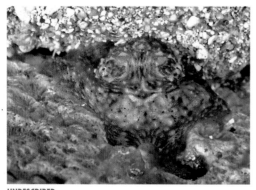

UNDESCRIBED
SIZE: to 3.5 cm (1½ in.)   Octopuses – Octopodidae
ID: Intriguing little undescribed octopus; grayish blue with tan markings; slit pupils appear to be vertical rather than horizonal. Appear to mimic a top shell [right]. Photographs taken at 40 ft. in Cayman Islands.

ATLANTIC WHITE-SPOTTED OCTOPUS
Octopus macropus
Octopuses – Octopodidae
SIZE: to 50 cm (20 in.)
ID: Brown to brick red; **often display a series of large white spots;** commonly erect skin papillae; can be quite animated. Sand and rubble near reefs from 15 to 75 ft. Nocturnal; forage for crustaceans; often bury. Identification tentative. Uncommon Florida, Bahamas, Caribbean.

VIOLET BLANKET OCTOPUS
Tremoctopus violaceus
Blanket Octopuses – Tremoctopodidae
SIZE: to 2 m (6 ft.)
ID: Female [pictured]; thin translucent veil-like web extends from 4 long front arms; reddish violet to violet or purple upper body; and occasionally shades of brown to orange; two long dorsal arms, usually edged with white; cream below.. Inhabit surface water; swim by water propulsion; feed primarily on fishes; tiny males, measuring only an inch or so, attach to females. Pelagic from the surface to 35 ft. Circumtropical.

Phylum Echinodermata

(Ee-KINE-oh-DER-ma-tuh / Gr. spiny skin)

Sea Stars, Sea Urchins & Sea Cucumbers

All echinoderms are marine and have a hard, internal skeleton composed of small calcareous plates called ossicles. Often, the ossicles have projections that give the body surface a spiny appearance. Members of the phylum have five body sections of equal size that are arranged around a central axis. Most have hundreds of small tube feet, called podia, that work in unison, either to move the animal over the bottom, or to capture food.

Feather Stars

CLASS: Crinoidea (Cry-noy-DEE-uh / L. a lily)

Feather stars, also known as crinoids, are the most ancient of echinoderms. These animals have changed little according to fossil records, and are sometimes referred to as "living fossils." They have small, flattened pentagon-shaped bodies with five arms that immediately fork one or more times, giving them a total of **ten or more long jointed arms** in multiples of five. Numerous short appendages extend along both sides of each arm creating a structure that resembles a feather. Skeletal ossicles give the arms a jointed appearance. Arms are used to sweep the water for particles of food. The arms adhere tightly, like Velcro, to anything that comes into contact with them and break easily. Fortunately, broken arms can be regenerated. Some crinoids can move short distances by swimming with coordinated arm movements, but most walk on jointed legs called cirri. Some species anchor inside narrow crevices with only their arms visible; others position themselves high atop coral heads and other reef structures.

Sea Stars

CLASS: Asteroidea (Ass-ter-OY-dee-uh / Gr. star form)

Asteroids have long been known as starfish, but a more modern and appropriate common name is sea stars. They usually have **five arms,** although a few species have more. The arms are triangular, merging at the base into the central disc. Broken arms can be regenerated, and in some species a new animal can form from a severed member. The mouth is located centrally on the undersurface, with anus on the top. Two or four rows of podia, tipped with suction discs, extend from the mouth down each arm. They are used both for movement and capturing prey. Some sea stars can invert their stomachs through their mouths to envelop and consume prey.

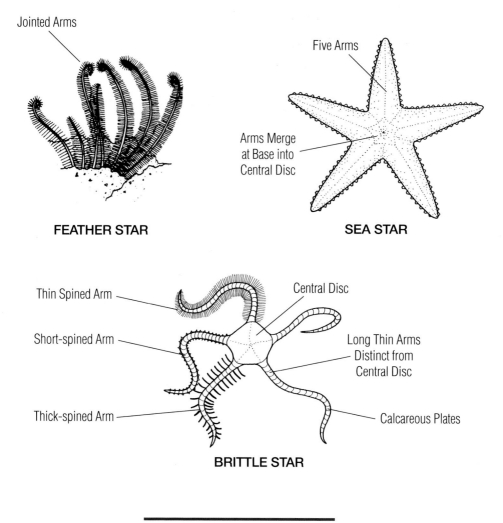

FEATHER STAR

Jointed Arms

SEA STAR

Five Arms

Arms Merge
at Base into
Central Disc

BRITTLE STAR

Thin Spined Arm

Short-spined Arm

Thick-spined Arm

Central Disc

Long Thin Arms
Distinct from
Central Disc

Calcareous Plates

Brittle & Basket Stars

CLASS: Ophiuroidea (Oh-fee-ER-OY-dee-uh / Gr. serpent tail in appearance)

Both orders in this class have **long, thin arms** that, unlike sea stars, do not widen as they approach the central disc. The central disc is a flattened, smooth and somewhat rounded pentagon. The mouth, centrally located on the underside, opens into the stomach; there is no intestine or anus.

Brittle Stars, Order Ophiurida, have a small **central disc** that rarely exceeds one inch in diameter, and five arms with numerous **spines** arranged in rows. The spines of different species can be distinct: they can be short or long, thin or thick, pointed or blunt. The tops of the arms are lined with large **calcareous plates** that allow only lateral movement. This armor results in arms that break off easily, giving rise to the common name. Severed arms, however, can be regenerated. In spite of their brittleness and restricted mobility, the arms allow the animal to move more rapidly than other members of the phylum. During the day brittle stars are occasionally seen clinging to sponges and gorgonian, but they generally hide under rocks and inside crevices, waiting for night before moving into the open to feed.

Basket Stars, Order Phrynophiurida, have **five arms that repeatedly subdivide into numerous branches,** resembling coiling tentacles. Unlike brittle stars, basket stars lack heavy arm shields and therefore can move their arms in all directions. During the day, the animals commonly cling to gorgonians, curling their network of arms into a tight ball. At night, they climb to the tops of gorgonians or other reef outcroppings, and spread their arms into the current to form a plankton net. Tiny, fine spines and tube feet work to transfer captured food to the mouth.

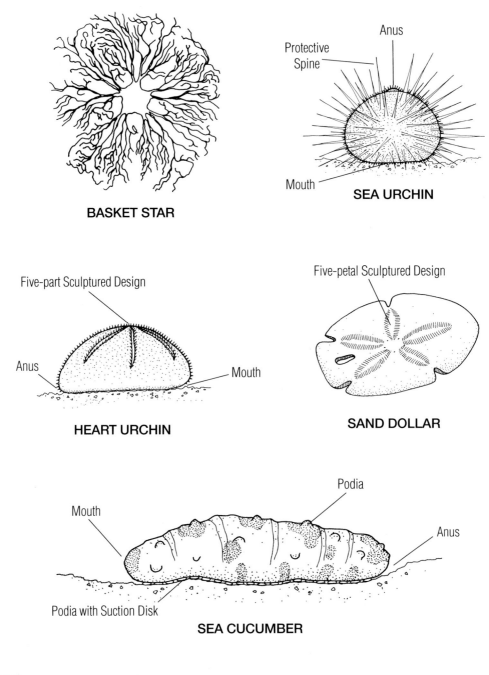

BASKET STAR

SEA URCHIN

Anus
Protective
Spine
Mouth

HEART URCHIN

Five-part Sculptured Design
Anus
Mouth

SAND DOLLAR

Five-petal Sculptured Design

SEA CUCUMBER

Mouth
Podia
Anus
Podia with Suction Disk

Sea Urchins, Heart Urchins, Sand Dollars & Sea Biscuits

CLASS: **Echinoidea** (Eck-ih-NOY-dee-uh / L. spiny)

A skeleton of ten fused calcareous plates, covered with numerous spines, encases the body of echinoids. They are characterized into two basic groups, regular and irregular.

Sea Urchins, regular echinoids, typically have spherical bodies with long **protective spines** and tube feet. The **mouth** is centrally located on the underside and the **anus on the top.** The mouth is a complicated arrangement of five teeth, called Aristotle's Lantern, used for scraping algae and other organic food from rocks. The spines of some species are long, sharp and needlelike, while others are stubby and blunt. Long, pointed spines easily puncture the skin, and are difficult to remove because the shaft is covered with recurved spinelets that function as miniature fish hooks. This causes a rather painful wound which should be treated to prevent infection.

Heart Urchins, Order Spatangoida, are irregular echinoids. Their bodies are non-spherical, shaped more like an **oval dome.** The **mouth,** which lacks Aristotle's Lantern, is in front, the **anus at the rear.** On top is a distinct **five-part sculptured design.** The body is covered with short, tightly packed spines well-adapted for burrowing; tube feet are degenerate or absent. They spend most of their lives buried in sand or mud where they feed on organic material. Although common, heart urchins are seldom seen. If the animal is spotted in the open at all, it is usually at night. Skeletal remains are occasionally found on the sand.

Sand Dollars and **Sea Biscuits,** Order Clypeasteroida, are also irregular echinoids. Their bodies are disc-shaped, with a **five-petal sculptured design** on the back. The mouth, which has an Aristotle's Lantern, is centered on the underside, with the anus toward the rear. The very short, compacted spines that cover the body appear as fuzz, and are well adapted for burrowing. Like heart urchins, they live under the sand and are rarely sighted in the open. Their skeletal remains, rather than the living animals, are usually found.

Sea Cucumbers

CLASS: **Holothuroidea** (Hoe-low-ther-OY-dee-uh / Gr. plantlike in appearance)

Sea Cucumbers have sausage-shaped bodies, with a **mouth in front and anus at the rear.** The five body-sections common to all echinoderms are not visible in these animals, but are part of their internal structure. They also have no external spines or arms, and the skeletal plates are reduced to microscopic size and buried in the leathery body wall. The shape of these hidden plates is the key to scientific classification, and thus many species cannot be positively identified underwater. **Podia** on the underside are tipped with suction discs; those on the back have been modified into a variety of shapes and sizes. These are often the visual clue to underwater identification. Sea cucumbers are usually sighted slowly crawling across sand or reef, scooping up organic debris.

Feather Stars

GOLDEN CRINOID
Davidaster rubiginosus
Feather Stars – Comasteridae
SIZE: arms to 37 cm (15 in.)
ID: Twenty to 40 arms; arms and side branches typically golden; arms occasionally yellow, tan, or black; side branches occasionally black or black with orange tips. Coral reefs with mild current from 330 ft.; attach inside recesses exposing only outstretched arms. Common to occasional E. Caribbean. Numbers have declined during the past two decades in many historic population centers; presently occasional to rare in remainder of Caribbean, S. Florida, Bahamas.

BLACK & WHITE CRINOID
Nemaster grandis
Feather Stars – Comasteridae
SIZE: arms to 25 cm (10 in.)
ID: Black with white-tipped side branches. Reefs; attach with sets of curved legs to tops of sponges and other reef structures from 40 to 130 ft. Occasional S. Caribbean; occasional to uncommon central Caribbean; rare N. Caribbean.

BEADED CRINOID   *Davidaster discoideus*
SIZE: arms to 15 cm (6 in.)   Feather Stars – Comasteridae
ID: Twenty golden arms; silver-gray side branches (occasionally with black tips) have **beaded appearance**. Deep reefs from 60 to 130 ft; attach inside recesses exposing only outstretched arms. Occasional Caribbean, Bahamas; rare S. Florida.

SWIMMING CRINOID
Analcidometra armata
Feather Stars – Colobometridae
SIZE: arms to 9 cm (3½ in.)
ID: Small; five paired sets of white arms with red and white side branches extend from small central disc. Attach to sea plumes, sea rods and sea whips from 10 to 450 ft, most frequent below 40 ft.; ability to coordinate arm movements enables animal to swim in open water. Occasional to uncommon Florida Keys, Bahamas, Caribbean.

261

Sea Stars

NINE-ARMED SEA STAR
Luidia senegalensis
Sea Stars – Luidiidae
SIZE: to 30 cm (12 in.)
ID: Nine long tapered tan to yellow arms with beadlike pattern forming rows; arms with wide lavender to blue or black central stripe. **MR-** Juvenile: Nine reddish brown and tan blunt arms tipped with orange. Nocturnal; sand and mud bottoms to 150 ft; often bury. Uncommon Florida, Caribbean.

BANDED SEA STAR
Luidia alternata
Sea Stars – Luidiidae
SIZE: to 30 cm (12 in.)
ID: Five long white to tan tapered arms with **wide reddish to dark brown chevron-shaped bands** (bands occasionally indistinct and can be dark green to purple); arms lined with fringe of tapering conical spines. Ventral surface yellowish; tube feet orange. Nocturnal; often bury. Sand and mud from 10 to 160 ft. Occasional Florida, Caribbean.

LINED SEA STAR *Luidia clathrata*
SIZE: to 28 cm (11 in.) Sea Stars – Luidiidae
ID: Five long flat tapering white arms with wide yellow, brown or black central stripe often paralleled with thin stripes; arms with beadlike pattern fringed with white spines. Sand to 130 ft; often bury. Common to occasional Florida, Bahamas, Caribbean.

BEADED SEA STAR *Astropecten articulatus*
SIZE: to 15 cm (6 in.) Sea Stars – Astropectinidae
ID: Five tapered arms bordered with elongate tan to yellow beadlike marginal plates; fringe of flat white spines, two to a plate; light brown to bluish central area with netlike pattern. Sand and mud to 540 ft.; bury. Occasional Florida, Bahamas, Caribbean.

TWO-SPINED SEA STAR
Astropecten duplicatus
Sea Stars – Astropectinidae
SIZE: to 20 cm (8 in.)
ID: Five flat tapering arms bordered with rectangular beadlike marginal plates; flat granular surface between plates covered with tiny spines; tan, lavender, reddish yellow, brown and black; flat white slightly curved spines two to a plate. Nocturnal; sand and mud to 65 ft; often bury. Occasional Florida, Bahamas, Caribbean.

Sea Stars

COMMON COMET STAR
Linckia guildingi
Sea Stars – Ophidiasteridae
SIZE: to 20 cm (8 in.)
ID: Four to seven slender tubular arms with rounded tips often of unequal lengths; uniform reddish to yellowish brown, tan, or violet; surface covered with small swollen plates covered with smooth granules. Reefs and hard bottoms from 20 to 130 ft. **MR-** Reproduce asexually by detaching arms which regenerate new individuals by forming starlike bud at broken base, known as comets. Common to occasional Florida, Bahamas, Caribbean; also circumtropical.

GUILDING'S SEA STAR
Ophidiaster guildingi
Sea Stars – Ophidiasteridae
SIZE: to 10 cm (4 in.)
ID: Five tubular arms with **reddish upturned tips;** slightly elongate surface nodules form distinct rows (similar Common Comet Star [previous] surface nodules more rounded and randomly spaced); highly variable from red to orange or pale yellow; young tend to be purple; often blotched with darker shading. Shallow reefs and rubble to 20 ft.; cryptic, often beneath rocks and inside recesses. Uncommon S. Florida, Caribbean.

MOTTLED SEA STAR
Copidaster lymani
Sea Stars – Ophidiasteridae
SIZE: to 30 cm (12 in.)
ID: Five slender tubular arms of equal or occasionally unequal length with rounded tips; small surface pits form rows extending length of arms; slimy to the touch; reddish orange with red mottling and irregular banding. Patch reefs and rubble from 15 to 110 ft. Occasional W. Caribbean; rare Florida, Bahamas.

RED THORNY SEA STAR
Echinaster echinophorus
Sea Stars – Echinasteridae
SIZE: to 20 cm (8 in.)
ID: Rows of large conical spines extend length of five tubular arms; uniform shades of red to orange; arms with one or two irregular rows of large erect spines. Cryptic; commonly beneath coral and rubble to 180 ft., but more commonly shallow. Uncommon to rare S. Florida, Bahamas, Caribbean.

ORANGE-RIDGED SEA STAR *Echinaster spinulosus*
SIZE: to 13 cm (5 in.) Sea Stars – Echinasteridae
ID: Orange to orangish yellow spines form irregular ridges extending the length of five tubular arms with whitish valleys between. Reefs, sand and dock pilings to 130 ft. Occasional Florida, S. Caribbean.

CONICAL-SPINED SEA STAR *Echinaster sentus*
SIZE: to 18 cm (7 in.) Sea Stars – Echinasteridae
ID: Conical spines typically arranged in rows along five tubular arms with spines in regular rows; usually red to orangish brown with maroon to violet valleys between; orange tube feet. Sand, rubble and seagrass to 50 ft. Occasional S. Florida, Bahamas.

265

Sea Stars

CUSHION SEA STAR
Oreaster reticulatus
Sea Stars – Oreasteridae
SIZE: to 50 cm (20 in.)
ID: Five short stout tapered arms extend from thick body; knobby spines form geometric designs; typically tan to orangish brown with yellow to dark brown spines and occasional lines; a few individuals gray. Sand and seagrass from 3 to 120 ft.; often form clusters. **BL&BR-** Juvenile: Flatter bodies than adults; colors and designs highly variable, yellow, white, tan and gray with contrasting mottled patterns. Common to occasional Florida, Bahamas, Caribbean.

STUDDED SEA STAR
Mithrodia sp.
Sea Stars – Mithrodiidae
SIZE: to 13 cm (5 in.)
ID: Five tubular arms attached to small central disc; prominent conical spines; white with brown bands on arms. Note: Species in genus *Mithrodia* known primarily from deep water, well below safe scuba diving depths and are rarely reported in Western Atlantic. Photographed at night in 25 ft. in Belize and 45 ft. in Utila, Honduras.

RED MINIATURE SEA STAR   *Poraniella echinulata*
SIZE: to 3 cm (1¼ in.)   Sea Stars – Asteropseidae
ID: Small; red with occasional white markings near center of disc and **black lining tips of arms.** Cryptic; beneath coral and rubble from 10 to 1,000 ft. Rare Florida, Bahamas, Caribbean.

BLUNT-ARMED SEA STAR   *Asterinides folium*
SIZE: to 2.5 cm (1 in.)   Sea Stars – Asterinidae
ID: Small; five short triangular arms emerge from raised central disc; white, tan, yellow, red, blue and olive. Reefs, rubble and sand to 50 ft. Cryptic; beneath rocks and rubble or inside crevices. Uncommon to rare Florida, Bahamas, Caribbean.

TESSELLATED CUSHION STAR   *Goniaster tessellatus*
SIZE: to 15 cm (6 in.)   Sea Stars – Goniasteridae
ID: Flat with five short wide triangular arms; shades of red; prominent conical spines on central disc; perimeter lined with marginal nodules. Sand from 70 to 1,400 ft. Occasional to rare Florida, Bahamas, Caribbean.

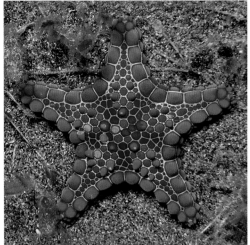

Brittle Stars

SIZE: arms to 13 cm (5 in.)

ID: Red and white bands on arms lined with short spines; disc solid red, patterned or mottled with rounded granules covering surface. **MR-** Juvenile. Cryptic; hide within recesses of reefs from 3 to 100 ft. Occasional S. Florida, Bahamas, Caribbean.

CIRCLE-MARKED BRITTLE STAR   *Ophioderma cinerea*
SIZE: arms to 15 cm (6 in.)   Brittle Stars – Ophiodermatidae
ID: Ten dark-outlined circles on edge of disc with occasional gold spotting; gray to brown; posterior arm plates wide with three short spines below; arms often banded. Cryptic; reefs and seagrass to 80 ft. Occasional Florida, Bahamas, Caribbean.

GAUDY BRITTLE STAR *Ophioderma ensifera*
SIZE: arms to 10 cm (4 in.) Brittle Stars – Ophiodermatidae
ID: Pink disc with some spotting; yellow arms can be bright or pale. Cryptic; deep reefs and slopes from 50 to 100 ft. Rare Bahamas, Turks & Caicos and W. Caribbean.

SMOOTH BRITTLE STAR *Ophioderma phoenium*
SIZE: arms to 9 cm (3¹/₂ in.) Brittle Stars – Ophiodermatidae
ID: Smooth red to brown disc with **arms of contrasting colors** of brown, pink, gray or green with dark bands; arms with series of tiny spines on vertical side plates. Cryptic; reefs, rubble, sand from 3 to 45 ft. Uncommon S. Florida, Bahamas, Caribbean.

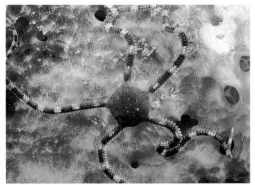

BANDEDARM BRITTLE STAR *Ophioderma appressa*
SIZE: arms to 13 cm (5 in.) Brittle Stars – Ophiodermatidae
ID: Green to gray with light and dark banded arms; disc covered with small rounded granules and some dark or white speckling and occasionally dramatic irregular patterns. Cryptic; reefs and rocks to 160 ft. Common Florida, Bahamas, Caribbean.

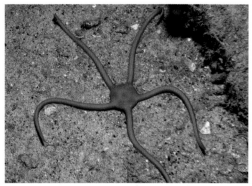

SHORT-ARMED BRITTLE STAR *Ophioderma brevicauda*
SIZE: arms to 7.5 cm (3 in.) Brittle Stars – Ophiodermatidae
ID: Granulated pentagonal disc and short arms; disc usually green with red to brown mottling; arms typically banded green, gray and white. Cryptic; reefs, rocks, seagrass; usually less than 60 ft., but to 210 ft. Uncommon S. Florida, Bahamas, Caribbean.

RED SERPENT STAR *Ophioderma squamosissima*
SIZE: arms to 20 cm (8 in.) Brittle Stars – Ophiodermatidae
ID: Large solid red to slightly orange disc and legs; smaller individuals may have pale orange patches; flat polygonal granules on disc; smooth arms. Cryptic; beneath rocks or inside reef crevices. Uncommon S. Florida, Bahamas, Caribbean.

Brittle Stars

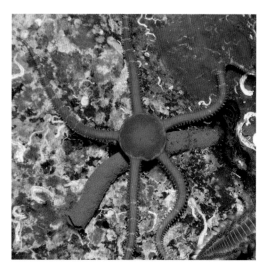

SLIMY BRITTLE STAR *Ophiomyxa flaccida*
SIZE: arms to 13 cm (5 in.)   Brittle Stars – Ophiomyxidae
ID: Rounded yellow, orange, red, brown or green; disc slimy with rounded nodules along edge; arms often lightly banded; disc can be solid, flecked or mottled with white, yellow or green. Reefs and seagrass to 330 ft. Common S. Florida, Bahamas, Caribbean.

ANTILLES BRITTLE STAR *Ophioblenna antillensis*
SIZE: arms to 13 cm (5 in.)   Brittle Stars – Ophiomyxidae
ID: Domed tan disc with reddish brown variegation occasionally with spotting; tan legs with brown, reddish brown to purple bands. Cryptic; reefs and rubble to 80 ft.; pictured specimen feeding on coral spawn. Uncommon Caribbean.

SPINY BRITTLE STAR *Ophiocoma paucigranulata*
SIZE: arms 15 cm (6 in.)   Brittle Stars – Ophiocomidae
ID: Shades of brown; arms with numerous long pointed spines; broad pale central stripe on arms extends onto disc; similar *O. wendtii* [next] has red highlights. Reefs with living coral from 5 to 80 ft. Uncommon S. Florida, Bahamas, N. W.

WENDT'S BRITTLE STAR *Ophiocoma wendtii*
SIZE: arms 18 cm (7 in.)   Brittle Stars – Ophiocomidae
ID: Reddish brown to black with granule-covered disc; arm spines long with swollen tips. **MR-** Juvenile: Brown disc with thin spiny orange legs. Cryptic; often extend arm tips to feed. Common, but seldom seen S. Florida, Bahamas, Caribbean.

BLUNT-SPINED BRITTLE STAR *Ophiocoma echinata*
SIZE: arms to 15 cm (6 in.) Brittle Stars – Ophiocomidae
ID: Long heavy blunt arm spines; tan, gray or brown disk with tiny granules; occasionally white to tan petal pattern; legs with vague banding. Cryptic; reef and rubble from 10 to 80 ft. Common Florida, Bahamas, Caribbean.

ANGULAR BRITTLE STAR
Ophiothrix angulata
Brittle Stars –
Ophiothricidae
SIZE: arms to 13 cm (5 in.)
ID: Small disc with prominent rounded lobes; discs and arms can be the same or different colors including pink, red, orange, green, blue, gray or brown; numerous long spines on thin arm often with central stripe, a lacy pattern and some banding. **BR-** Juvenile. Most habitats from shallow to deep. Common Florida, Bahamas, Caribbean.

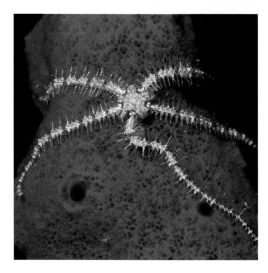

Brittle Stars

OERSTED'S BRITTLE STAR *Ophiothrix oerstedii*
SIZE: arms to 6.5 cm (2½ in.) Brittle Stars – Ophiothricidae
ID: Arms with thin white and black bands separated by wider colored bands and pairs of adjacent yellow spots; numerous long spines; colors variable. **TR-** Female with ripe gonads. Cryptic; reefs. Abundant S. Florida, Bahamas, Caribbean.

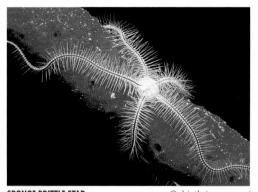

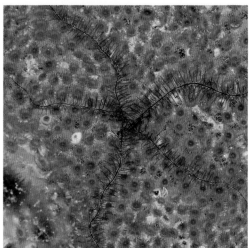

SPONGE BRITTLE STAR *Ophiothrix suensoni*
SIZE: arms to 9 cm (3½ in.) Brittle Stars – Ophiothricidae
ID: Wispy; small disc and thin heavily spined arms with distinct dark central line; yellow, brown, gray or black; spines and arms often different colors. **BR-** Juvenile. In open on sponges, fire coral, gorgonians to 200 ft. Common S. Florida, Bahamas, Caribbean.

RETICULATED BRITTLE STAR *Ophionereis reticulata*
SIZE: arms to 25 cm (10 in.)   Brittle Stars – Ophionereididae
ID: Light green to tan; pentagonal disc with thin dark reticulated lines; long arms with dark banding. Cryptic; sand and reefs; extend arms from hiding place to feed. Common Florida, Bahamas, Caribbean.

CREVICE BRITTLE STAR
Ophiopsila riisei
Brittle Stars – Ophiocomidae
SIZE: arms to 16 cm (6¼ in.)
ID: Long thin heavily spined arms vaguely banded; extend arms from crevices at night to feed. Identification tentative. Cryptic; quickly retract when illuminated by light; arms luminesce when touched, believe to deter shrimp and crab predators. Reefs and rubble; can be locally abundant with many individual inhabiting area. Abundant to occasional Florida, Bahamas, Caribbean.

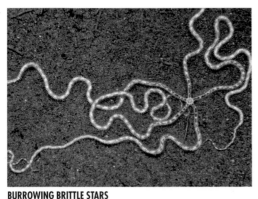

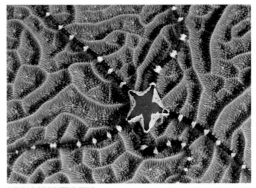

BURROWING BRITTLE STARS
SIZE: arms to 25 cm (10 in.)   Brittle Stars – Amphiuridae
ID: Numerous species in family burrow in mud extending a few long thin arms from opening of mucus-lined burrow to feed in water column. At times emerge from burrows for unknown reason. Mud to 20 ft. Occasional Florida, Bahamas, Caribbean.

REDBADGE BRITTLE STAR *Ophiurochaeta littoralis*
SIZE: arms to 4 cm (1½ in.) Brittle Stars – Ophiodermatidae
ID: Small; thin banded arms extend from thin star-shaped white disc with red star pattern (red star is occasionally indistinct or absent); short spines. Reefs from 30 to 160 ft. Rare S. Florida, Bahamas, W. & central Caribbean.

Brittle Stars

SIZE: arms to 2.5 cm (1 in.)

ID: Tiny quarter-inch disc with dark and light shades of cream, pink, purple or reddish brown; tapered arms with tiny spines. During day wrap arms around branches of Rose Lace Coral, *Stylaster roseus*, at night arms open to feed. Protected areas of reefs from 15 to 100 ft. Uncommon Bahamas, Caribbean; also Gulf of Mexico.

YELLOW SIXARM BRITTLE STAR   *Ophiothela mirabilis*
SIZE: arms to 2.5 cm (1 in.)   Brittle Stars – Ophiotrichidae
ID: Tiny; six spiny orangish yellow arms extend from quarter-inch disc; wrap arms around branches of numerous hosts, primarily gorgonians. Invasive species native to Pacific first reported from Brazil 2000, reported from St. Vincent 2012.

RINGED BRITTLE STAR
Asteroporpa annulata
Brittle Stars –
Gorgonocephalidae

SIZE: arms to 18 cm (7 in.)

ID: Five rounded and spineless brown and white banded arms; banded disc elevated in rounded humps where arms join disc. Attach to hard and soft corals, crinoids from 120 to 1000 ft. Rare E. Florida, Bahamas, Caribbean; also Gulf of Mexico.

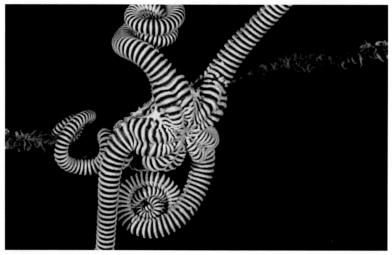

SEA ROD BASKET STAR   *Schizostella bifurcata*
SIZE: arms to 5 cm (2 in.) Brittle Stars – Gorgonocephalidae
ID: Thin arms with only one or two branches; reddish brown with thin white bands. Attach to gorgonians especially sea rods on deep fore reefs from 40 to 150 ft.; open to feed at night. Occasional S. Florida, Caribbean.

GIANT BASKET STAR
Astrophyton muricatum
Brittle Stars –
Gorgonocephalidae
SIZE: arms to 45 cm (18 in.)

ID: Large; numerous thin branching arms extend at night to form a plankton net. **BL-** During day arms tightly contract to form a fist-sized ball; tan, orange to dark brown. Commonly attach to gorgonians and sponges from 2 to 230 ft. Climb to top of elevated feeding perches at night to feed; often retreat to protective recess during day. **BR-** Occasionally intertwine within flexible arms of gorgonians during day. Common S. Florida, Bahamas, Caribbean.

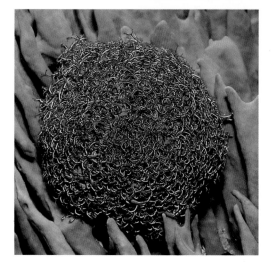

Sea Urchins

LONG-SPINED URCHIN
Diadema antillarum
Sea Urchins – Diadematidae
SIZE: spines to 20 cm (8 in.)
ID: Numerous long thin, extremely sharp spines; black, occasionally white spines. **BL&BR-** Juveniles: Black banded white spines; test with some white. Regularly form aggregations along rocky shorelines; typically take shelter during day, forage at night. Brittle needlelike spines easily puncture skin and break off leaving dark discoloration beneath skin from dye in spines. Treat for infection; difficult to remove, but dissolve within days. Sand, seagrass, reefs to 165 ft. Abundant to occasional S. Florida, Bahamas, Caribbean.

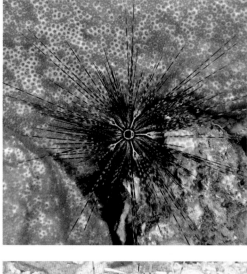

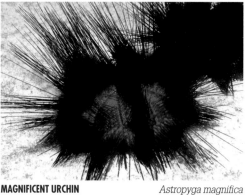

MAGNIFICENT URCHIN
Astropyga magnifica
SIZE: body to 15 cm (6 in.)   Sea Urchins – Diadematidae
ID: Black spines on dark red body; clusters of spines separated at body plates. **BR-** Juvenile: Reddish and cream with banded spines; blue spotting. Prefer deeper water to 290 ft. Occasional E. Caribbean; rare Florida and remainder of Caribbean.

ROCK-BORING URCHIN
Echinometra lucunter
Sea Urchins –
Echinometridae
SIZE: body to 7.5 cm (3 in.)
ID: Short thick spines black, olive, tan, red and reddish orange. Nocturnal; bore holes in substrate where they remain during day. Most common in rocky tidal areas, but found to 150 ft. Occasional to uncommon Florida, Bahamas, Caribbean.

REEF URCHIN
Echinometra viridis
Sea Urchins –
Echinometridae
SIZE: body to 5 cm (2 in.)
ID: Thick pointed spines with violet to dark brown tips and white ring around base; body red to maroon. Nocturnal; hide during day often in Lettuce Coral, *Agaricia tenuifolia*. Prefer shallow reefs, but to 130 ft. Occasional to uncommon S. Florida, Bahamas, Caribbean.

Sea Urchins

PURPLE URCHIN
Arbacia punctulata
Sea Urchins – Arbaciidae
SIZE: body to 10 cm (4 in.)
ID: Stout pointed spines; shades of red, brown and purple; spines lighter color than body. Seagrass, algae, reefs and rubble to 160 ft. Nocturnal; hide during day. Occasional continental shelf of Florida, Caribbean; also Cuba.

VARIEGATED URCHIN   *Lytechinus variegatus*
SIZE: body to 10 cm (4 in.)   Sea Urchins – Toxopneustidae
ID: Dense covering of short spines arranged in rows or clusters; body white; spines white, red, green, blue or lavender. Sand, seagrass to 160 ft. Often covered with debris.
BR- Juvenile: Common Florida, Bahamas, Caribbean.

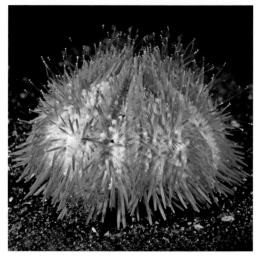

JEWEL URCHIN   *Lytechinus williamsi*
SIZE: body to 5 cm (2 in.)   Sea Urchins – Toxopneustidae
ID: Tan to white body with **reddish lines between plates;** spines green, white, brown; dark reddish ball-like structures used to remove debris (distinctive of species). Prefer shallow reefs, but to 300 ft. Cryptic. Rare to occasional S. Florida, Caribbean.

WEST INDIAN SEA EGG
Tripneustes ventricosus
Sea Urchins –
Toxopneustidae
SIZE: body to 13 cm (5 in.)
ID: Reddish brown, occasionally white body, with dense covering of short white spines; occasionally spines separated into clusters along joints of body plates. Seagrass, sand and shallow reefs to 30 ft. Often covered with seagrass blades and debris as shade. Common to uncommon Florida, Bahamas, Caribbean.

SLATEPENCIL URCHIN   *Eucidaris tribuloides*
SIZE: body to 5 cm (2 in.)   Sea Urchins – Cidaridae
ID: Thick blunt spines reddish white with reddish brown banding, often encrusted appearing gray; short white secondary spines. Nocturnal; wedge inside recesses during day. Reefs, seagrass to 150 ft. Common to uncommon Florida, Bahamas, Caribbean.

Heart Urchins & Sand Dollars

LONG-SPINED SEA BISCUIT
Plagiobrissus grandis
Heart Urchins – Brissidae
SIZE: to 20 cm (8 in.)
ID: Oval dome-shaped body covered with tan hairlike spines, those on top long and can be raised in defense; underside flat. Sand to 210 ft. Typically burrow two inches beneath surface. Occasional Florida, Bahamas, Caribbean.

RED HEART URCHIN   *Meoma ventricosa*
SIZE: to 15 cm (6 in.)   Heart Urchins – Brissidae
ID: Dome-shaped body with **indented pentagonal petal design on back;** densely covered with short brown spines. Sand, seagrass. **MR-** Typically bury beneath surface. Common Florida, Bahamas, Caribbean.

INFLATED SEA BISCUIT
Clypeaster rosaceus
Sand Dollars – Clypeasteridae
SIZE: to 20 cm (8 in.)
ID: Large brown to reddish brown slightly elongate biscuit-shaped body with **raised pentagonal petal design on back;** thick covering of short spines. Nocturnal; shallow seagrass beds, sand, rubble, but to 900 ft.; often covered with grass blades and debris as shade; does not bury. Common to occasional S. Florida, Caribbean; also Gulf of Mexico.

SAND DOLLAR
Clypeaster subdepressus
Sand Dollars –
Clypeasteridae
SIZE: to 30 cm (12 in.)
ID: Disc in shades of brown with dense covering of tiny spines; pentagonal petal design on back of equal size **(no notches in margin or holes in body);** shells of dead specimens gray. Sand and shell rubble with little seagrass to 150 ft.; burrow beneath surface. Occasional Florida, Bahamas, Caribbean.

MOSAIC SAND DOLLAR   *Clypeaster luetkeni*
SIZE: to 10 cm (4 in.)   Sand Dollars – Clypeasteridae
ID: Gray disc with **mosaic netlike pattern of white lines** (no notches in margin or holes in body); pentagonal petal design on back. Bury beneath sand. Rare S. Florida, Caribbean.

NOTCHED SAND DOLLAR   *Encope aberrans*
SIZE: to 15 cm (6 in.)   Sand Dollars – Mellitidae
ID: Dark brown to purplish disc with **single oval hole and two notches in disc margin;** pentagonal petal design on back; dense covering of tiny spines. Bury beneath sand, rubble from 30 to 300 ft. Occasional Florida, Bahamas; also Gulf of Mexico.

FIVE-KEYHOLE SAND DOLLAR   *Mellita quinquiesperforata*
SIZE: to 15 cm (6 in.)   Sand Dollars – Mellitidae
ID: Yellow-brown to brown or gray disc with **five oval holes;** pentagonal petal design on back; dense covering of tiny spines. Shallow sand near reefs, but to 150 ft. Occasional Florida Caribbean; also Gulf of Mexico.

SIX-KEYHOLE SAND DOLLAR   *Leodia sexiesperforata*
SIZE: to 10 cm (4 in.)   Sand Dollars – Mellitidae
ID: Brown to silvery gray disc with **six oval holes;** pentagonal petal design on back; dense covering of tiny spines. Shallow sand near reefs, but to 150 ft. Occasional Florida, Bahamas, Caribbean.

Sea Cucumbers

SIZE: to 36 cm (14 in.)

ID: Dark gray to black with deep creases; sole rose to white with scattered brown podia. Seagrass, sand, reefs to 120 ft. Common Caribbean; occasional to uncommon S. Florida, Bahamas.

IMPATIENT SEA CUCUMBER   *Holothuria impatiens*
SIZE: to 20 cm (8 in.)   Sea Cucumbers – Holothuriidae
ID: Slender mottled gray, brown, reddish and purple wrinkled body; often narrower toward mouth creating flask shape; collar of papillae surrounds mouth; rows of cone-shaped papillae. Tidepools, sand and reefs to 90 ft. Occasional Florida, Bahamas, Caribbean.

FLORIDA SEA CUCUMBER   *Holothuria floridana*
SIZE: to 25 cm (10 in.)   Sea Cucumbers – Holothuriidae
ID: Slender tapered body with numerous folds and conical podia with pointed tips; shades of gray, brown, yellow or red, often mottled. Sand, seagrass, algae, mangroves from 3 to 15 ft. Occasional Florida, Bahamas, Caribbean.

PRINCEPS SEA CUCUMBER   *Holothuria princeps*
SIZE: to 30 cm (12 in.)   Sea Cucumbers – Holothuriidae
ID: Mottled brown, tan and white; tapered body, more to the posterior than toward mouth; numerous warts of varying sizes with tiny papilla on tips; two rows of brown to black blotches on back. Sand to 750 ft. Occasional Florida, Bahamas, C. & S. Caribbean.

TIGER TAIL SEA CUCUMBER
Holothuria thomasi
Sea Cucumbers –
Holothuriidae
SIZE: to 2 m (6 ft.)
ID: Extend anterior portion of elongate bodies from holdfast in reef recesses; yellow to golden brown often with irregular brown banding; mouth on bottom of anterior end encircled by 20 flattened feeding tentacles. Feed primarily at night in sand near reefs from 10 to 100 ft. Common to occasional S. Florida, Bahamas, Caribbean.

GRAY SEA CUCUMBER   *Holothuria grisea*
SIZE: to 25 cm (10 in.)   Sea Cucumbers – Holothuriidae
ID: White to red with brown mottling; upper body covered with cone-shaped papillae; flattened sole; yellowish-tipped tube feet. Identification tentative. Lagoons with seagrass, hard bottoms to 40 ft. Occasional Florida, Bahamas, Caribbean.

GRUB SEA CUCUMBER   *Holothuria cubana*
SIZE: to 15 cm (6 in.)   Sea Cucumbers – Holothuriidae
ID: Brown to grayish white with numerous small podia; two rows of brown blotches on back (often obscured by sand coating); thick body tapering to blunt ends. Cryptic; reefs and rubble to 30 ft. Occasional Florida, Bahamas, Caribbean.

FIVE-TOOTHED SEA CUCUMBER
Actinopyga agassizi
Sea Cucumbers –
Holothuriidae
SIZE: to 25 cm (10 in.)
ID: Mottled yellow-brown to brown or cream with whitish sole; small knobby podia on back, those along sole large and conical; somewhat flattened sides; body occasionally creased. Sand and seagrass to 125 ft. Occasional Florida, Bahamas, Caribbean.

Sea Cucumbers

THREE ROWED SEA CUCUMBER
Isostichopus badionotus
Sea Cucumbers –
Stichopodidae
SIZE: to 40 cm (16 in.)
ID: Highly variable colors and markings from earth-tones to golden yellow and orange; knoblike podia on exposed surface often of contrasting colors; three rows of podia on sole, center row wide and split by a seam. **BR-** Juvenile: Cream to yellow with large knobs and some reddish markings. Sand, seagrass, reefs to 200 ft. Occasional Florida, Bahamas, Caribbean.

FURRY SEA CUCUMBER *Astichopus multifidus*
SIZE: to 40 cm (16 in.) Sea Cucumbers – Stichopodidae
ID: Cream to white with scattered brown blotches; back covered with short podia, some long and pointed; skirt of pointed podia encircles body. Sand from 10 to 120 ft. Occasional Florida, Bahamas, Caribbean.

CONICAL SEA CUCUMBER *Eostichopus arnesoni*
SIZE: to 40 cm (16 in.) Sea Cucumbers – Stichopodidae
ID: Reddish brown covered with prominent tan cone-shaped podia; **white area just above red skirt encircling body.** Sand and rubble from 25 to 75 ft. Uncommon Caribbean.

BEADED SEA CUCUMBER *Euapta lappa*
SIZE: to 1 m (3 ft.) Sea Cucumbers – Synaptidae
ID: Long wormlike with encircling sections of knobs; crown of featherlike feeding tentacles; highly variable, usually tan, brown, gray often with blotching and stripes. Nocturnal; sand, rubble, seagrass to 80 ft. Occasional S. Florida, Bahamas, Caribbean.

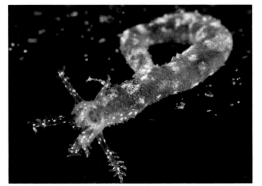

SEAWEED CUCUMBER *Synaptula hydriformis*
SIZE: to 10 cm (4 in.) Sea Cucumbers – Synaptidae
ID: Small thin elastic and sticky; crown of 12 featherlike feeding tentacles; adults dull green to reddish brown with white patches; juveniles semi-transparent. Solitary or in clusters; algae, seagrass, mangroves to 20 ft. Occasional S. Florida, Caribbean.

HIDDEN SEA CUCUMBER *Pseudothyone belli*
SIZE: to 5 cm (2 in.) Sea Cucumbers – Sclerodactylidae
ID: Mouth surrounded by 8 long highly branched tentacles and a single short pair; white with brown or maroon. Body attaches below sand or in crevices with feeing tentacles exposed to capture food. Sand, reefs to 120 ft. Uncommon Florida, Caribbean.

Phylum Chordata

(Core-DOT-uh / Gr. string)

Subphylum Urochordata

(Your-oh-CORE-dot-uh / Gr. tail string)

Tunicates

Most chordates have backbones and are called vertebrates; urochordates do not have backbones, but are included because they have four important characteristics that are shared by all members of the phylum — at some point in their life cycle all have a tail, dorsal central nerve cord, pharyngeal gill clefts and notochord. The latter functions as a support system for the dorsal nerve cord and is replaced by bone in vertebrates. The subphylum's common name, tunicate, comes from a body covering of cellulose material called a **tunic.**

Tunicates

CLASS: Ascidiacea (Ah-sid-EE-aa-see-uh / Gr. little bottle)

Although tunicates are among the most common marine invertebrates, they are probably the least recognized. In most cases, they are simply overlooked, ignored or mistaken for sponges. They are attached to the substrate at one end; at the opposite end they have two siphons. Water is drawn in through the **incurrent** or buccal **siphon,** pumped through a **gill net** in the body, where food and oxygen are extracted, and then discharged through an **excurrent** or atrial **siphon.** Body shape, as well as size, varies considerably among species; some are only a quarter inch in length while others may exceed five inches. Tunicates come in a dazzling array of colors that is often enhanced by a translucent quality of the tunic.

When the animal is disturbed, muscular bands rapidly close the siphons. This ability easily distinguishes tunicates from sponges, which either cannot close their openings, or do so very slowly. In spite of their spongelike appearance, tunicates are complicated animals with nervous, digestive, reproductive and circulatory systems.

Solitary tunicates are called **simple ascidians,** and include most of the larger species. Many of the smaller species grow in varying degrees of colonialism and are called **compound tunicates.** In some species individuals are joined only at their bases, while in more intimate associations, numerous individuals are completely embedded in a **common tunic** and the individuals are recognizable only by their two siphons. The most specialized colonies are those in which the individuals are not only imbedded in a common tunic, but their excurrent siphons open into a large common chamber or cloaca. Some of these colonies form geometric designs with the **incurrent siphons** evenly spaced around a **central outflow opening** or cloacal orifice. Others have incurrent siphons scattered randomly around larger **outflow openings.** Compound colonies often cover an area, appearing much like an encrusting sponge.

Pelagic Tunicates

CLASS: Thaliacea (Thal-ee-AA-see-uh / Gr. to flourish or bloom)

Members of this class are pelagic, free-swimming tunicates found in open water that occasionally swim over reefs. They are translucent-to-transparent animals that resemble a jet engine pod in both appearance and function. The **incurrent** or buccal and **excurrent** or atrial **siphons** are at opposite ends of the pod. Water is pushed through the body by muscular contractions, moving the animal by water jet propulsion. Orange **cerebral ganglions** can usually be seen at the top, near the buccal siphon.

Members of the genera *Salpa* and *Doliolumn* are solitary adults that reproduce by asexual budding. Occasionally, buds are seen connected in long chains or other patterns. When mature, an individual detaches and swims free.

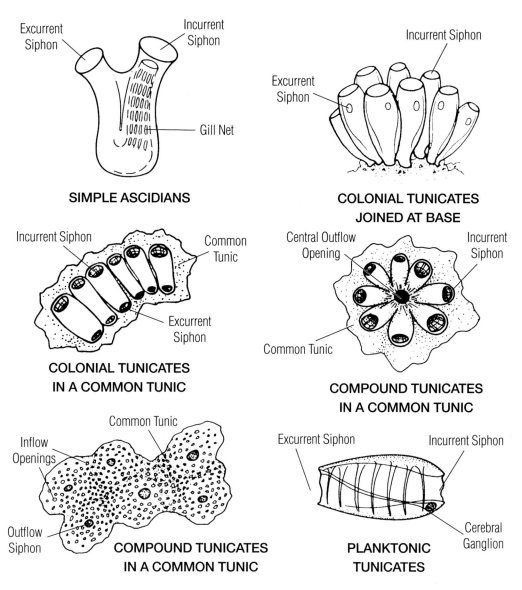

SIMPLE ASCIDIANS

COLONIAL TUNICATES
JOINED AT BASE

COLONIAL TUNICATES
IN A COMMON TUNIC

COMPOUND TUNICATES
IN A COMMON TUNIC

COMPOUND TUNICATES
IN A COMMON TUNIC

PLANKTONIC
TUNICATES

Tunicates

PAINTED TUNICATE
Clavelina picta
Tunicates – Clavelinidae
SIZE: to 2 cm (³/₄ in.)
ID: Translucent with white, red or purple shading; siphon rims and internal body parts typically carmine to purple. Grow in clusters from a few to over 1,000 individuals on reefs and walls from 15 to 100 ft. Often attach to gornonians, black coral and sponges. Common to occasional Florida, Bahamas, Caribbean.

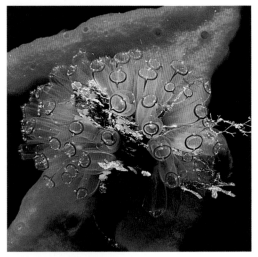

BLUEBELL TUNICATE
Clavelina puertosecensis
Tunicates – Clavelinidae
SIZE: to 1.2 cm (¹/₂ in.)
ID: Deep blue; siphon rims white; smallest member of genus in Caribbean; may display other colors not reported in scientific literature. Reefs from 20 to 100 ft. Occasional Caribbean.

BULB TUNICATES
Clavelina spp.
Tunicates – Clavelinidae
SIZE: to 2 cm (³/₄ in.)
ID: Translucent bulb shape in various shades; pair of large apex siphons. Colors and markings of genus members vary considerably and are not well established in scientific literature. Identification to species requires microscopic examination of internal body parts. Clusters attach to a variety of substrates on reefs from 15 to 130 ft. Common to occasional Florida, Bahamas, Caribbean.

MANGROVE TUNICATE
Ecteinascidia turbinata
Tunicates – Perophoridae
SIZE: to 5 cm (2 in.)
ID: Translucent orange, occasionally yellow or pink, body and internal parts; pair of large apex siphons. Grow in clusters numbering from a few to hundreds. Mangroves, seagrass, and occasionally shallow reefs to 40 ft. A few Painted Tunicates [previous] in shades of red and lavender also appear in photograph. Common Florida, Bahamas, Caribbean.

Tunicates

GIANT TUNICATE
Polycarpa spongiabilis
Tunicates – Styelidae
SIZE: to 10 cm (4 in.)
ID: Two large tan to brown protruding siphons; interior of incurrent siphon ringed with bristlelike unbranched tentacles. Two similar species, *Microcosmus exasperatus* and *Pyura vittata*, can be distinguished from the Giant Tunicate by noting branched tentacles inside incurrent siphon. Reefs and walls from 25 to 100 ft. Occasional Florida, Bahamas, Caribbean.

REEF TUNICATE   *Rhopalaea abdominalis*
SIZE: to 4 cm (1½ in.)   Tunicates – Diazonidae
ID: Solitary thick gelatinous body; lavender to dark purple or brown, may appear black at depth. Reefs; often grow in tight crevices with only upper body and siphons exposed. Occasional S. Florida, Bahamas, Caribbean.

GREENTUBE TUNICATE   *Ascidia sydneiensis*
SIZE: length to 10 cm (4 in.)   Tunicates – Ascidiidae
ID: Long tubular yellow to yellow-green incurrent siphon extends from recesses in reefs from 30 to 130 ft.; much of body and excurrent siphon hidden from view. Occasional Caribbean.

BLACK CONDOMINIUM TUNICATE   *Eudistoma obscuratum*
SIZE: to 10 cm (4 in.)   Tunicates – Polycitoridae
ID: Numerous small tunicates embedded in a firm **black globular common tunic;** individuals appear as two slightly protruding siphon openings outlined in white. Reefs from 25 to 75 ft. Identification tentative. Occasional Florida, Bahamas, Caribbean.

WHITE CONDOMINIUM TUNICATES   *Eudistoma* sp.1
SIZE: to 10 cm (4 in.)   Tunicates – Polycitoridae
ID: Numerous small tunicates embedded in a firm **white globular common tunic;** individuals appear as two slightly protruding openings. Reefs from 25 to 75 ft. Identification tentative. Occasional Florida, Bahamas, Caribbean.

STRAWBERRY TUNICATE
Eudistoma sp.2
Tunicates – Polycitoridae
SIZE: to 4 cm (1 1/2 in.)
ID: Numerous small tunicates embedded in a **firm common berrylike tunic attached to the substrate by a short stalk;** vary from violet to red to orange; individuals appear as two small siphons outlined in darker shade. Occasional Florida, Bahamas, Caribbean.

ENCRUSTING SOCIAL TUNICATE　　　　　　*Symplegma viride*
SIZE: to 7 mm (1/4 in.)　　　　　　Tunicates – Styelidae
ID: Clusters of tiny tunicates attached to common encrusting tunic at base; variable from yellow-green, orange and purple, possibly other colors; interiors often of contrasting shade. Reefs and walls from 15 to 100 ft. Common Florida, Bahamas, Caribbean.

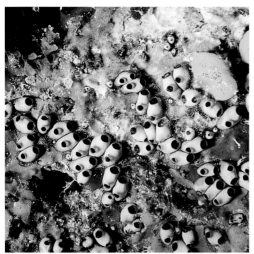

MOTTLED SOCIAL TUNICATE　　　　　　*Polycarpa tumida*
SIZE: to 1.2 cm (1/2 in.)　　　　　　Tunicates – Styelidae
ID: Individual tunicates grow in clusters; brown apex becomes pale toward base; occasionally with pale or mottled siphons. Identification tentative. Dead areas of reefs and shipwrecks from 25 to 75 ft. Occasional Florida, Bahamas, Caribbean.

291

Tunicates

FLAT TUNICATE
Botrylloides nigrum
Tunicates – Styelidae
SIZE: to 6 mm (¹/₄ in.)
ID: Within a common tunic numerous tiny elongated tunicates cluster around large central outflow siphons; typically brick red and yellow, although occasionally black to bright orange; individuals can be recognized by their small incurrent siphons. Grow on a variety of substrates including dead coral, shipwrecks, dock pilings and seagrass. Occasional Florida, Bahamas, Caribbean.

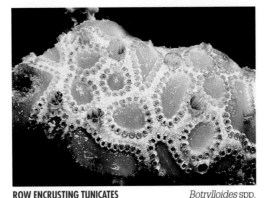

ROW ENCRUSTING TUNICATES *Botrylloides* spp.
SIZE: to 6 mm (¹/₄ in.) Tunicates – Styelidae
ID: Several species of the genus can be recognized by meandering rows of tunicates forming wide pathways with large common outflow openings; rows occasionally encircle areas of translucent tunic. Reefs from 5 to 100 ft. Occasional Florida, Bahamas, Caribbean.

GEOMETRIC ENCRUSTING TUNICATES *Botryllus* spp.
SIZE: to 6 mm (¹/₄ in.) Tunicates – Styelidae
ID: Tunicates cluster in circular patterns around central outflow openings forming various geometric patterns. Visual characteristics of genus members not consistent making species identification impractical. From 5 to 100 ft. Occasional Florida, Bahamas, Caribbean.

MOTTLED ENCRUSTING TUNICATE *Distaplia bermudensis*
SIZE: to 6 mm (¹/₄ in.) Tunicates – Holozoidae
ID: Tiny tunicates form circles or ovals around central outflow openings within common tunic; soft to the touch; mottled in a variety of colors including brown, pink, red and blue. Reefs from 25 to 65 ft. Occasional Florida, Bahamas, Caribbean.

BUTTON TUNICATES *Distaplia corolla*
SIZE: to 6 mm (¹/₄ in.) Tunicates – Holozoidae
ID: Tiny tunicates form circles or ovals around central outflow openings within common tunic; orange or purple buttonlike colonies usually grow in small clusters. Reefs from 25 to 75 ft. Occasional Florida, Bahamas, Caribbean.

GLOBULAR ENCRUSTING TUNICATE
Diplosoma glandulosum
Tunicates – Didemnidae
SIZE: to 10 cm (4 in.)
ID: Numerous tiny tunicates embedded in a soft thin globular tunic; excurrent siphons empty into a swollen interior chamber with large randomly spaced outflow openings; colors include yellow, orange, green, brown, and gray; often white outlines around tiny incurrent siphons; soft to the touch. Reefs from 25 to 100 ft. Common Caribbean.

WHITESPECK TUNICATE
Didemnum conchyliatum
SIZE: to 5 cm (2 in.)
Tunicates – Didemnidae
ID: Numerous tunicates embedded in a thin encrusting tunic; typically orange with white specks, occasionally white; one or several outflow openings; often form meandering chains. Reefs to 100 ft. Common Caribbean; occasional S. Florida, Bahamas.

BLACK OVERGROWING TUNICATE
Didemnum vanderhorsti
SIZE: to 10 cm (4 in.)
Tunicates – Didemnidae
ID: Dark gray with numerous tiny tunicates embedded in a soft thin tunic; tiny incurrent siphons are scattered over surface; large randomly spaced outflow openings. Often in protected areas of reefs from 20 to 75 ft. Occasional Caribbean.

OVERGROWING MAT TUNICATE
Trididemnum solidum
Tunicates – Didemnidae
SIZE: to 1 m (3 ft.)
ID: Numerous tiny tunicates embedded in a tough leathery tunic with relatively small outflow openings; tiny incurrent siphons scattered over surface; typically gray, but also blue-green, green or white. Shallow reefs from 10 to 40 ft; often overgrow living corals. Common Florida, Bahamas, Caribbean.

Tunicates & Planktonic Tunicates

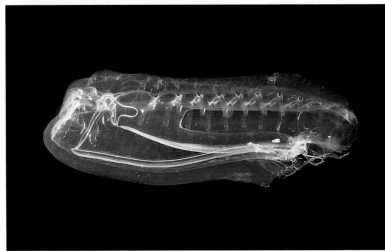

**Planktonic Tunicates:
Chains and Other
Formations**

T, ML, MR & BL- Chain
formations.

BR- Reproductive budding
in process.

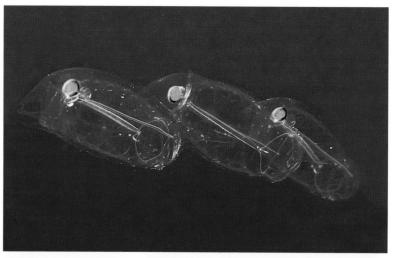

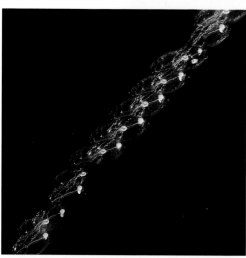

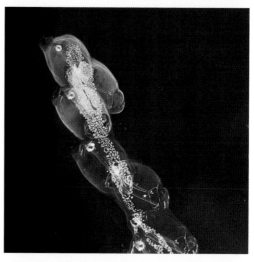

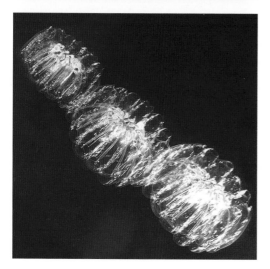

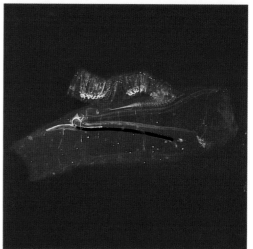

COMMON NAME INDEX

SCIENTIFIC NAME INDEX

NOTES

NOTES